SMASHING THE ATLANTIC WALL

PATRICK DELAFORCE

SMASHING THE ATLANTIC WALL

THE DESTRUCTION OF HITLER'S COASTAL FORTRESSES

Pen & Sword
MILITARY

First published in Great Britain in 2001 by Cassell & Co.
Published in 2005, reprinted in this format in 2006 by
Pen & Sword Military
An imprint of
Pen & Sword Books Ltd
47 Church Street
Barnsley
South Yorkshire
S70 2AS

Copyright © Patrick Delaforce, 2001, 2005, 2006

ISBN 1 84415 371 1

A CIP catalogue record for this book is
available from the British Library

Printed and bound in England
By CPI UK

Pen & Sword Books Ltd incorporates the Imprints of Pen & Sword Aviation,
Pen & Sword Maritime, Pen & Sword Military, Wharncliffe Local history,
Pen & Sword Select, Pen & Sword Military Classics and Leo Cooper.

For a complete list of Pen & Sword titles please contact
PEN & SWORD BOOKS LIMITED
47 Church Street, Barnsley, South Yorkshire, S70 2AS, England
E-mail: enquiries@pen-and-sword.co.uk
Website: www.pen-and-sword.co.uk

CONTENTS

The Maps

The Cinderella War

THE FIVE YEARS OF GLOBAL WARFARE DURING WORLD WAR TWO can be likened to a three-dimensional deadly game of chess. The killing fields were on the beaches, in the bocage, swamps and polders, and terrible battles took place in the air, and on and under the sea. Many of those campaigns have been well documented, but this book is about a crucial series of battles rarely chronicled. Prime Minister Winston Churchill and the Führer, Adolf Hitler, were both agreed on the final chess move and where (but not when) it would take place.

After the launch of Operation Barbarossa, the unexpected invasion of Russia in June 1941, Hitler knew with absolute certainty that his Achilles heel would be the successful opening up of the Second Front in Western Europe. He and Winston Churchill both knew that a successful attack and lodgement (requiring one or two *larger* ports in good working order) by the Allied armies on the western flank would eventually spell the end of the Third Reich. Despite the enormous manpower available to the Axis armies (including press-ganged Russian, Hungarian, French, Dutch and Belgians), they could not hope to win the war fighting the Russian hordes in the east and the Allied armies in the west. On the eastern front Hitler launched his Panzer armies—the 'bishops' and 'knights' of his chessboard. On the western front he created a dozen or more powerful fortresses, 'castles', to defend his vulnerable major ports and harbours. Hitler's secret edicts by which he created the Atlantic Wall, are detailed in this book. In the winter of 1941 the vast Todt organization (mainly slave labour) were tasked by the Führer to build the long line of some 1,500 steel and concrete defensive strongpoints—spread over four country coastlines—Denmark, Holland, Belgium and, most vitally, in France.

According to size, the strongpoints were called Widerstansnest, Stützpunkt, Blockhaus, and Verteidigungs Bereiche. Hitler realised he was powerless to prevent raids by the 'pawns' on the chessboard but he intended that his fortresses (Festung) would defend and dominate the vital ports and, by total destruction, deny them to his enemies. He personally supervised the detailed plans for their defences; the amount and quality of the concrete and steel required; the type and number of guns (German, French, Belgian, Czech, Russian, Yugoslav or British) needed for their defence. (He switched Panther tanks from the Russian front to be integrated into the defensive rings of strongpoints in the west). He personally selected the (usually) dedicated fortress commandants, met them face to face, briefed them about their duties and made them swear an oath of allegiance to him, their Führer and to the Third Reich. They had to promise to fight to the last man and the last 'stone' of the defence walls!

Should the worst come to the worst, the commandants were ordered to oversee the *total* destruction of their port and wreck all the harbour facilities, leaving deadly mines hidden in the water and sunken ships blocking the entrance. On several occasions he sent Iron Crosses to heavily beleaguered commandants to issue to key defenders. He maintained direct radio control and issued them with (often unnecessary) orders. This book details the key secret edicts which promulgated the precise rules of engagement and the responsibilities of each fortress commandant. His trusted generals and advisers also give their viewpoints: Walther Warlimont, Blumentritt, Jodl, Rommel and also Albert Speer, his close friend, architect, city planner and head of the huge Todt construction organization (from 1942).

The opening of the Second Front—Operation Overlord—in June 1944 was probably one of the most dramatic events of the twentieth century. Brilliant planning and intense co-operation between the American, British and Canadian armed forces on sea, land and in the air produced, eventually, a stunning victory. A year later, the Allied forces met the Russian armies on the Baltic, Berlin had been captured and the Third Reich was finished. And Adolf Hitler, the Führer, committed suicide. After bitter attritional fighting in Normandy during June and July 1944, the Allied armies broke through the German defences in the notorious killing grounds around Falaise and Argentan. General Patton sent his armour through Brittany towards Paris and Field Marshal Bernard Montgomery unleashed his three armoured divisions in the famous 'Great Swan' to seize Brussels, Antwerp and Ghent.

Many experts were sure that the war would be over by Christmas. Hitler's generals fighting desperate battles on the Russian front still managed to cobble together scores of battlegroups and halt the British in Holland and the Americans in the Metz-Nancy region.

The Allies had far outstripped their coastal supply points. Petrol and ammunition were severely rationed because, quite simply, the fanatical defences of Hitler's dozen fortress-ports had thwarted the Allied plans.

The two secret man-made Mulberry harbours on the Normandy coast had performed superbly and supplied the bridgeheads with everything then needed. Now the front lines were stretched 300 miles away and one, but preferably two, major ports were urgently needed, if the Siegfried line and the Ruhr defences were to be breached.

Just before Operation Market Garden, the famous 'bridge too far', took place in mid-September, Prime Minister Winston Churchill was writing, 'This was the end of the great pursuit. For the next few months we could only advance after very hard fighting. Everywhere enemy resistance was stiffening and our supplies had been stretched to the limit. These had to be restored and the forward troops reinforced and replenished for the coming autumn battles.' To the Chief of Staffs Committee he wrote on 8 September 1944, 'Apart from Cherbourg and Arromanches [Mulberry] we have not yet obtained any large harbours. The Germans intend to defend the mouth of the Scheldt and are still resisting in the northern suburbs of Antwerp. Brest has not been taken in spite of very heavy fighting. Lorient still holds out. No attempt has been made to take and clear the port of St Nazaire which is about twice as good as Brest and twice as easy to take. No attempt has been made to get hold of Bordeaux. Unless the *situation changes remarkably* the Allies will still be short of port accommodation when the equinoctial gales are due.... No one can tell what the future may bring forth. Will the Allies be able to advance in strength through the Siegfried line into Germany during September or will their forces be so limited by supply conditions and *the lack of ports* as to enable the Germans to consolidate on the Siegfried line?'

Although the great commanders made light of it afterwards in their memoirs it was a desperate situation. Besides the very serious lack of supplies, the German secret weapons, V-1s and V-2s were taking a savage toll of life in southeast England. Besides opening—come what may—a number of vital ports the Allies were determined to winkle out and subdue the scores of rocket launching sites in northwest France and parts of Holland.

Left behind and almost forgotten in the mad stampede into the Low Countries, American, Canadian and British forces with great support from the RAF/USAAF and the Royal Navy and US Navy, were fighting a score of brutal 'little' battles. On the western flank in Brittany, American forces seized Cherbourg, quickly took St Malo, invested Brest and surrounded Lorient and St Nazaire. (All classified by Hitler as 'fortress-ports'). On the eastern flank, Canadian and British forces took Rouen, Dieppe, besieged Calais, Boulogne and Dunkirk, and in a classic all-arms attack captured Le Havre. In a bravado armoured dash, British armoured forces captured Antwerp. Beside himself with rage, the Führer declared Flushing and the island of Walcheren to be 'Fortress Scheldt' to deny access to Antwerp.

Many famous names connected with Overlord are imprinted in the history books of World War Two, the famous D-Day beaches of Juno, Sword and Gold, and to the west Omaha and Utah, and the bitter attritional battles fought after D-Day: Epsom, Mitten, Jupiter, Greenline, Charnwood, Goodwood, Bluecoat, Totalize, Tractable and Cobra. But who now knows about Astonia, Wellhit, Undergo, Infatuate, Switchback, Vitality and Calendar? Those were the operational code names for the combined assaults on Hitler's fortress-ports, attacks by land, sea and air to secure and open harbours to get the supplies moving again. Some of those forces involved referred to themselves as the 'Cinderella' units. This is the story of the Cinderella War.

None of the Allied generals: Eisenhower, Montgomery, Bradley, Patton, Crerar or Horrocks, were interested in the slow, horrible, grinding battles to invest and reduce Hitler's fortresses. There was no glamour attached (Montgomery admitted this), no fame and few press headlines in the dreary, attritional fighting and the equally hard and deadly work, after their capture, of restoring the harbours to working order. The heroes in this book are the men of the forgotten armies who fought in the Cinderella War.

A Dedication

The Americans   To the 'Lightning' Joe Collins GIs who slogged their way up the Cotentin peninsula to capture Cherbourg; to Macon's men, who caught the Nazi 'Mad Major' in St Malo; and to Patton's 'stepchildren' who eventually seized Brest; and not forgetting the green GIs, who invested German garrisons, many times their size, in the 'mousetrap' war around St Nazaire and Lorient.

The Canadians   To Crerar's 'Canooks' who with set-piece attacks took Dieppe, Boulogne, Cap Gris Nez, Calais, invested Dunkirk and as the 'water-rats', in dreadful conditions, occupied the watery polders in the Breskens pocket and the Beveland Islands.

The British   To the Scottish Lowlanders who were first blooded at Flushing, Beveland and Walcheren; and to the Highland (51st) and Polar Bears (49th) divisions who jointly captured Le Havre in a classic all-arms masterpiece of planning and determination. To Hobart's terrible 'zoo' of Funnies who flamed, flailed, petarded and carried British and Canadian troops in a score of encounters; and to the dashing Black Bull (11th Armoured Division) who captured Antwerp single-handed and upset all the Führer's plans.

The Air Forces   To the RAF and USAAF who dropped tens of thousands of bombs in support of all the Cinderella War sieges. They had little effect on U-boat and E-boat pens or the impregnable gun casements, but they breached vital sea-walls and were a great morale booster.

The Royal Navy   To the trio HMS *Warspite*, *Erebus* and *Roberts* sent to bombard most of the fortress-ports, and RN cruisers who joined the US Navy off Cherbourg and Brest. To the gallant Royal Marine commando brigade who stormed the Westkapelle fortress on Walcheren—an epic encounter. To the RN port-clearance parties, who cleared up mines and wreckage in every devastated port, working closely with their opposite American teams. To the crews of the 100 RN minesweepers, who eventually cleared 55 miles of Scheldt river estuary and Antwerp harbour. And the small ships, destroyers, frigates and motor torpedo boats who fought—and won—a score of dashing, savage little battles off the Channel ports against enemy R-boats, E-boats, AF barges, minesweepers and submarine chasers.

The Cinderella War lasted six months. It involved American, Canadian and British formations and was fought in appalling conditions on the ground, in the air and on the seas.

CHAPTER ONE

Adolf Hitler's Fortress-Ports and the Secret Edicts

THE FIRST STRATEGIC ORDERS OF THE GERMAN FÜHRER WERE promulgated in June 1936. Just before the Anschluss with Austria in March 1938 a numbered series called Führer Weisungen, or Führer directives, were issued. They were intended quite clearly to be his orders, some of an immediate, some of a long-term, nature. Number One was for the occupation of Austria, and on the same day Number Two was for the actual (bloodless) invasion of that country. Poor Czechoslovakia was the subject of 'Fall Green' (Case Green) for Edicts Numbers Three and Four respectively in May and October 1939. But after the attack on Poland, Hitler began a new numbered series of Führer Weisungen.

Around Christmas 1940, months after the defeat of the British Expeditionary Force (BEF), and the successful evacuation of most of the British and some of the French armies from Dunkirk, Hitler made a tour of the western front. Operation Sealion (the invasion of England) had been scaled down and then cancelled. Dr Felix Todt's vast organization of mainly slave workers had constructed huge, casemented big-gun coastal batteries around Calais, Cap Gris-Nez and Dunkirk called *Grosser Kurfurst* (Great Elector), 'Siegfried' and 'Gneisenau'. His special inspection train was ambushed by the RAF on 23 December 1940 near Boulogne and had to be rapidly shunted into a long safe railway tunnel guarded by anti-aircraft (AA) guns at each end. By September 1940 Churchill noted the growth of the German heavy batteries along the Channel coast:

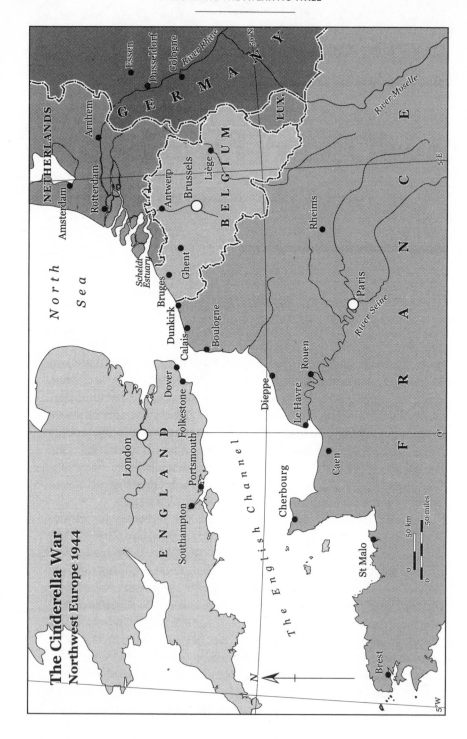

The Cinderella War
Northwest Europe 1944

a) Siegfried battery south of Gris-Nez, four 38 cm guns
b) Friedrich August battery, north of Boulogne, three 30.5 cm guns
c) Grosser Kurfurst battery at Gris-Nez, four 28 cm guns
d) Prinz Heinrich battery between Calais and Blanc-Nez, two 28 cm guns
e) Oldenburg battery, east of Calais, two 24 cm guns
f) M1, M2, M3, M4 batteries Griz-Nez–Calais, fourteen 17 cm guns and a further 35 heavy and medium batteries plus seven batteries of captured guns sited along French coast.

(*Their Finest Hour* Vol 2 of *The Second World War*)

These almost impregnable coastal batteries were intended not only to harass Channel convoys, but were the first steps towards the building of the famous Atlantic Wall. Hitler knew that Britain and the Allies would be back in Europe sooner or later. A week before Operation Barbarossa, the invasion of Russia started in June 1941, he sent Hermann Goering's deputy, Field Marshal Erhard Milch to ensure urgent reinforcements were in place along the Dutch coastal ports to prevent or deter a British attack.

Edict Number 39 in July 1941 related to the defeat of his initial blitzkrieg in Russia. He wrote, 'We are justified in risking a purely temporary weakening of our forces in France during the winter. Battle-tried officers, NCOs and men from the divisions in the east which are to be relieved may be posted to the divisions in the west. Beyond this I will decide whether divisions in the west which cannot be employed in the east as *full* divisions should be disbanded and employed to reinforce seasoned divisions on the eastern front. *At all events* the strength of the army in the west must be maintained so that it is capable of coastal defence and of carrying out Undertaking Attila. Young workers classified as essential will be released from their employment on a large scale and will be replaced by prisoners and Russian civilian workers, employed in groups. The High Command of the Armed Forces will issue special orders in this respect.' On 20 October 1941 on his own initiative Hitler issued an OKW (Wehrmachtfuhr-ungsstab, Abt Landesverteidigung) order, 'large-scale English operations against the western occupied areas remain unlikely... but account must be taken of the possibility that the English may at any time carry out isolated attacks as the result of pressure from their eastern allies and for political and propaganda reasons.' He was sure that the Channel Islands would be recaptured, 'Of considerable importance for our escort traffic.' Hitler did not use the term 'fortress' on this occasion but he personally went into great detail specifying the number, calibre and type of the coastal batteries, the details of the heavily reinforced concrete works and the thickness of the casement walls in millimetres. The Todt organization had to render monthly construction reports. The Führer had an immense collection of large-scale maps which he kept locked up in his own desk for his own personal scrutiny.

On 14 December 1941 Hitler decided to expand, in grandiose fashion, the quick achievements in the Channel Islands into what became known as Hitler's West Wall. The *whole* Atlantic coastline was now the almost impossible objective, 'Construction of a new west wall to assure the protection of the Arctic, North Sea and Atlantic coasts.' The strategy was, 'To assure protection against any leading operation even of very considerable strength with the employment of the smallest possible number of *static* forces.' In order of priority and urgency of construction, curiously enough, Norway was made first. Perhaps the Führer thought that Churchill wanted revenge for the fiasco of the British-French operations in the winter of 1939–40. Next came the coasts of Belgium and France which according to General Walther Warlimont (head of the 'national defence' section of the OKW), by agreement with Section Land, the high commands of the services, were divided into the following sectors. In the first category was the area between the mouths of the River Seine and the Scheldt, plus the area south of Brest and the area from Quiberon to the Gironde (protecting, of course, the great U-boat pens). In the second category were the Normandy and Brittany peninsulas. Third place was allotted to the coasts of Holland and the western and northern coast of Jutland. Finally came the German Bight. Fortifications on the coasts of the Baltic were to be dismantled and only the approaches through the Kattegat were to remain blocked. This was the initial plan for Hitler's subsequent 'Fortress Europa', based on the assumption that Russia would soon be rendered hors de combat.

By March 1942 the possible threats in the west were deemed much greater and Directive Number 40 was issued, now quoted in full.

The Führer and Supreme Commander   **Führer Headquarters**
of the Armed Forces   **23 March 1942**

         25 copies

OKW/WFST/OpNo 001031
        Directive Number 40
Ref. Competence of Commanders in coastal areas
I. *General considerations:*

The coastline of Europe will, in the coming months, be exposed to the danger of an enemy landing in force.

The time and place of the landing operations will not be dictated to the enemy by operational considerations alone. Failure in other theatres of war, obligations to allies, and political considerations may persuade him to take decisions which appear unlikely from a purely military point of view.

Even enemy *landings with limited objectives* can interfere seriously with our own plans if they result in the enemy gaining any kind of foothold on the coast. They can interrupt our coastal sea traffic, and pin down strong forces of our army and air force, which will therefore have to be withdrawn from areas of crucial importance. It would be particularly dangerous should the enemy succeed in capturing our airfields or in establishing his own in areas which he has occupied.

The many important military and industrial establishments on the coast or in its neighbourhood, some of them equipped with particularly valuable plant, may moreover tempt the enemy *to undertake surprise attacks of a local nature.*

Particular attention must be paid to English *preparations for landings* on the open coast, for which they have at their disposal many armoured landing craft, built to carry armoured fighting vehicles and heavy weapons. The possibility of *parachute and airborne attacks* on a large scale must also be envisaged.

II *General operational instructions for coastal defence:*

1. *Coastal defence is a task for all armed forces,* calling for particularly close and complete co-operation by all units.

2. The intelligence service, as well as the day-to-day reconnaissance by the *navy* and the *air force,* must strive to obtain early information of enemy *readiness and approach preparations* for a landing operation.

   All suitable sea and air forces will then concentrate on enemy points of embarkation and convoys, with the aim of destroying the enemy as far from the coast as possible.

   It is however possible that the enemy, by skilful camouflage and by taking advantage of unpredictable weather conditions, may achieve a complete surprise attack. *All troops* who may be exposed to such surprise attacks must be in *a state of permanent readiness.*

One of the most important duties of commanding officers will be to overcome the lack of vigilance among the troops which, as experience has shown, increases with the passage of time.

3. *In defending the coast*—and this includes *coastal waters* within range of medium coastal artillery—*responsibility for the planning and implementation of defensive measures* must, as recent battle experience dictates, lie unequivocally and reservedly in the hands of a single commander.

The commander responsible must make use of all available forces and weapons of the branches of the armed forces, of organizations and units outside the armed forces, and of our civil headquarters in the area, for the destruction of enemy transports and landing forces. He will use them so that the attack collapses *if possible before it can reach the coast, at the latest on the coast itself.*

Enemy forces which have landed must be destroyed or thrown back into the sea by immediate counterattack. All personnel bearing arms—irrespective to which branch of the armed forces or to which non-service organization they may belong—will be employed for this. Moreover, the required working capacity of the naval shore supply establishments must be guaranteed, insofar as they are not involved in the land fighting themselves. The same applies to the readiness for action of the air force ground staff and the anti-aircraft defence of airfields.

No headquarters or formation is to initiate withdrawal in such circumstances. All German troops stationed on or near the coast must be armed and trained for battle.

The enemy must be prevented from securing a foothold on all islands which could present a threat to the mainland or coastal shipping.

4. *The distribution of forces and the extension of defensive works* must be so carried out that our strongest defence points are situated in those sectors most likely to be chosen by the enemy for landings (fortified areas).

Other coastal sectors which may be threatened by small-scale surprise attacks will be defended by a series of strong-points, supported if possible by the coastal batteries. All military and industrial plant of importance to the war effort will be included within these strongpoints.

The same principles will apply to offshore islands.

Less-threatened sectors will be kept under observation.

5. *The division of the coast into sectors* will be decided by the three services in mutual agreement, or, should the situation demand it, by the responsible commander (referred to here in paragraph III, 1), whose decision will be final.

6. *The fortified areas and strong points* must be able, by proper distribution of forces, by completion of all-round defence, and by their supply situation, to hold out for some time even against superior enemy forces.

Fortified areas and strong points will be defended to the last man. They must never be forced to surrender from lack of ammunition, rations, or water.

7. The responsible commander (referred to here in paragraph III, 2) will issue orders for keeping the coast under constant observation, and ensure that reconnaissance reports from all services are quickly evaluated, co-ordinated, and transmitted to the headquarters and civilian authorities concerned.

As soon as there is any evidence that an operation by the enemy is imminent, the commander is authorized to issue the necessary instructions for co-ordinated and complementary reconnaissance on sea and land.

8. There can be no question of peace-time privileges for any headquarters or formation of the armed forces in coastal areas, or for nonmilitary organizations and units. Their accommodation, security precautions, equipment, immediate readiness for action, and the use they make of the terrain, will be entirely dependent upon the necessity of meeting any enemy attack as swiftly and in as great strength as possible. Where the military situation requires it, the civilian population will be immediately evacuated.

III. *Competence of commanders*

1. The following are responsible for the preparation and execution of coastal defence in the *areas under German command:*

(a) In the eastern area of operations (excluding Finland):
The army commanders appointed by the High Command of the Army.

(b) In the coastal area of Army High Command Lapland:
Commander-in-Chief Army High Command Lapland.

(c) In Norway:
Commander Armed Forces Norway.

(d) In Denmark:
The Commander of German troops in Denmark.

(e) In the occupied western territories (including the Netherlands):
Commander-in-Chief West.

For coastal defence the responsible commanders in (d) and (e) will be directly subordinate to the High Command of the Armed Forces.

(f) In the Balkans (including the occupied islands):
Commander Armed Forces Southeast.

(g) In the Baltic Territories and the Ukraine:
Commander Armed Forces Baltic Territories and Ukraine.

(h) In the home theatre of war: the commanding admirals.

2. The commanders named in paragraph III, 1 will have for these tasks full powers of command over the staffs commanding all armed forces, the German civil authorities, and the nonmilitary units and organizations in their area.

In exercising their authority they will issue the necessary tactical, administrative, and supply instructions, and will ensure that they are complied with. In all matters relating to land fighting, training of units will follow their ruling, and all necessary information will be put at their disposal.

3. Among the orders to be given and measure to be taken, the following must *be given first place.*

(a) The inclusion within fortified areas of strongpoints of all important military and industrial establishments connected with defence, particularly those of the navy (submarine bases) and the air force.

(b) The co-ordination of coastal reconnaissance.

(c) The defence of fortified areas and strong-points by infantry.

(d) The defence by infantry of all isolated positions outside the fortified areas and strong points—e.g., coastal lookout points and air-attack warning-posts.

(e) Artillery defence against land targets. (The navy has priority in the installation of new batteries, or the conversion of existing batteries.)

(f) The defensive readiness, development, and supply facilities of installations, as well as of isolated positions away from these installations. (This includes being equipped with all weapons needed for defence: mines, hand-grenades, flame-throwers, barbed wire, etc.)

(g) The signals network.

(h) Methods for ensuring that troops are always on the alert, and that infantry and gunnery training is being carried out in accordance with the special defence requirements.

4. *The same authority is conferred upon local commanders up to sector commanders*, insofar as they are responsible for the defence of a part of the coast.

The commanders designated in paragraph III, 1 will, in general, appoint commanders of *army divisions* employed in coastal defence as local commanders with full powers. In Crete the Fortress Commandant Crete will appoint them.

As far as their other duties allow, local commandants or commanders of the air force and navy will be made responsible for the general defence of individual sectors or subsectors, particularly air and naval strongpoints.

5. *All naval and air units employed in strategic warfare* are subordinate to the navy or air force. In the event of enemy attacks on the coast, however, they are required to comply, insofar as tactical considerations allow, with the orders for the commanders responsible for defence. They must therefore be included in the distribution of such information as they require for their duties, and close liaison will be maintained with their headquarters.

IV *Special duties of the branches of the armed forces in the field of coastal defence.*

1. *Navy*

(a) Organization and protection of coastal traffic.

(b) Training and employment of all coastal artillery against targets at sea.

(c) Employment of naval forces.

2. *Air Force*

(a) Air defence of coastal areas. The use against enemy landings of suitable and available anti-aircraft guns, under the orders of the commander responsible for local defence, will not be affected.

(b) The completion of ground organizations and their protection against air attack and surprise attack by land; the latter in cases where airfields are not included in the coastal defences and are therefore insufficiently protected.

(c) Operational employment of air forces. Attention will be paid to the duplication of command implied by these special duties.

V Orders and instructions which run contrary to this directive are cancelled from 1 April 1942.

New operation orders, which will be issued by commanders on the basis of my directive, are to be submitted to me through the High Command of the Armed Forces (OKW).

Signed: ADOLF HITLER

It may have been coincidence or efficient Abwehr espionage information received, but on 27 March Hitler was convinced that the Cherbourg and Brest peninsulas might be on Churchill's 'setting Europe alight' list of targets. He thus ordered all available reserves immediately to the area west of Caen and further west, to St Nazaire. The U-boat base there was heavily reinforced. The next morning a combined Royal Naval and commando raid with the old destroyer *Campbelltown* took place. Many commandoes were killed or taken prisoner, but the docks were put out of action—for the time being. Hitler ordered the Atlantic defences still further strengthened. Directive Number 41, dated 5 April was mainly concerned with new offensives in the east but Hitler also stressed, 'At the same time, the security of occupied territories in Western and Northern Europe, *especially along the coast* will be ensured in all circumstances.'

Minister of Armaments Albert Speer, perhaps one of the closest 'Führer observers', wrote of Hitler, 'Amateurishness was one of Hitler's dominant traits. He had never learned a profession and basically had always remained an outsider to all fields of endeavour. Like many self-taught people, he had no idea what real specialized knowledge meant. Without any sense of the complexities of any great task he boldly assumed one function after another... the victories of the early years of the war can literally be attributed to Hitler's ignorance of the rules of the game and his layman's delight in decision making. Since the opposing side was trained to apply rules which Hitler's self-taught autocratic mind did not know and did not use, he achieved surprises. These audacities, *coupled with military superiority*, were the basis of his early successes. But as soon as setbacks occurred he suffered shipwreck, like most untrained people. Hitler made himself into an armaments and tank 'expert'. He had a large book, according to Albert Speer, in a red binding with broad yellow stripes. It was a catalogue of 30–50 different types of ordnance and ammunition, constantly updated and was the book he kept on his bedroom night table.

Albert Speer was convinced that Hitler's technical knowledge and ideas were based on his First World War experience of traditional weapons. He had little inclination to pursue development of modern radar, rocketry, jet fighters or crucially the atom bomb. He changed his mind several times on the jet fighter and muddled up Operation Waterfall at Peenemüde on the V-1 and V-2 rockets, as Speer points out in his memoirs. Speer noted that 5,000 long-range rockets, five months production, would produce the equivalent of only 3,750 tons of bombs, whereas a *single* attack by the RAF and USAAF could deliver 8,000 tons.

During the summer of 1942 Luftwaffe photographs showed that between Portsmouth and Portland Bay 3,000 small craft had been assembled. In occupied France, the Resistance movement was sabotaging railroads causing Hitler to worry that reserve troops would be held up in the event of a probable invasion. When General Franz Halder, Chief of General Staff, suggested sending an armoured panzer division to the west, Hitler agreed and ordered three others already in reserve to stay in place and available.

A conference was held on 29 June with Field Marshal Von Rundstedt's new chief of staff in the west (General Zeitler) and with Albert Speer (who had taken over from Todt) and Alfred Jacob (in charge of fortifications and engineering). Hitler felt that a major Anglo-US invasion was now being planned. On 9 July he predicted that areas within Allied fighter range and suitable for small craft landings could be attacked. He also predicted a landing in Normandy or between Dieppe and Le Havre. He wrote, 'In the event of an Allied invasion I will proceed to the west and take command myself.' Abwehr agents in Madrid reported that the Allies had assembled 2,400 landing craft for a strong combined operation towards the end of August 1942. On 13 August an Abwehr agent in England reported that the target would be Dieppe. The ill-fated Operation Rutter, renamed Jubilee, supported by Admiral Mountbatten (but not by General Montgomery) took place on 19 August. Two brigades of Canadian troops, British Commandos, 30 tanks and the full might of the RAF and Royal Navy were bloodily repulsed. Some 4,000 troops were casualties, 100 RAF planes were lost and a destroyer and 33 landing craft destroyed.

That same month on the 13th in the Werewolf Hitler's field HQ at Rastenburg, East Prussia Führer Protokoll, Point 48 was issued to Albert Speer, Adjutant Colonel Schmidt, Field Marshal Wilhelm Keitel, Admiral Krancke, General of Engineers Jacob and the head engineer of Todt (Xavier Dorsch). Hitler's requirements for the Atlantic Wall were formidable. In order to deter a beach head in Western Europe, 15,000 concrete bunkers must be built, many at 50 metre intervals to protect the ten most vital war bases or 'fortresses'. The rest would be positioned at 100 metre intervals along the entire coast. An armed force of 500,000 troops with 150,000 in reserve would be needed. Field Marshal Von Rundstedt had by mid-August 29 divisions in the west including the 'Gross Deutschland', the 'Hermann Goering', plus two parachute, two SS and four panzer divisions.

Hitler had done his homework. He had studied carefully all the coastal area maps and had sent his staff movie cameraman, Walther Frentz to tour the *whole* coastline. Mile after mile was shown to be totally undefended! Hitler wrote, 'Our most costly substance is the German man. The blood these fortifications will spare is worth the billions.' Barbed-wire defences, extensive minefields, and enfilading bunkers would cover the beaches. Decoy sites would be designed to attract attention but the main coastal batteries and the U-boat pens were to be built to withstand *any* bombs or naval shells. The ceilings and walls would have four metres of concrete and all the coastal troops would be under cover. So too would the anti-tank guns, tanks and heavy machine guns, as Hitler now knew of the power of the RAF and Royal Navy. He wrote, 'It is wisest to consider our own Luftwaffe so weak in the west as to be nonexistent.' Hitler considered that the Allies might use gas, napalm bombs, or flame-throwers and that the main invasion would have a parachute and glider troop attack at night to seize vital canals, aerodromes, and rail stations preceded by very heavy bomber attacks. He was sure the invasion would come at dawn with thousands of landing craft under cover of an enormous air force and naval armada. This vital planning operation took place five days before the Dieppe raid! The Atlantic Wall had to be finished by the end of April 1943.

The Todt organization constructed three types of coastal defence works. The smallest was a single self-contained post for up to platoon strength, known as Widerstandsnest, a 'resistance nest'. Several of these combined for co-ordinated defence for a larger sector, up to company strength with heavy weapons was known as a Stuepunkt. A pillbox was known as a Blockhaus. Heavily casemented defence areas in ports, submarine pens or mouths of river/port estuaries were called Verteidigungs Bereiche, manned by appropriate local reserves. The heavy gun batteries, *batterie*, had priority for quantity and quality of steel-reinforced concrete, often up to twenty feet in depth. They were impregnable except to a direct hit by an RAF 6 ton Tallboy bomb. The German navy and army differed on siting and design of coastal batteries. The navy believed they should be sited forward on the coastline in heavily protected casements of steel and concrete to engage ships at sea by *direct* fire. The army felt casements should be concealed further back with wide fields of fire, able to bring down *indirect* fire on the beaches and on landing craft approaching. Disputes between navy and army on the building of the Atlantic Wall were referred to Hitler. He gave no decision but favoured the naval system which sacrificed a wide field of fire for protection in closed casements.

Engineer Eisenrieth inspected the Todt workers fortifying St Malo and noted French, Polish Czech, Dutch, Belgian, Algerian and Spanish workers employed. Work in shifts went on nonstop through the night and day, week after week. In the Channel Islands the extensive fortifications required 250,000 cubic metres of excavation, consumed over 500,000 cubic metres of reinforced concrete, 250,000 metric tons of cement and over 37,000 tons of reinforcing steel. More than 40 million man hours of labour was required.

Albert Speer wrote in his memoirs *Inside the Third Reich,*

As early as August 1942, Hitler had assured the naval leadership that the Allies could not make a successful invasion unless they were *able to take a sizeable port.* Without one, he pointed out, an enemy landing at any point on the coast could not receive sufficient supplies long enough to withstand counterattacks by the German forces. Given the great length of the French, Belgian and Dutch coasts, a complete line of pillboxes spaced close enough to offer mutual protection would have far exceeded the capacity of the German construction industry. Moreover, there were not enough soldiers available to man such a large number of pillboxes. Consequently, the larger ports were ringed with pillboxes, while the intervening coastal areas were only protected by observation bunkers at long intervals. Some 15,000 smaller bunkers were intended to shelter the soldiers during the shelling prior to an attack. As Hitler conceived it, however, during the actual attack the soldiers would come out into the open, since a protected position undermines those qualities of courage and personal initiative which were essential for battle.

Hitler planned these defensive installations down to the smallest details. He even designed the various types of bunkers and pillboxes, usually in the hours of the night. The designs were only sketches, but they were executed with precision. Never sparing in self-praise, he often remarked that his designs ideally met all the requirements of a frontline soldier. They were adopted almost without revision by the general of the Corps of Engineers.

For this task we consumed, in barely two years of intensive building, 17,300,000 cubic yards of concrete worth 3.7 billion DM. In addition the armaments factories were deprived of 1.2 million metric tons of iron. All this expenditure and effort was sheer waste. By means of a single brilliant technical idea the enemy bypassed these defences within two weeks after the first landing. For as is well known, the invasion troops brought their own port with them. At Arromanches and Omaha Beach they built loading ramps and other installations on the open coast, following carefully laid out plans. Thus they were able to assure their supplies of ammunition, implements, and rations, as well as the landing of reinforcements. Our whole plan of defence had proved irrelevant.

In fact Luftwaffe aerial photographs of southern England showed large contraptions lying in the Thames estuary. The experts in Berlin estimated they were anything from floating grain elevators to substitute piers for use in a captured harbour. Correct interpretation plus interdiction bombing by the Luftwaffe might have delayed Overlord by many months.

General Jacob thought that the Führer's orders for permanent coastal fortifications were 'impossible demands'. In the autumn of 1942 Admiral Wilhelm Canaris, the Abwehr chief, produced reports that the Allies were planning a Second Front against the Cherbourg peninsula.

On 29 September in the Chancellery's Cabinet room, Hitler reminded Von Rundstedt, Albert Speer, Hermann Goering and several of his generals, 'Let us be quite plain about one point, a major enemy landing in the west could precipitate a real crisis.' It was a three-hour long secret speech about the 'only one remaining danger for the outcome of the war....the emergence of a Second Front in the west, as the fighting in the east and the home base would be directly endangered by this....if we can prevent (an invasion in the west) until the spring (of 1943 when the Atlantic Wall would be prepared) nothing can happen to us any longer.'

In February 1943 Adolf Hitler predicted a simultaneous invasion of the Channel and the Atlantic coastlines where his Atlantic Wall—clearly identified by RAF photographic planes—could be seen to be some months short of completion. He warned Von Rundstedt to expect possible mass parachute landings in the rear of the coastal defences. 1943 was a traumatic year for the Führer, with disasters in Russia, North Africa, Sicily and Italy. A third Russian winter would be too much for human blood and flesh. And the dreaded Second Front was imminent.

On 25 October Field Marshal Von Rundstedt submitted a lengthy report to the Führer. He wrote that the defence of France would stand or fall at the Atlantic Wall, but the wall itself was largely bluff and propaganda. Any German retreat there would provide the enemy with the harbours that they needed and deprive Germany of her U-boat bases and coastal convoys. His (Von Rundstedt's) divisions were too weak in both men and equipment to fight a war of movement against a superior enemy. At a conference with Hitler on 30 October Jodl supported Von Rundstedt's main contention, that whatever else the Allies might undertake in Scandinavia or the Balkans, a spring 1944 invasion of France was a certainty, because only the loss of the Ruhr would finally defeat Germany. Also Churchill would certainly neutralize the A-4 (V-2) missile sites in northern France. Jodl demanded a massive effort using impressed French labour and prisoners of war to reinforce the Channel defences. Hitler agreed and on 3 November issued the last of his *numbered* directives, Number 51.

The Führer **Führer Headquarters**

3 November 1943
27 copies

OKW/WFST/OpNo 662656/43
Directive Number 51

The hard and costly struggle against Bolshevism during the last two and a half years, which has involved the bulk of our military strength in the east, has demanded extreme exertions. The greatness of the danger and the general situation demanded it. But the situation has since changed. The danger in the east remains, but a greater danger now appears in the west: an Anglo-Saxon landing! In the east, the vast extent of the territory makes it possible for us to lose ground, even on a large scale, without a fatal blow being dealt to the nervous system of Germany.

It is very different in the west! Should the enemy succeed in breaching our defences on a wide front here, the immediate consequences would be unpredictable. Everything indicates that the enemy will launch an offensive against the western front of Europe, at the latest in the spring, perhaps even earlier.

I can therefore no longer take responsibility for further weakening the west, in favour of other theatres of war. I have therefore decided to reinforce its defences, particularly those places from which the long range bombardment of England will begin. For it is here that the enemy must and will attack, and it is here—unless all indications are misleading—that the decisive battle against the landing forces will be fought.

Holding and diversionary attacks are to be expected on other fronts. A large-scale attack on Denmark is also not out of the question. From a naval point of view such an attack would be more difficult to deliver, nor could it be as effectively supported by air, but if successful, its political and operational repercussions would be very great.

At the beginning of the battle the whole offensive strength of the enemy is bound to be thrown against our forces holding the coastline. Only by intensive construction, which means straining our available manpower and materials at home and in the occupied territories to the limit, can we strengthen our coastal defences in the short time which probably remains.

The ground weapons which will shortly reach Denmark and the occupied areas in the west (heavy anti-tank guns, immobile tanks to be sunk in emplacements, coastal artillery, artillery against landing troops, mines, etc.) will be concentrated at strongpoints in the most threatened areas on the coast. Because of this, we must face the fact that the defences of less-threatened sectors cannot be improved in the near future.

Should the enemy, by assembling all his forces, succeed in landing, he must be met with a counterattack delivered with all our weight. The problem will be by the rapid concentration of adequate forces and material, and by intensive training, to form the large units available to us into an offensive reserve of high fighting quality, attacking power, and mobility, whose counterattack will prevent the enemy from exploiting the landing, and throw him back into the sea.

Moreover, careful and detailed emergency plans must be drawn up so that everything we have in Germany, and in the coastal areas which have not been attacked, and which is in any way capable of action, is hurled immediately against the invading enemy.

The air force and navy must go into action against the heavy attacks which we must expect by air and sea with all the forces at their disposal, regardless of the losses.

I therefore order as follows:

A. Army
1. *The Chief of the Army General Staff and the Inspector General of Armoured Forces* will submit to me without delay a plan for the distribution, within the next three months, of weapons, tanks, self-propelled guns, motor vehicles, and ammunition on the western front and in Denmark, in accordance with the requirements of the new situation.

   The plan will rest on the following basic principles:
   (a) All armoured and armoured grenadier divisions in the west will be assured of adequate mobility, and each will be equipped with 93 Mark IV tanks or self-propelled guns and with strong anti-tank weapons by the end of December 1943.

   The 20th Air Force Field Division will be converted into an effective mobile offensive formation by the allocation of self-propelled artillery before the end of 1943.

   SS Armoured Grenadier division 'HJ' [Hitler Youth], 21st Armoured Divison, and the infantry and reserve divisions stationed in Jutland will be brought up to full armed strength with speed.
   (b) There will be a further reinforcement with Mark IV self-propelled guns and heavy anti-tank guns of armoured divisions in reserve in the west and in Denmark, and of the self-propelled artillery training unit in Denmark.
   (c) A monthly allocation of 100 heavy anti-tank guns Marks 40 and 43 (of which half will be mobile), for the months of November and December, in addition to the heavy anti-tank guns, will be made to the newly raised formations in the west.

(d) An increased allocation of weapons (including about 1,000 machine guns) will be made to improve the equipment of ground forces engaged in coastal defence in the west and in Denmark, and to co-ordinate the equipment of units which are to be withdrawn from sectors not under attack.

(e) A liberal supply of short range anti-tank weapons will be granted to formations stationed in threatened areas.

(f) The fire power in artillery and anti-tank guns of formation stationed in Denmark and on the coasts of occupied territories in the west, will be increased, and army artillery will be strengthened.

2. No units or formations stationed in the west and in Denmark, nor any of the newly raised self-propelled armoured artillery or anti-tank units in the west, will be withdrawn to other fronts without my approval.

   The Chief of the Army General Staff and the Inspector General of Armoured Forces will report to me, through the high command of the armed forces (operations staff), when the equipment of armoured units, self-propelled artillery units, and light anti-tank units and companies is complete.

3. Commander-in-Chief West will decide which additional formations from sectors of the front that have not been under attack can be moved up and made capable of an offensive role, by a timetable of exercises in the field and similar training measures. In this connection, I insist that areas unlikely to be threatened should be ruthlessly stripped of all except the smallest forces essential for guard duties. In areas from which these reserves are drawn, units will be formed from security and emergency forces for duties of surveillance and protection. Our labour units employed on construction will open the lines of communication which will probably be destroyed by the enemy, employing for this the help of the local population on an extensive scale.

4. The Commander of German troops in Denmark will adopt the measures outlined in paragraph 3 for the area under his command.

5. The Chief of Army Equipment and Commander of the Replacement Army will raise battle groups of regimental strength in the home defence area from training depots,

troops under instruction, army schools, training locations and recuperative establishments. These will form security and engineer-construction battalions, and will be ready, on receipt of special orders, to move within forty-eight hours of being called up.

In addition, all further personnel available will be incorporated in infantry units and equipped with such weapons as are available, so that they may immediately replace the heavy casualties to be expected.

B. *Air Force*

In view of the new situation, the offensive and defensive power of formations of the air force stationed in the west and in Denmark will be increased. Plans will be drawn up to ensure that all forces available and suitable for defensive operations will be taken from flying units and mobile anti-aircraft artillery units engaged in home defence, from schools and training units in the home defence area, and will be employed in the west and if necessary in Denmark.

Ground establishments in southern Norway, Denmark, northwestern Germany and the west will be organized and supplied so that, by the largest possible degree of decentralization, our own units are not exposed to enemy bombing at the beginning of large-scale operations, and the weight of the enemy attack will be effectively broken up. This applies particularly to our fighter forces, whose ability to go into action must be increased by the establishment of a number of emergency airfields. Particular attention will be paid to good camouflage. In this connection also I expect all possible forces to be made available for action regardless of the circumstances, by stripping less-threatened areas of their troops.

C. *Navy*

The navy will draw up plans for bringing into action naval forces capable of attacking the enemy landing fleet with all their strength. Coastal defences under construction will be completed with all possible speed, and the establishment of additional coastal batteries and the laying of further obstacles on the flanks will be considered.

Preparations will be made for the employment of all ranks capable of fighting, from schools, training establishments and other land establishments, so that they may be deployed with the least possible delay, if only on security duties, in the battle area where enemy landings have taken place.

In the naval plans for strengthening defences in the west, special attention will be given to defence against enemy landings in Norway or Denmark. In this connection, I attach particular importance to plans for using large numbers of submarines in the northern sea areas. A temporary diminution of submarine forces in the Atlantic must be accepted.

D. *SS*

The Reichsführer SS will test the preparedness of units of the Waffen-SS and police for operational, security, and guard duties. Preparations will be made to raise battle-trained formations for operational and security duties from training, reserve, and recuperative establishments, and from schools and other units in the home defence area.

E. Commanders-in-chief of the branches of the armed forces, the Reichsführer SS, the Chief of the Army General Staff, Commander-in-Chief West, the Chief of Army Equipment and Commander of the Replacement Army, the Inspector-General of Armoured Forces, and the Commander of German troops in Denmark will report to me by 15 November the steps taken and those which they propose to take.

I expect all staffs concerned to exert every effort during the time which still remains in preparation for the *expected decisive battle in the west.*

All those responsible will ensure that time and manpower are not wasted in dealing with questions of jurisdiction, but that they are employed in increasing our powers of defence and attack.

Signed: ADOLF HITLER

Two days later, on 5 November, Field Marshal Erwin Rommel was safely back from the debacle with the Afrika Korps. After a month or so inspecting the defences in northern Italy he was entrusted with a new role—the defence of the Atlantic Wall. Von Rundstedt noted, 'I had over 3,000 miles of coastline to cover from the Italian frontier in the south to the German frontier in the north and only 60 divisions with which to defend it. Most of them were low-grade divisions and some of them were skeletons.' Rommel took his new army group staff to inspect the western coastal defences and to suggest ways in which they could be improved. His group also studied methods and plans to mount counterattacks to demolish enemy beachheads on the Western European front. General Warlimont, OKW Chief of Staff, heard Hitler say, 'Now the danger in the east remains *but an even greater one is emerging in the west*....the Anglo-American invasion...I can no longer tolerate the weakening of the west in favour of other theatres of war.' Hitler went on, 'If the Allied invasion established a beachhead, the war was lost for Germany.' He expected the enemy to invade in the spring of 1944, probably landing near the V-2 rocket sites and V-1 flying bomb catapult sites in the Pas de Calais.

On 12 December Hitler ordered Field Marshal Keitel to prepare a report on the fighting qualities of the Anglo-Saxon forces. OKW then drew up a tabulation of armed forces to be furnished in the event of a major landing. At his briefing conference on 20 December Hitler stated 'There is no doubt that an attack in the west will come in the spring; that is entirely beyond question.... There is no doubt that they have made their decision. The attack in the west will take place any time from the middle of February or early March.' But General Buhle, who as a staff officer had to get the appropriate formations to their correct positions, complained, 'If by January [1944] we can in fact get the tank battalions for the west then nothing untoward can happen there, but if we take everything away from the west, we can only hope! No sooner have I got something together [troop formations] than it's gone.' Hitler was distinctly unamused but he was not in total control of his generals. The OKW had to protest that personnel and equipment were being quietly withdrawn from the west to feed the eastern front, and Hitler on 28 December issued an explicit instruction that no more withdrawals were to take place without his own personal authorization.

The Luftwaffe aerial photographs of the troop concentrations in southern England indicated probable landings as early as mid-February. Hitler ordered troops to concentrate on the front held by Fifteenth Army (Pas de Calais) and the right flank of Seventh Army (guarding the Cotentin/Cherbourg Peninsula in Normandy), where he now expected the main attack. On the last day of the year Rommel heard Hitler say. 'If only they would land half a million men and then foul weather and storms cut them off in the rear—then everything would be all right.'

General Gunther Blumentritt, chief of staff with the Commander-in-Chief West told Liddell Hart immediately after the war, 'Rumours grew stronger throughout 1943 that an invasion was coming. They reached us largely from foreign diplomatic sources—from the Rumanian, Hungarian and Japanese military attachés as well as from Vichy quarters.' Blumentritt noted that the French Resistance was now very formidable, 'And was causing us many casualties as well as serious strain. The Communists, Gaullists and Giraudists were now united with Britain directing their operations and supplying them with arms by air.' By the end of 1943 permanent coast defence divisions were formed but the officers and men were mostly older and their armaments on a lower scale than the active divisions. Their weaponry included much captured French, Polish and Yugoslav equipment. Most divisions only had two infantry regiments with two field batteries (24 pieces in all) and one medium battery of 12 pieces—all horse-drawn with little mobility. The coastal artillery, whether naval or military, came under the naval command causing friction with the army command. Rommel had now completed his inspection of the defences in Denmark and moved into France over Christmas—into Field Marshal Von Rundstedt's sphere of command. As Rommel reported directly to the Führer and as his ideas on coastal defence clashed with those of Von Rundstedt, a compromise was urgently needed.

General Johannes Blaskowitz's Army Group G, the 1st Army, now controlled the Bay of Biscay and the Pyrenees, and the 19th Army, the Mediterranean coast. Rommel took command of Army Group B, with the Fifteenth Army in Holland, the Pas de Calais to the Seine and the Seventh Army from the Seine to the Loire. But another problem soon arose. General Geyr von Schweppenburg was now commander of Panzer Group West, and all armoured forces in France. Rommel wanted panzer divisions relatively close to the main landing areas to fight the invaders *before* a beachhead consolidated. Von Schweppenburg supported by Field Marshal Guderian, Inspector-General of Panzer Forces, wanted his formations concentrated and this obvious conflict placed von Rundstedt in a dilemma. Eventually another compromise was reached and Rommel had access to panzer formations. The 'Desert Fox' with enormous energy and determination now demanded the provision of millions of mines *per month* to be laid along the coastlines, above and below high tide. With the Todt chief engineer Xavier Dorsch, a huge range of beach defences were prepared: barbed wire, Element 'C', Tetrahada, wooden poles with mines facing out to sea, curved steel rails, metal hedgehogs and large minefields on the coastal lateral roads. Cash rewards were given to the local French population and their womenfolk made rush matting for sandtraps, or helped erect anti-paratroop defences. Rommel said, 'They worked with a will and finished each day singing lustily!' But Rommel made it clear to his Führer that many of the 15,000 fortifications were incomplete. When the invasion came 12,247 were completed, with 500,000 beach obstacles laid—a great tribute to Rommel's power and influence. It helped that General Jodl had completed his separate tour of the Atlantic Wall and reported on 14 January similar findings direct to Hitler. The latter insisted that scores of Panther tanks reputedly ineffective on the Russian front were to be dug in as coastal gun batteries along the French coast. Hitler issued instructions that 3,000 new anti-tank guns be installed in appropriate concrete pillboxes to be built by the end of April 1944—at the latest. From 12 January to the end of February Rommel stood in for von Rundstedt as Commander-in-Chief West and thus was able to secure some panzer support within close range of the likely landings.

In the autumn of 1943 Hitler had let the OKW into the secret of the V-weapons which he hoped would win the war in the west. Now General Warlimont noted, however, 'The quantity of high explosive which can be delivered daily by the V-weapons is less than that which could be dropped in a major air attack.' But in February 1944 it was known that due to technical difficulties and RAF interdiction the launch dates for both V-1s and V-2s would be delayed. Rommel was discouraged by his meetings with Field Marshal Sperrle, Commander-in-Chief, Third Air Force based in Paris, whose Luftwaffe resources seemed to be very limited. Indeed Jodl wrote in his diary early in the New Year, 'How on earth is the air war against the invasion going to be conducted? Major action against the enemy air forces is not possible. We must not accept battle with the enemy air force.'

On 19 January 1944 Hitler designated a number of areas from Holland to the Gironde estuary in southwest France as fortresses and had issued special instructions for their defence. A week earlier Jodl had noted in his diary (and had probably reported to the Führer) that, 'There is chaos in Cherbourg with the three services alongside each other.... Situation in Brest bad.' A little later Hitler assembled the commandants of the fortresses at his headquarters and personally briefed them on their duties. However, despite prompting from the OKW, he could not bring himself to invest the fortress commandants with *full* powers of command. But Hitler was convinced that his fortresses and particularly the port areas—

La Rochelle, Lorient, St Nazaire, Brest, St Malo, Cherbourg, Le Havre, Boulogne, Calais, Dunkirk and, later, when Antwerp had been captured, 'Fortress Scheldt' of Walcheren and Flushing—were all absolutely vital to the defence of his 'Atlantic Wall'. On 8 March he spelt out his directive in no uncertain terms.

The Führer   Führer Headquarters
High Command of the Army   8 March 1944

FÜHRER ORDER NUMBER 11

(COMMANDANTS OF FORTIFIED AREAS AND BATTLE COMMANDANTS)

In view of various incidents, I issue the following orders:

1. A distinction will be made between 'fortified areas' [feste Pläze] each under a 'fortified area commandant', and 'local strongpoints' [Ortsstützpunkte], each under a 'battle commandant'.

   The *'fortified areas'* will fulfil the function of fortresses in former historical times. They will ensure that the enemy does not occupy these areas of decisive operational importance. *They will allow themselves to be surrounded, thereby holding down the largest possible number of enemy forces, and establishing conditions favourable for successful counterattacks.*

   'Local strongpoints' are strongpoints deep in the battle area, which will be tenaciously defended in the event of enemy penetration. By being included in the main line of battle they will act as a reserve of defence and should the enemy break through, as hinges and cornerstones for the front, forming positions from which counterattacks can be launched.

2. Each *'fortified area commandant' should be a specially selected, hardened soldier, preferably of general's rank*. He will be appointed by the army group concerned. Fortified area commandants will be personally responsible to the commander-in-chief of the army group.

   Fortified area commandants will pledge their honour as soldiers to carry out their duties to the last.

   Only the commander-in-chief of an army group in person may, with my approval, relieve the fortified area commandants of his duties and perhaps order the surrender of the fortified area.

   Fortified area commandants are subordinate to the commander of the army group, or army, in whose sector the

---

fortified area is situated. Further delegation of command to general officers commanding formations will not take place.

Apart from the garrison and its security forces, all persons within a fortified area, or who have been collected there, are under the orders of the commandant, irrespective of whether they are soldiers or civilians and without regard to their rank or appointment.

The fortified area commandant has the military rights and disciplinary powers of a commanding general. In the performance of his duties he will have at his disposal mobile courts martial and civilian courts.

The staff of fortified area commandants will be appointed by the army group concerned. The chiefs of staff will be appointed by high command of the army, in accordance with suggestions made by the army group.

3. The *garrison* of a fortified area comprises the security garrison, and the general garrison.

   The security garrison must be inside the fortified area at all times. Its strength will be laid down by the Commander-in-Chief Army Group, and will be determined by the size of the area and the tasks to be fulfilled (preparation and completion of defences, holding the fortified area against raids or local attacks by the enemy).

   The general garrison must be made available to the commandant of the fortified area in sufficient time for the men to have taken up defensive positions and be installed when a full-scale enemy attack threatens. Its strength will be laid down by the Commander-in-Chief Army Group, in accordance with the size of the fortified area and the task which is to be performed (total defence of the fortified area).

4. The *'battle commandant'* comes under the orders of the local forces commander. He will be appointed by him, will be subordinate to him, and will receive operation orders from him. His rank will depend upon the importance of the position in the battle area and the strength of the garrison. His duties call for specially energetic officers whose qualities have been proved in crisis.

5. *The strength of the garrison* of a 'local strongpoint' will be determined by the importance of the position and the forces

available. It will receive its orders from the authorities to which the battle commandant is subordinate.

6. *The duties* of 'fortified area commandants' and 'battle commandants' as well as a list of fortified areas and of reports on them submitted by army groups, are contained in the appendices.

7. All previous orders concerning battle commandants are hereby cancelled.

signed: *ADOLF HITLER*

General Blumentritt told Liddell Hart just after the end of hostilities, 'Our naval staff always insisted that the Allies would land near a big port. They anticipated an attack on Le Havre—not only because of its value as a port but because it was the base for our midget submarines. We soldiers did not agree with their view. We doubted whether the Allies would make a *direct* attack on such a well-fortified place. Moreover we had information about a big exercise carried out in southern England, where the troops had been disembarked on a *flat* and *open* coastline. From this we deduced that the Allies would not try to attack a port at the outset: we thought you were probably intending to lay your ships side by side, to form a bridge over which stores could be unloaded and carried ashore to the beaches.' Von Rundstedt told Liddell Hart 'I thought the invasion would come across the narrower part of the Channel, between Le Havre and Calais—rather than between Caen and Cherbourg. I expected the landing might take place on the west side, between Le Tréport and Le Havre, followed by a further landing between the Somme and Calais—the quickest route to the Rhine. I reckoned you could get there in four days.' Von Rundstedt then said, 'The strength of the defences was absurdly over-rated. The "Atlantic Wall" was an illusion conjured up by propaganda—to deceive the German people as well as the Allies. Hitler himself never came to visit it and see what it really was.' But General Blumentritt revealed, 'At the end of March OKW issued instructions which showed that Hitler expected an invasion of Normandy. From that time onward we received repeated warnings about it, starting with the words: "The Führer fears...." I don't know what led him to that conclusion. But as a result, the 91st Air-landing Division with some tank squadrons was moved down there and posted in reserve behind the Cherbourg Peninsula—near Carentan.' General Warlimont's OKW view was, 'As regards the site of the landing Hitler was the first who came to the conclusion that Normandy was the most probable spot.'

The conference at the Berghof, 1,500 feet high at Berchtesgaden on 20 March gave Rommel control of the Fifteenth and Seventh Armies and influence over the armoured divisions, leaving von Rundstedt only the tactical reserve. Rommel was delighted, saying 'We have the utmost confidence that we'll get by in the west.' Hitler told all his generals, and von Rundstedt, Rommel, Kleist and Manstein, 'The enemy will establish their main beachheads either in Normandy or Brittany' [i.e., not near the Pas de Calais]. On 6 April, looking at the coastline map of Normandy, Hitler was heard to say, 'I am for bringing all our strength in here, particularly the forces we don't absolutely have to have anywhere else.' He ordered the crack Das Reich Division to be moved into Normandy. And on 1 May Jodl's staff told both von Rundstedt and Rommel, firmly, that the Führer expected the invasion in the Seventh Army's area, not in the 15th (i.e., the Pas de Calais) [known as Kanalkueste]. The next day Hitler ordered anti-aircraft and anti-tank weapons to be reinforced throughout that sector. His view was based on calculations from intelligence received as to troop movements in Britain, the British troops in the southeast and American troops in the southwest. Warlimont noted, 'The situation of the Americans, in particular, led Hitler to anticipate an attack launched against the western part of Normandy. Hitler based his conclusion on the consideration that the Allies, from the outset, would need a big port situated as to be quickly protected by a rather short front line, essentially met by the port of Cherbourg and the Cotentin peninsula. We [the generals] were not convinced that Hitler was right but he kept harping on it and demanded more and more reinforcements for the Normandy sector. We generals figured along the lines of our regular military education, whereas Hitler figured, as he always did, out of intuition.' Warlimont continued, 'Hitler became more and more firm in his conviction, but he believed furthermore, previous to, and also for a long time after the invasion, that a second landing would take place on the Channel coast. Small operational reserves were kept back around Paris.... This was the more fateful as Hitler repeatedly reiterated in my presence. "If we do not stop the invasion and do not drive the enemy back into the sea, the war will be lost".' However, he refused to allow any reduction in the strength of the Fifteenth Army in the Pas de Calais. On 19 May Rommel wrote to his son, 'The last months and weeks we have achieved the impossible but we are still not as ready as I would have liked, more mines, even deeper submerged obstacles, better anti-paratroop defences, even more artillery. AA guns, mortars and rockets. So far their [the RAF and USAAF] bombing of the Atlantic Wall has not had much effect, damage and casualties have been slight.' And ten days later, 'The nonstop Anglo-American bombardment is continuing. The French are suffering cruelly—3,000 civilians dead in 48 hours, our casualties are mostly low.' By the end of the month there were 59 German divisions in the west—eight being stationed in Holland and Belgium. More than half the total were coastal defence or training divisions. Of the 27 field divisions, ten were armoured, with three in the south and one near Antwerp. Rommel chose to place the 21st Panzer Division close to Caen. In Africa his tanks were often too far back for the counterattacks required at critical moments. If the panzer reserves were kept too far inland their move up would be savaged by the Allied air forces. In fact General Freiherr Von Geyr, the armoured forces GOC had persuaded Hitler that four armoured divisions in the west were to be kept as an OKW strategic reserve near Paris. Von Rundstedt wanted to evacuate the whole of southern France up to the Loire and bring back ten to 12 infantry divisions and both armoured divisions to fight a mobile battle in the west, but 'I could not move one of them without Hitler's permission.'

By the end of 1943 Operation Barbarossa had cost the Wehrmacht a staggering 3,500,000 casualties, killed, missing and wounded. The OKH order of battle on the Russian front listed 151 army divisions, of which 50 infantry and ten panzer divisions had been so decimated as to be operationally worthless. Hitler's dilemma was clear. The eastern front was stretched to breaking point. The Italian front, with its 12 full divisions, was intact but slowly conceding ground whilst OB West was now to be threatened by the Anglo-Amercian avalanche. The appalling losses had been partially offset by the OKH 'employment' of Volksdeutschen, so-called racial Germans, recruited from occupied territories, which included Russia, Poland, France and Italy. By May 1944 those from the eastern front, many of them prisoners of war were called Osttruppen (troops from the east). In May 1944 the Seventh Army had no less than 23 Osttruppen battalions of infantry, many serving as fortress garrison troops.

OKW planned to move south three infantry divisions from Norway and Denmark, another from Italy and four mobile or jaeger divisions from the Balkans to OB west if the main invasion area was in the Normandy/Brittany area. Admiral Theodor Krancke had studied recent aerial photographs taken by the Luftwaffe over southern England. In April he noted little naval activity in the ports of southeast England or at the mouth of the Thames. He [rightly] concluded that there seemed to be no obvious threat to the Pas de Calais area. Moreover the RAF/USAAF air attacks against radar installations and coastal batteries were mainly concentrated between Cherbourg and Boulogne. Inland bombing of bridges and railway junctions had been directed against roads and rail transport to the Channel coast and not the Atlantic area. What was a new factor was the omission of the Boulogne-Dunkirk area as a possible landing area. Krancke felt that the main attack would come against the Cotentin Peninsula, or the mouth of the Seine or the mouth of the Somme. But in the next month of May his view hardened *that the great ports of Le Havre and Cherbourg seemed to be prime targets for the Anglo-American forces.* Curiously enough RAF/USAAF air bombing of those ports was *much less* than might have been expected! As a result the defences in the Cotentin were considerably reinforced. These two Hitler fortress-ports were destined to be stormed by American, British and Canadian forces in the Cinderella War.

CHAPTER TWO

Churchill and the Second Front

IN THE AUTUMN OF 1941 CAPTAIN LORD LOUIS MOUNTBATTEN was appointed head of Combined Operations. In October he was summoned to see the Prime Minster and was told: 'You are to prepare for the invasion of Europe for unless we can go and land and fight Hitler and beat his forces on land, we shall never win this war. You must devise and design the appliances, the landing craft and the technique to enable us to effect landing against opposition and to maintain ourselves there. You must take the most brilliant officers from the Navy, Army and Air Force to help as planners to plan this great operation. You must take bases to use as training establishments where you can train the Navy, Army and Air Force to work a *single* entity. The whole of the south coast of England is a bastion of defence against the invasion of Hitler; you've got to turn it into the springboard for our attack.' Shortly after the evacuation of the BEF from Dunkirk, the intrepid Prime Minister had established Combined Operations staff to 'set Europe alight' with Commando raids against German-occupied Europe. Now a year later he was planning a cross-Channel attack!

In the spring of 1941 General George C. Marshall, US Army Chief of Staff, had sent Major General James Chaney as a special observer in case the United States came into the war. The British also exchanged military missions in Washington for the same reason. In January 1942 when Germany declared war on the USA the collaboration was extended with the formation of the Combined Chiefs of Staff. In the same month General

Sir Bernard Paget, Commander-in-Chief Home Forces studied a cross-Channel attack plan produced by the British Joint Planners. Operation Roundup was planned on the assumption that German forces were withdrawing to concentrate on the defence of the Fatherland. An area between Calais and the Seine nearly 100 miles deep would be invaded by a dozen British divisions. Operation Sledgehammer was planned for a summer 1942 invasion to secure the high ground north of the Seine and Oise rivers, initially by British troops, but with rapidly built up American participation.

There were many insoluble problems. In April 1942 the General Marshall's OPD (Operations Division of the War Department) produced a detailed Sledgehammer plan for a 1943 cross-Channel attack with the seizure of bridgeheads between Le Havre and Boulogne. The invasion force would total 48 divisions with 5,800 combat aircraft in support. Initial landings would be between Etretat, north of Le Havre, and Cap Gris-Nez, near Calais. When the bridgeheads linked up, the capture of Le Havre would be a major objective. The lack of landing craft and the scarcity of long-range aircraft were the two main problems. Operation Bolero was the US commitment to land 1 million servicemen and weapons, and specifically to mount an air offensive in late 1942 and a cross-Channel operation in 1943. Meanwhile Stalin was pressing Churchill and Roosevelt for urgent action—the Second Front—in northwest Europe to take pressure off the eastern front.

In July Churchill was writing to Roosevelt, 'I have found no one who regards Sledgehammer as possible.' However, General Marshall's chief planner was a certain Brigadier General Dwight D. Eisenhower, whose moment of fame was soon to come.

The next month there took place the ill-fated Operation Rutter/Jubilee inspired by Mountbatten, on the Dieppe town and harbour. On 19 August the day-long raid saw the loss of nearly 4,000 brave young Canadian troops. It was a disaster but Churchill, as usual, put on a brave face: 'It was a costly but not unfruitful reconnaissance in force. Tactically it was a mine of experience. It shed revealing light on many shortcomings in our outlook. It taught us to build in good time various new types of craft and appliances for later use. We learnt again the value of powerful support by heavy naval guns in an opposed landing and our bombardment technique, both marine and aerial was therefore improved....team work was the secret of success. All these lessons were taken to heart.' With his memories of the Somme and Passchendaele and the many fatal frontal attacks on the German lines in the First World War, Churchill was always haunted by the fear of similar heavy casualties when the Second Front was being planned. He knew that concrete and steel fortifications with well-trained troop defenders and adequate weaponry would inflict grievous losses on the invaders. 'Channel tides running red with Allied blood,' was one of his phrases at the time. Certainly the results from the Dieppe raid did not actively encourage the cross-Channel planners.

Churchill reflected after Dieppe that success depended on various factors: on surprise in time and place; on development of new and mechanical devices, such as tanks 'swimming' onto the beaches, and of landing craft for tanks to land on the beaches; on special 'bombard' tanks to blast the concrete and steel pillboxes; and an artificial harbour (Mulberry) of 'caissons' or empty floating barges or ships to form an artificial harbour when placed in position and sunk. In WWI he had *personally* advocated several of these concepts for planned amphibious attacks on the Heligoland Bight. He had drafted a memorandum to Mountbatten in May 1942 entitled 'Piers for use on Beaches', which instructed that 'they must float up or down on the tide.'

What was now crystal clear to the Allied planners (but not apparently to the German planners) was that a head-on attack against a well-defended port was suicidal. Churchill now proposed other operations in Africa and the Mediterranean, first Torch and then Husky. The newly appointed Lieutenant General Frederick Morgan, commander of the British First Corps gave added impetus to the plans for the Second Front. COSSAC (Chief of Staff to the Supreme Allied Commander) was to become an outstanding success and, despite many obvious difficulties, a triumph of British-American integrated planning. In his book *Overture to Overlord* Morgan revealed the complex task of surmounting the traditional rivalries, not just between the disparate traditions of US and British military 'top brass', but the inevitable interservice rivalry, as each branch of the forces scrambled to maintain pole position. Fortunately Morgan's role was later changed from being purely 'planning' to 'control'. Churchill wrote, 'General Morgan and his advisers recommended the Normandy coast [for the invasion landings] which from the first had been advocated by Mountbatten. There can be no doubt now that this decision was sound. Normandy gave us the greatest hope. The defences were not so strong as in the Pas de Calais. The seas and the beaches were on the whole suitable. The hinterland favoured the rapid deployment of large forces and was sufficiently remote from the main strength of the enemy. *The port of Cherbourg could be isolated and captured early in the operation. Brest could be outflanked and taken later.'* Churchill believed that the German

High Command would think, 'This is a good sector for raids up to 10 or 20,000 men but unless Cherbourg is taken in working order no army in any way equal to the task of an invasion can be landed or supplied. It is a coast for raids, but not for wider operations.'

Morgan, on behalf of COSSAC, in July 1943 defined his very clear brief: 'The object of Overlord is to mount and carry out an operation with forces and equipment established in the United Kingdom and with target date the 1 May 1944, to secure a lodgement area on the Continent from which further offensive operations can be developed. The lodgement area *must contain sufficient port facilities to maintain a force of some 26 to 30 divisions* and enable that force to be augmented by follow-up shipments from the United States or elsewhere of additional divisions and supporting units at the rate of three to five divisions per month.'

COSSAC had decided that only the Pas de Calais and Caen-Cotentin regions were acceptable and agreed with Mountbatten's conclusion (after Dieppe) that it was useless to count on captured ports, which would almost certainly be blocked up by the Germans and damaged by Allied air and sea bombardments. Other factors studied were weather, tides, beaches, the length of sea voyage, dangers from U-boats, E-boats and the Luftwaffe, the provision of air cover by RAF/USAAF, the quantity and quality of the enemy defences, and of course, vitally, an area where a large port could be seized quickly, and the time needed to repair and restore harbour facilities.

In August 1943 Churchill gave his approval for the construction of the Mulberry harbours. 'The whole project was majestic. On the beaches themselves would be the great piers with their seaward ends afloat and sheltered. At these piers coasters and landing craft would be able to discharge at all states of the tide.' At the major conference held in Teheran in November 1943, Stalin pressed the Anglo-Americans (Churchill and President Roosevelt) for specific details about Overlord: the date, of course, the overall commander-in-chief and the size of the invasion force. Churchill specified 16 British and 19 US divisions would be available for the assault, but he reminded Stalin that there were three key conditions (apart from the landing craft problem). Firstly a noticeable reduction in the Luftwaffe strength in northwest Europe leading up to the assault was necessary; secondly, on the day of the assault the Wehrmacht full strength *first-quality mobile* divisions would not exceed about a dozen in number; and thirdly, in the two months after the assault German reinforcements from other fronts must *not* exceed 15 first-quality divisions. At the end of the conference Stalin asked Churchill, 'Do the Prime Minster and the British

Staff *really* believe in Overlord?' Churchill replied to the effect that if the three conditions were in fact met 'When the time comes, it will be our stern duty to hurl across the Channel against the Germans every sinew of our strength.'

Roosevelt was reluctant for General Marshall to leave Washington—his most valuable and trusted military chieftain—to become supremo in northwest Europe. On 6 December 1943 the appointment of Dwight Eisenhower was made as the supreme commander. Marshall was happy as 'Ike' was his protégé. Alan Brooke, the CIGS, although disappointed that he was not selected was now pleased because 'Ike' had some command experience in wartime. Churchill was pleased too. 'We had the warmest regard for General Eisenhower and would trust our fortunes to his direction with hearty goodwill.' Perhaps the most relieved and pleased individual was Lieutenant General Morgan, who for eight months had been planning in a vacuum without a leader in the great enterprise. Next to be decided was the post of commander of the British Liberation Army for Overlord. On 11 December Alan Brooke and Eisenhower met in Tunis. Both Churchill and Eisenhower favoured the appointment of General Harold Alexander, but Alan Brooke and the War Cabinet favoured General Bernard Montgomery. Churchill himself, after weeks of travel to Cairo and Teheran, was very ill with pneumonia 'stranded amid the ruins of Carthage'. However, he cabled President Roosevelt on 18 December, 'I propose to you that Air Chief Marshall Tedder shall be Eisenhower's Deputy Supreme Commander on account of the great part the air will play in this operation and this is most agreeable to Eisenhower. The War Cabinet desires that Montgomery should command the first expeditionary group of armies. I feel the Cabinet are right as Montgomery is a public hero and will give confidence among our people, not unshared by yours.' However, Eisenhower badly wanted Alexander, with whom he was much in sympathy. It was already clear from Monty's meteoric and abrasive rise to fame after Alamein, Tunis, Sicily (Husky) and initially in Italy that he was (a) a very successful military commander, (b) extremely popular with his troops, (c) almost impossible to work with, and (d) absolutely impossible to control. Montgomery was notified on 24 December by the War Office of his new appointment. Three days later he met Eisenhower and his Chief of Staff, Major General Walter Bedell Smith.

The COSSAC planners had been working in handcuffs, in that the lack of landing craft had reduced their D-Day invasion force to but three divisions. Eisenhower and Montgomery both agreed that a five-division assault was essential. Bedell Smith said later 'Freddy Morgan wanted more [divisions] but he had to work with what he had.' Montgomery then flew to see Churchill, still ill, but now in Marrakesh and stressed that a five-division D-Day attack was vital for any chance of success. Montgomery was now made temporary Commander-in-Chief of all Allied ground forces for the invasion. SHAEF (Supreme Headquarters Allied Expeditionary Force) soon took over from COSSAC. Morgan had done a superb job.

Montgomery soon stamped his strong views on the Overlord plan and ordered that, 'The American Army will clear the Cherbourg peninsula and capture the port of Cherbourg. They will subsequently develop their operations to the south and west. The British Army will operate to the south to prevent any interference with the American Army from the east. It is hoped eventually to get a firm lodgement from Caen to Nantes with the British Army being built up through the Cherbourg peninsula and the American Army through Brittany.' On 21 January 1944 the first major conference took place in St James's Square. He emphasised the five-division assault, with one airborne division to land on the right flank of the Cotentin. In due course one British and two American airborne divisions took part on D-Day. Montgomery wanted a landing to take place on the eastern side of the Cotentin, to allow for a rapid capture of Cherbourg by General Omar Bradley's US First Army. Then they were to push into Brittany, towards Brest and the Loire ports. The area from Bayeux eastwards to the Orne river should be British (and Canadian) and from Bayeux westwards, American. Neither the two navies nor air forces were happy with the expanded plan, with additional responsibility for escort, sealift and air support. Soon there was considerable debate about Anvil, an American invasion planned for the south of France and requiring landing crafts badly needed for Overlord. Many deception plans were launched to mislead the enemy. Heavy bombing took place on the Pas de Calais defences and General George Patton commanded a 'phantom' army in southeast England—Operation Fortitude—with extensive radio usage, obviously destined for an assault on Calais and Boulogne. Exercise Thunderclap took place on 7 April 1944 in St Paul's School and General Montgomery spoke first for over an hour. Amongst many decisions he had made was that the Canadian First Army would take over the extreme left sector of the lodgement area and Patton's US Third Army would clear Brittany and cover the southern flank. The US First Army would turn east to drive towards the Seine and Paris. On 15 May a great dress rehearsal was held at St Paul's School in front of HM King George VI, Field Marshal Smuts, Churchill, Eisenhower, Tedder, Montgomery, Admiral Ramsay,

Air Marshal Leigh-Mallory, the CIGS Alan Brooke and a glittering array of red-tabbed officers of all services down to divisional commander rank. The VIPs sat on a row of armchairs in the dark, damp and uninspiring lecture room. The rest sat on hard wooden forms from 10.00 a.m. to 5.00 p.m. with an hour for lunch! General George Patton predictably arrived late after the main doors were barred and guarded. Monty was brilliant, dressed in smart battledress, looking trim and businesslike, repeating key phrases but quiet, deliberate, full of confidence, not complacent and sure he had the measure of his old adversary, Field Marshal Erwin Rommel.

The final COSSAC plans stated

Point 27. After the capture of Cherbourg the Supreme Allied Commander will have to decide whether to initiate operations to seize the Seine ports or whether he must content himself with first occupying the Brittany ports. In this decision he will have to be guided largely by the situation of the enemy forces. If the German resistance is sufficiently weak, an immediate advance could be made to seize Le Havre and Rouen. On the other hand the more probable situation is that the Germans will have retired with the bulk of their forces to hold Paris and the line of the Seine....Elsewhere they may move a few divisions from Southern France to hold the crossings of the [river] Loire and will leave the existing defensive divisions in Brittany. It will therefore most probably be necessary for us to seize the Brittany ports, first, in order to build up sufficient forces with which we can eventually force the passage of the [river] Seine. *Point 29*. A force would be employed in capturing the Brittany ports. The first step being a thrust southwards to seize Nantes and St Nazaire, followed by subsidiary operations to capture Brest and the various small ports of the Brittany peninsula. *Point 30*. This action would complete the occupation of our initial lodgement area and would secure sufficient major ports for the maintenance of at least 30 divisions. As soon as the organisation of the lines of communication in this lodgement area allowed and sufficient air forces had been established, operations would then be begun to force the line of the [river] Seine and to capture Paris and the Seine ports. As opportunity offered, subsidiary action would also be taken to clear the Germans from the Biscay ports to facilitate the entry of additional American troops and the feeding of the French population.

COSSAC and SHAEF realized the immense importance of capturing as many French ports as possible, as quickly as possible. Adolf Hitler, of course, had been aware of this objective for several years.

A month before D-Day, Eisenhower lunched privately with Churchill, who told him, 'I am in this thing with you to the end, and if it fails we will go down together.' At the end of the lunch Churchill said to Ike, 'And, my dear General, if by the time the snow flies you can have restored her liberty to our beautiful Paris, I shall proclaim to the world that this has been the best conceived and most remarkably successful operation of all history.' And that is the way it turned out.

CHAPTER THREE

Operation Neptune: Naval Operation Orders

The naval aspect of the planning for Overlord was predictably codenamed Neptune. Admiral Sir Bertram Ramsay was selected by the British Admiralty as naval commander, Allied Expeditionary Force. A veteran of the First World War and with much experience of amphibious warfare, he was responsible for not only the planning but the actual oversight of all naval aspects of the invasion programme. Rear Admiral Alan Kirk was the senior US Navy officer who worked closely with Ramsay. Initially there was a major disagreement with the American Admiral Ernest King, the difficult and fiery Commander-in-Chief US Fleet based in the States, about allocations of LSTs (Landing Ship Tanks), LCI (Landing Craft Infantry) and LCTs (Landing Craft Tanks). The Pacific theatre of war needed considerable quantities as did the proposed Anvil/ Dragoon invasion of southern France. On D-Day the huge Allied armada consisted of:

	Battleships	Cruisers	Destroyers	Coastal Craft	Frigates, etc.
Royal Navy	3	17	65	360	447
US Navy	3	3	34	111	49

The amphibious fleet of various landing craft totalled 4,126 of which 3,261 were British and 865 were American, and the Merchant Navy contribution was 1,260 vessels, including 59 block ships.

On 10 April 1944 Operation Neptune Naval Operation Orders were issued by Admiral Ramsay's Headquarters with 22 separate sections coded (ON1-22) which amounted to 1,100 pages. The following list is a very brief summary. ON1 was Ramsay's introduction. ON2 was the mine-laying operations by RN and RAF off enemy ports from the Bay of Biscay to the Baltic from D minus 45 days. ON3 were naval, with air support, diversions against the Pas de Calais to continue to deceive the enemy (part of Operation Fortitude). ON4 was the assembly of the vast fleet of 4,000 vessels in comprehensive detail.

The five separate assault forces would assemble and land with escorts and minesweepers in south coast ports with two follow-up forces scattered from Felixstowe, the Thames Estuary, to west of Plymouth. The British forces would be brought together and landed in the Thames Estuary and the Americans in the Bristol Channel. The heavy bombardment forces started mainly from Belfast Loch and the Clyde Estuary. The unwieldy Mulberry harbours were brought together between Felixstowe and Portland. ON5 covered the deployment at sea of the protective naval escorts against U-boats, German destroyers, E-boats and R-boats (motor minesweepers). ON6 covered mine-sweeping operations by 255 RN and USN sweepers. ON7 covered various eventualities: 'friendly' fire; procedures to take if vessels were sighted out of their expected positions; and procedures for final approach and landing of each assault force in 16 planned stages from H-Hour minus 120 minutes to H-Hour plus 105 minutes (H-Hour was the designated start time). The earliest to arrive would be the first landing craft tank (LCT) groups loaded with amphibious Dual-Duplex 'swimming' Sherman tanks; then bombarding ships to open fire; the first group of rocket-equipped LCTs to open fire; and amphibious tanks to touch down on the beach. At H-Hour itself, the infantry assault, assault craft were detailed to bring in the first infantry reserves; the obstacle clearance units; the LCTs with standard tanks; LCTs with self-propelled artillery and priority motor transport to touch down. ON8 related to the bombardment forces to engage hostile coast defences and support assault operations ashore; it included Air Force heavy bomber attacks in the run-up to D-Day with planned drops of 4,200 tons of bombs. ON9 covered orders to the task and assault forces for the rest of D-Day. ON10 dealt with the follow-up forces, Force L (British) in five groups and Force B (American) in three groups. ON11 was the air plan by RAF/USAAF to concentrate their bombers against the French road and rail networks inland; 5,886 Allied planes

(3,612 American and 2,274 British) would overwhelm the Luftwaffe with their estimated total strength in the west of 1,510 planes with 590 available over the Neptune area.

Amongst the other eleven Operation Neptune instructions were ON16, which dealt with the complicated procedures for getting the component parts of Mulberry (Bombardons, Phoenixes, Gooseberries and Whales) from the UK to their final destination. Of special note, however, was ON19, which dealt in detail with procedures for opening captured ports, starting initially with the nine small fishing or yachting harbours along the invasion coast. But ON19 included plans for the opening of the major ports of Cherbourg, Brest, Le Havre, Dieppe, St Nazaire etc. The exact sequence of events was specified from the first arrival of a joint navy-army reconnaissance team, through to the work of the main port parties.

Thus Operation Neptune was launched. Lieutenant Commander J.D. Hayes, the Resident Naval Officer for the small port of Ouistreham deployed his port party on D+1 under enemy fire. Commander Cowley Thomas was Naval Officer Dock Command of Port-en-Bessin which soon unloaded an average 1,000 tons of equipment a day. Courseulles was opened on D+2 and also handled 1,000 tons per day. The Americans opened the minor ports of Grandcamp and Isigny.

The port reconstruction companies were military units responsible for the repair of quays, jetties and lock gates. The naval port clearance parties (or 'P' parties) had a more dangerous task. There were four of them, Numbers 1571, 1572, 1573 and 1574, each consisting of an officer and 21 ratings including eight specialist divers trained to detect and make safe underwater mines in enemy harbours.

Captain Anthony Kimmins, RN described in early October 1944 how the Royal Navy had 'cleared up' captured enemy ports.

> On 8 August Field Marshal von Kluge sent the following message to the German High Command: "A breakthrough has occurred at Caen, the like of which we have never seen" [*Von Kluge actually said this to General Hausser, Commander of the German Seventh Army.*] Those were the actual words—"the like of which we have never seen"—very strong words for an experienced general. But quite clear in their meaning. In spite of foul weather conditions the Mulberries, coupled with heroic efforts across open beaches, had done the trick. The first phase in the battle of the ports—for it is on that battle that the whole of our operations on the Continent depend—had proved a clear victory for the Allies.

There was only one hope for the Germans. With each mile of the Allied advance, lines of communication were becoming more and more stretched to the limit, and the original ports were soon hundreds of miles from the front line. In order to keep up their pressure, the Allied armies must employ the closer Channel ports such as Dieppe, Boulogne, Calais, Ostend and Zeebrugge.

Orders went out from the Führer that those ports were to be held to the last man, and, if captured, to be so demolished as to be unusable.

That demolition wasn't a very difficult job. They were all similar in character. Small ports; approaches ideal for mining; narrow entrances perfect for blockships; quays—mostly constructed on wooden piles—easy to destroy. Observers on the south coast of England saw enormous flashes and a few moments later felt their windows shake with the concussion. Those explosions were our urgently needed quays and harbour installations going west! There was only one answer: superhuman efforts of clearance and reconstruction the moment these ports had fallen into our hands.

On this side of the Channel minesweepers were waiting to clear the approaches—wreck-raising ships and salvage vessels were standing by to get busy the moment the word came. But obviously there was nothing much they could do until effective measures had been taken by men working inside the ports themselves.

There were two main organisations for this. The Army Port Construction parties of sappers and pioneers under the command of the Port Commandant, whose job it is to clear and repair the quays, get the cranes working, get electric light and power going, repair the bridges, clear the roads, and the thousand and one other jobs ashore; and the naval Port parties under the NOIC—the Naval Officer-in-Charge—whose job it is to clear the entrances, force a passage through the blockships, sweep all the mines, raise or remove the wrecks alongside the quays so that ships can enter the harbour, berth alongside, and unload in safety.

Watch them now as they wait behind the artillery carrying out the final bombardment. There are two little groups of jeeps—the NOIC and his reconnaissance party in one; the Army Port Commandant and his reconnaissance party in the other.

The main units of men will follow in later—but an early reconnaissance by both the Naval and Military Port parties is vital to the whole future of the campaign.

At last as the tanks and infantry go forward for the final assault, they find themselves well up in the queue of ingoing vehicles. But soon, as the piles of rubble grow higher and higher, they have to desert their jeeps and do the rest of the journey on foot. As they scramble across the ruined lock gates a sudden whine of bullets sends them sprawling to the ground. But there is no time to waste. They work their way on towards a good vantage point.

At last they reach the top of a wrecked E-boat pen. Yes, they've chosen well. It's a perfect spot. Out come notebooks and they start to make diagrams and notes of what they observe. Their heads turn automatically towards the narrow entrance between the breakwaters, and those of you who crossed the Channel before the war will remember them well. The rows of blue-smocked fishermen, the children waving handkerchiefs. You sniffed the first smells of THE CONTINENT; you had arrived.

But what a difference now! Those breakwaters are no longer nice and solid and friendly. Splintered wood lies everywhere and large gaps have been torn in them. And in the narrow waters between, a jumble of masts and funnels clearly indicates the large number of tugs, freighters, dredgers, and other ships which have been sunk to block the entrance.

A few jottings in their notebooks, and they turn their attention to the quays. The cranes lie drunkenly sprawling into the water. Between them barges and lighters have been sunk to stop ships berthing alongside, and the quays themselves have been blown to smithereens.

Everywhere they look it's the same—chaos, rubble, and destruction.

An occasional side of a building with BYRRH or DUBONNET in those enormous letters may just remind them of the good old days. But only just. All they are interested in is that this is a port.

A mouth of a river fitted out to receive men and supplies from across the water, but now... they glance at their notebooks... 'At least fifteen blockships in main channel... all principal quays blown ... cranes demolished...lockgates....'

Well, the Naval Officer-in-Charge of this caricature of a harbour closes his notebook and puts it in his pocket. 'That's about all we can do for the moment. Let's go and chat it over with the Army.' And so starts the first Port Conference. There will be one every day until the port is in full running order. Later they will be held around a table in comparative comfort and with detailed charts and plans. But this evening it's a case of a few figures clustered at some prearranged corner and swapping pages out of dirty notebooks.

That night some very weary men swallow their iron rations and curl up to sleep wherever they can find cover. Tomorrow their job starts in earnest.

Now how that job is done I defy anyone to describe. There are certain landmarks, yes. The enormous explosions as blockships are removed, others as the remains of a lock gate are destroyed; the significant moment when the first minesweepers arrive and clear the approaches, when a repaired bridge is opened to traffic, when the electric light supply is suddenly restored, when the first motor minesweeper creeps in through the narrow entrance in the blockships and starts to sweep inside; and of course the greatest moment of all when the first supply ship is berthed alongside and her precious cargo is hoisted inshore.

But taking it by and large, it isn't so much a series of marked events, but each day—almost imperceptibly—the whole thing grows and then suddenly... the port is working.

But of all those little groups—the minesweepers, the pioneers, the salvage parties, the sappers, the wreck raisers, the signalmen, and the many others who are setting about their jobs under dangerous and incredibly difficult conditions, there's one little group which I must single out.

You'll see them on a quay with a couple of lorries close by, from one of which blares out dance music. At first sight they look as idle as a bunch of WW Jacobs' longshoremen, sitting there on bollards staring down into the water below. They appear to be looking at nothing—which in a way is true—because their interest is concentrated in their mates who are groping about in the darkness some thirty feet below the surface.

No obviously I mustn't go into any details of how they work, but let me assure you that of all the acts of bravery that I have seen in this war, theirs, for sheer cold-blooded guts, is one of the greatest.

To put it in a nutshell, their job is to go down below in diving suits, grope about in the darkness amongst twisted girders, dead horses and corpses, and search for any wrecks which might prevent ships coming alongside—and don't forget that some of those wrecks may contain thousands of pounds of explosive itching to go off at a false touch. In pitch darkness, mind you, and in all the difficulties of slithering about in black oozy mud against the pressure of thirty feet of water.

There are two of them to each team. A youngster—specially chosen for his physical fitness and usually under twenty-one—who actually does the job, and his dresser or link with the surface—chosen for reliability and usually well over forty—who watches every move.

Now those are the men—the dressers—whom you saw staring in to the water from the quayside. They weren't idle... far from it. On their attendance depended the life of the kid down below and they were feeling the strain far more than he was.

Suddenly there's a rustle of excitement, a hauling in of ropes, and a kid comes to the surface. His 'Pop'—that's really the only word for him—is immediately down to the water's edge finding out what he has got to report. Obviously the kid can't talk, but those two have a sign language between them which puts all normal efforts at dumb crambo or other similar games to shame. In a moment the news is being passed on to the Officer-in-Charge and the kid disappears back into the depths.

Meanwhile, other teams are waiting up top for their turn. There's the same, you know, rather hilarious, vaguely unreal, slightly high-pitched conversation going on which one has heard so often before—pilots before a raid, soldiers before an assault, submariners before an attack—whenever the future is in the balance. Great, great heroes—all of them.

So give a thought—not just sometimes, but very often—not only to the diving lads but to the thousands of others—both Army and Navy—who make up the Port Clearance Parties.

The headlines are very naturally and properly about the advance of our soldiers at the front. But they cannot advance without supplies. Those supplies must come through the ports.

It's on the Battle of the Ports that everything depends.

On 20 July Winston Churchill flew in a US Army Dakota to a landing ground on the Cherbourg peninsula and was taken around the harbour by the US Army GOC. He examined a flying bomb launching point, an elaborate affair, and was shocked by the damage the Germans had done to town and harbour. 'The basins of the harbour were thickly sown with contact mines,' he wrote afterwards and, 'A handful of devoted British divers were at work day and night disconnecting these at their mortal peril. Warm tributes were paid to them by their American comrades.' There was also one other unorthodox formation. The 30th Assault Unit was a joint Royal Navy and Royal Marine unit. Their task was the capture and skilful utilization of enemy documents and secret equipment, under the operational control of ANCXF (Allied Naval CinC Expeditionary Forces). 30th Assault Unit was based initially in Littlehampton, Sussex, under command of Lieutenant Commander A. T. Hawkes. For the Overlord planning there were A, B and X troops, each about 40 strong, HQ troop, a naval wing under Lieutenant Commander McFee with naval ratings to deal with underwater weaponry. Also Lieutenant Colonel Jambie US Navy, Flight Lieutenant Nutting RAFVR—an all-arms group. Their two main tasks in Overlord were coded Pikeforce and Curtforce for the D-day landings, and Woolforce (Lt Col Woolley) and Nutforce (Flight Lt Nutting) for the objective of Villa Meurice. This was the centre for covert survellance and German Headquarters in Cherbourg, expected to fall on D+8, and another target was the liquidation of the 'ski-sites' or platforms in the Cotentin peninsula for launching guided missiles onto southern England. RAFVR's first selected target was the station at Douvres-la-Deliverande, but it was so stoutly defended that it held out for two weeks despite being a mile or so inland from the captured beaches.

The second task on D+4 was to land on Utah American Beach and to be in at the 'kill' of the vital port of Cherbourg. On 26 June Captain Hargreaves-Heap RN helped capture the naval headquarters in the arsenal and the naval headquarters in the port and examined explosives, port plans and mining depots. He then helped start the complicated plans for the clearance of the vital port.

CHAPTER FOUR

The Capture of Cherbourg:
'A field of devastation'

The Neptune plan had envisaged the capture of the first of Hitler's fortress-ports taking place on D+8, i.e., 14 June. Cherbourg was the base for the 5th and 9th Motor Torpedo Flotillas of E-boats, which patrolled off Cape Barfleur and west of Cape de la Hague. Before D-Day they numbered 21, plus 20 small patrol vessels, and up to 10 minesweeper-trawlers. The survivors after the RN/USN, RAF/USAAF had taken them on fled to St Malo a week before Cherbourg was captured. It took a further two weeks before Cherbourg's surrender.

Utah Beach where the US 4th Division landed at 06.30 hours on 6 June (2,000 yards south of their beach objective) was only twenty miles southeast of Cherbourg. The assault went well against weak opposition and by 18.00 hours Admiral Moon's task force had landed over 21,000 troops, 1,700 vehicles and 1,700 tons of supplies. Casualties during the day were light, 12 killed in action and 106 wounded.

Hitler was 'sure' that the Cotentin peninsula would be a key objective and had sent 91st Air Landing Division to occupy the centre of the southern part of the peninsula. The tough 6th Parachute Regiment and a panzer battalion were added south of Carentan. Rommel thought the Cotentin 'bocage' country could be an airborne objective and most parachute drop zones were 'seeded' with 'Rommel's Asparagus', poles about two metres high to block glider landings.

With additional aircraft available, the Operation Neptune plan was for two American airborne landings to take place inland. Major General

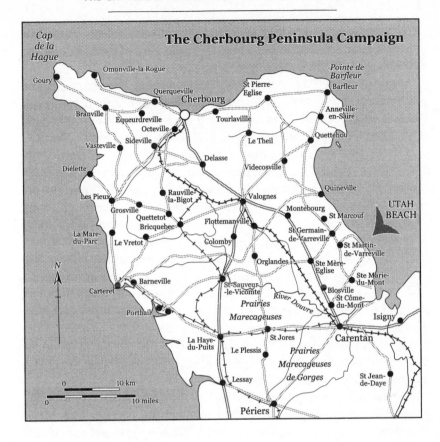

The Cherbourg Peninsula Campaign

Maxwell Taylor's 101st 'Screaming Eagles', dropped at 01.30 hours on D-Day around the western exits to Utah Beach to help cut the peninsula. Heavy winds and inexperienced glider pilots caused the 6,600 parachute or glider troops to be widely scattered over a 28 by 17 mile area. Within two hours of dropping there were nearly 1,740 dead, captured, drowned or injured on impact. But by 13.00 hours the four exits from Utah, causeways over flooded land, were captured. The 82nd Airborne, under Major General Matthew Ridgway dropped an hour later at 02.30, again widely scattered. The small town of Ste Mère Eglise inland was captured from the 101st drop. Many units were dropped into flooded marshland along the River Merderet and failed to establish bridgeheads over two important causeways at La Fière and Chef-du-Pont; 82nd Airborne also lost about 2,000 casualties in the first day. By the end of D-Day a complete set of Overlord plans was in enemy hands, obtained from an American small craft sunk just offshore which had drifted out of control. General

Dollmann, Commander of the German Seventh Army ordered immediate counterattacks by his 91st and 709th Divisions west of the Merderet and 6th Parachute Regiment south in Carentan.

Major General Wilhem Falley, commanding the 91st Luftland (Airlanding) Division was ambushed and killed on D-Day. His successor Colonel Eugen Koenig, was responsible for heavy counterattacks with 1057 Grenadier Regiment at La Fière and the crossroads at Le Motey.

For the next few days confused fighting went on inland from Utah. The Führer sent the Commanding Officer of 6th Parachute Regiment Lieutenant Colonel Baron von der Heydte a message on 9 June 'You are to defend Carentan to the last man and the last bullet.' The tough young 18-year-old paratrooper gave 101st Airborne troops a hard time but under overwhelming air power, naval fire, artillery, mortars and tank destroyer guns the town was taken. On the night of 11 June von der Heydte had pulled his troops out to fight another day. Hitler was furious and sent a directive to all Wehrmacht commanders in Normandy, 'Explicit orders demand that everyone at strongpoints of resistance and other defensive positions surrounded by enemy units must defend the position to the last man and to the last bullet, in order to allow time for preparation for the counterattack and the reconquest of the [Normandy] coast. No orders to retreat will be issued [by any commander].'

The German defenders now fell back to the ridge between Quineville, Montebourg and Le Ham, which had many linked strongpoints. Major Friedrick Küppers commanded the Artillirie Gruppe Montebourg which had 19 powerful guns, the Flak Gruppe Konig, the 100th Mortar Regiment, the 919th Grenadier Regiment and combat groups from Lt General Heinz Hellmich's 243nd Division.

General Omar Bradley wrote in his memoirs, 'I assigned four divisions to Collins [Major General J. Lawton Collins] for the Cherbourg campaign, Barton's 4th Infantry, Ridgway's 82nd Airborne and two divisions recently arrived from England, Manton Eddy's veteran 9th and Jay MacKelvie's 90th.' The last was a very green and poorly trained formation and was soon replaced by 79th under General Ira Wyche. 'Collins jumped off on 14 June. His first goal was to drive 25 miles west to the Atlantic coast, sealing off the Cotentin Peninsula. Ridgway's 82nd and Eddy's 9th spearheaded the drive with Landrum (who had replaced MacKelvie) a lacklustre 90th bringing up the rear. From Enigma/Ultra we now knew that Rommel had reinforced the Cotentin with the 77th Division which joined up with elements of the mobile 91st and the static 243rd and 709th coastal divisions.'

On 16th June Hitler and OKW staff flew from Metz to Soissons. He sent another directive to Hans Spiedel (Rommel's chief of staff) and thence to Seventh Army Group Headquarters. 'The fortress Cherbourg is to be held at all costs. A retreat in one stage will *not* take place. German troops may make a fighting withdrawal into the fortress delaying the enemy's advance by obstacles, minefields and deception. Stock up Cherbourg for a long siege, demolish port facilities at once so the enemy could not use it.' Rommel now told his Führer 'Cherbourg will fall in a week.' The Luftwaffe and E-boats operating out of Brest and Cherbourg had been dropping new oyster-pressure sea mines for the first time. These caused unexpected losses to small ships supplying the beachhead via the two newly erected Mulberry harbours.

General Omar Bradley wrote 'Conflicting field orders to the German defences in the Cotentin resulted in confused and poor defensive deployment. In four days of brilliant manoeuvres, Joe Collins punched through to the Atlantic coast at Barneville-sur-Mer,' thus completely cutting the peninsula. Bradley ordered VIII Corps under Major General Troy Middleton to hold the 'anchor line' south of Collins's VII Corps. Middleton was assigned the 90th, and both Airborne divisions. 'Collins's VII Corps now consisting of the 4th, 9th and 79th Divisions thrust north on 19 June—the day the great storm wrecked Omaha beach [Mulberry]. Thereafter the VII Corps ammunition supply was severely rationed.' The French FFI resistance movement known as Centurie had supplied valuable information about the Cherbourg defence including accurate maps which were of great help. Major General Collins wrote in his autobiography,

As usual I based my scheme of manoeuvre on an analysis of the terrain and what we knew of the enemy's plans and potential. A relief map of the Contentin peninsula that Mason Young, our Corps Engineer, had prepared for me, showed that the Divette River and the upper reaches of the Douve divided the northern half of the peninsula into two broad compartments. The eastern compartment, in which the 4th Division had been fighting, contained two small cities, Montebourg and Valognes, whose solid stone houses could become strong enemy redoubts. The compartment west of the Douve was more open country, with fewer natural obstacles, and was not being held in strength. Ground rose steadily in both compartments to the hills ringing Cherbourg, broken only by the narrow Trotebec and Divette streams, both of which flowed into Cherbourg harbour. We knew from aerial photographs that the

Germans had organised this ring of hills, cresting four to five miles from the city, with a formidable series of mutually supporting strongpoints consisting of concrete machine gun, anti-tank, and 88 mm gun emplacements and tank barriers. Our able G-2, Colonel Leslie D Carter, estimated that the enemy would fight stubborn delaying actions until he withdrew within his ring defences. This was confirmed by capture of orders of the LXXXIV Corps and the 77th Division. The total enemy force, including coastal defence, anti-aircraft, and naval personnel and organised labour battalions, was estimated at from twenty five to forty thousand.

I decided to hit the enemy with three divisions abreast, in order from the east: 4th, 79th and 9th. The major effort of the Corps would be in the form of a double-pronged attack by the 4th and 9th Divisions, cutting in against the Cherbourg defences from east and west, with the 79th Division and the 4th Cavalry Squadron serving as a link between the two prongs.

Montebourg was attacked from both sides and by midnight on 19 June Valognes was encircled and captured. The next day General von Schlieben withdrew his forces into the outer-ring defence of Cherbourg. But the German Colonel Bernard Bacherer marched nearly 2,000 men of 77 Infantry Division *through* the lines of the exhausted US 9th Division south to La Haye du Puits. They kept going for 30 hours to the River Ollande, capturing 275 US prisoners of war en route!

Lieutenant David Nutting, Officer Commanding 'B' Troop 30th Assault Unit wrote of their advance up to the Cotentin peninsula:

We then began giving our allies a hand, slogging our way up north through the bocage towards Cherbourg, our ultimate target. On the way there, we confined ourselves to the bocage, never passing through a single town or village. It was only after we left Cherbourg, to go to Cartaret, that we saw the terrible damage inflicted on places such as Montbourg, Valognes, St Sauveur, etc.

American battle sectors are pretty disgusting. The dead are left, even the American dead, unburied for anything up to a couple of weeks until a burial party of PoWs comes round to load them into a lorry. The British bury theirs straight away, to be exhumed later and re-interred in a military cemetery. Some bodies even lay in the roads, with trucks driving over them. Quite disgusting. This was particularly the case when German transport had been caught on the open roads by Allied aircraft; the bodies were badly burned in most cases, in addition to being partially dismembered.

As usual, the US infantry was poorly trained. At first they tended to mill around looking lost or to amble aimlessly up the road. The survivors became very good. In the US Army, being posted to the infantry was regarded as having failed and there were some horribly inexperienced but gung-ho colonels who bravely accepted their men's casualties without turning a hair.

The US paratroops were a different kettle of fish. The majority of them were very good indeed. They had been, most of them, dropped well away from their designated landing zones and many of them just disappeared altogether. The remainder gradually gathered together into larger groups of varying sizes and went, as far as they could, for their planned targets or, failing those, for whatever targets appeared to be feasible with the resources they had. Large numbers fell into the flooded areas in the marshes behind the beaches and simply drowned under the weight of their kit (the latter could be the same as the man's bodyweight). They took considerable casualties in these operations but succeeded in holding Jerry away from the beaches until the main sea-borne forces arrived. When we landed, their bodies were lying everywhere, all too eloquent evidence of the bitterness of the fighting.

The other airborne forces came in gliders. Landing gliders in the Normandy bocage was a brutal decision for the planners to make, and many gliders just ran head-on into the earth banks, killing all aboard. However, surprising numbers of occupants survived, despite the virtually complete demolition of their transports, to join their parachutist comrades.

The US artillery was good. Their barrages were very effective, co-operation between airborne observers and their batteries was tight, and their barrages of air bursts were a joy to behold as we followed them up, the bursts almost touching each other.

When we besieged the fortress, Major Alan Evans called on the US Artillery to shell the rear access, which caused the Germans to come out with the white flag at the front, where 30AU was waiting.

We took some amazing prisoners. The first bunch looked like nothing we had ever seen before and, after trying all sorts of languages on them, it turned out that they were Georgians from Holy Mother Russia. They were not Hilfswillige (volunteers) doing non-combatant duties, but were armed combatants. Details in their paybooks were entered in Cyrillic script. After that we were no longer surprised as Poles, Romanians, Balts and the 'UN' itself fell into our bag.

Another surprise was to see French girls marching back along the road with the German prisoners. This really made us mad; what bare-faced cheek after we had gone to all that trouble to liberate them from the hands of the filthy and rapacious Hun. Understanding came later when we liberated a few more of them and saw what the rest of the population did to girls they thought had been fraternising with Jerry. Most unpleasant to see, but no sense in being judgmental; we had not experienced a foreign occupation ourselves.

Enemy snipers were a menace; they even sniped at medical personnel. One of our medics, Squinty Johnson, had been shot through the knee while attending one of our wounded, and there had been several near misses reported by the other SBAs. They became fed up with this and armed themselves with rifles to retaliate. I don't think the German troops were responsible for this; it was more likely to be the rubbish they had recruited from Eastern Europe, a belief made more concrete by our previous experiences in Yugoslavia.

There were the usual casualties through carelessness or stupidity. One chap was shot through the heart by another man cleaning his rifle with a bullet up the spout. Another chap had shot a rabbit on a minefield and went to collect it, thus stepping on a mine. Minefields were still marked with barbed wire fences on which were hung the skull and crossbone signs with 'Achtung—minen' written on them.

Two journalists joined Collins's VII Corps advance, and Robert Dunnett reported on 20 June 1944:

The American troops are moving so fast up practically the whole width of the Cherbourg peninsula that it's becoming quite a job to keep up with them. Tonight they're ringing the Germans round only a few miles from the city and port of Cherbourg. It's difficult to say at any given time exactly how near any of the advanced elements are to Cherbourg, but the nearest are probably now within four miles. The whole picture of the campaign in the peninsula has changed in the last three days. Then the Germans controlled about three quarters of the area of the peninsula. Today barely a

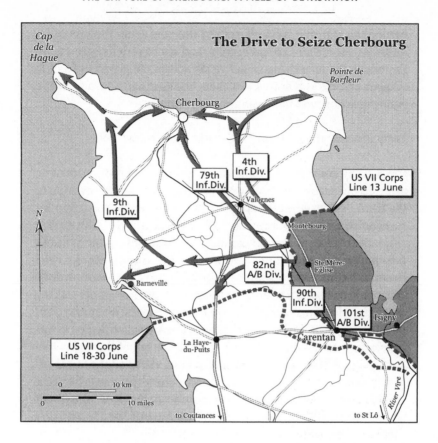

The Drive to Seize Cherbourg

quarter is left to them. The eastern side of the peninsula and the main national highway up through Montebourg and Valognes bears all the signs of a battlefield—roads cut by bombs, trees and houses splintered by fire, men and cattle dead in the fields. I drove through this skeleton town of Montebourg today, and I couldn't find one whole house. Five miles farther on along a road where, for the first time, I noticed places where the Germans had laid mines, we came to the shattered centre of Valognes. A fortnight ago this had been one of the main German headquarters in the peninsula; now, from the twisted and broken German field gun at the corner as we entered the city to the plaster-covered floor of the Commanding General's office in the main civic building, with a photograph of Hitler crooked on the wall, it was an example of the power of Allied bombing and American shelling. These two towns of Valognes and Montebourg, and the country to the south and east of them, have been the main battlefields. On the western side of the peninsula the picture is different. Here there are more hills, and after the dense growth on the plains it's refreshing to get vistas across the greenery to little villages and church spires. But here the Germans have fought a running action that has been mostly running.

Larry Lesueur reported for CBS on 20 June 1944:

Great credit for our surging advance towards Cherbourg must be given to our traffic control and truck transport. In all my trips to the front I've never seen a single American truck out of action for mechanical reasons. Our military police are all provided with explicit maps of their area, and do wonders rerouting our supply trucks into narrow wooded lanes and avoiding traffic snares. As each American command post moves forward to keep in touch with its advancing troops, our telephone linesmen work incessantly, taking down the wires and stringing them out anew to the most advanced positions. One of the favourite jokes of the American Signal Corps linesman is to call down scornfully from the top of the tallest tree and telegraph posts at our infantry trudging ahead on the duty road to wisecrack, 'Keep your heads down, boys, there are German snipers around'. The heavily loaded infantry just look up wearily and sheepishly at the linesmen outlined against the sky and give them an appreciative grin.

Up to midnight on 18 June, D+12, on the beaches and via the Mulberry harbours 314,547 men, 54,000 vehicles and 116,000 tons of supplies were landed. This was reduced after the great storm on the 19th to a trickle just at the time when shells were needed for the final onslaught on Cherbourg.

Hitler sent General Karl von Schlieben a message from Berchtesgaden 'You are hereby appointed Commander of Fortress Cherbourg. You will defend the city to the last man and the last bullet.' The four main German *gruppe* were commanded by Müller, Kiel, Küppers and Hoffmann. They all gave considerable heed to their Führer's orders.

A British presence was noted by the Americans—a special radio caravan/truck with many aerials known as Station X operated by the SLU. The Special Liaison Unit was partly RAF, partly Royal Corps of Signals. The unit constantly received secret messages from the Enigma/Ultra decoded by the Bletchley Park 'interceptions'. Many of the messages between Hitler, Rommel, von Rundstedt and the beleaguered von Schlieben were passed to General Bradley. One such was 'launch Operation Heinrich tonight', probably ordering the destruction of the Cherbourg harbour facilities.

General Bradley wrote, 'By the time Collins swung north for Cherbourg, Ultra had given us a good idea of the German Order of Battle. The 30,000 to 40,000 defenders were in disarray, falling back on Cherbourg helter-skelter. Our best opportunity lay in driving north at such speed as to prevent a consolidation of their defences. When the Channel storm abated, we launched a massive air and sea bombardment against Cherbourg in support of the VII Corps drive. In four days it was on the outskirts of the city.'

The inner port of Cherbourg was defended by Kapitan Weise with MAA (Marine Artillery) 260th and 1709th Artillery Regiments with seven casemented batteries. These were Hamburg (four 240 SKL 40 guns) under Ober Lt Gelbhaar; Gneisenau under Kapitan Le Vi (four 150 mm guns); Fort Central (four 94 mm guns); Arsenal/Bastion II (four 105 mm guns); Gare Maritime (two 105 mm guns); Brommy/Caplains (four 150 mm guns) and Fort Montagne du Roule (four 105 mm guns). Other batteries inland were Castel-Vendon at Tourville; Yorck at Amfreville, and also at Varouville, Cosqueville, Val Bourgin, La Judée, Digosville/ Tourlaville, Mesnil Val, Ozouville, Ste-Croix-Hague and Couples. Their main purpose, of course, was to deter an invasion by sea and not from the Cotentin peninsula to the south. But each was a self-contained little fortress and each needed a careful planned attack.

OKW HQ sent von Schlieben orders to 'Hold outer perimeter and belt of forts at all costs'; 'Hold on to Joburg peninsula NW corner at all costs', and 'Hold the hills round Brix'. Von Schlieben's four divisions were exhausted and depleted in numbers. The battlegroups of German defenders included Luftwaffe ground staff, naval gunners with no guns to fire, crews of Schnellboot (PT) boats, construction workers and unreliable Osttruppen battalions (Cossacks, Georgians, etc.). On the 21st von Schlieben ordered all his commanding officers 'Withdrawal from present positions is punishable by death. All leaders will shoot on sight anyone who leaves his post because of cowardice. The hour is serious.' Leaflets in various languages were dropped by the Americans over the town. 'Surrender is an honourable alternative to death.' On the night of 21 June Collins broadcast a message on 1520 kilocycles urging surrender. On the same night 4,200 acres of port jetties and quays were being dynamited and the Luftwaffe parachuted a special package for von Schlieben which contained several hundred Iron Crosses—morale-boosters from the Führer. On 22 June 375 American fighter bombers and 627 medium bombers plastered six main targets with white phosphorous bombs. The American line had been pulled back 1,000 yards—just in case of friendly fire. The massive bombardment started at 12.40 hours with P47s, P51s and British Typhoons. Major General Collins and Major General 'Pete' Quesada USAAF were strafed first by British Typhoons then by American P47s! At the same time Hitler sent a message 'I expect of you that you (von Schlieben) will conduct this action as Gneisenau once conducted the defence of Kolberg. As long as you still have the ammunition and rations every enemy attack must be shattered by your inflexibility, with the strength of your wisdom, your skill and the bravery of your troops. Even if the worst should happen, it is your duty to defend the last pillbox and to leave the enemy, not a harbour, but a field of devastation.' Originally the city had a population of 40,000. Most had fled to the countryside but 6,000 civilians sheltered in cellars. The Red Cross hospitals had by now 1,000 wounded Wehrmacht and several hundred wounded GI prisoners.

Collins launched the major attack at noon on the 22nd, with the 79th Division from the south, the 9th from the west and the 4th from the east. Under a massive artillery barrage, from 1,000 guns following the 1,000 bomber raid, it should have been a classic victory. Lieutenant Colonel Gunther Kiel with 919th Grenadier Regiment and the 7th Machine Gun Battalion, with Colonel Walter Koehn's 739th Regiment, and Colonel Helmuth Rohrbach's combat group put up a terrific resistance. Early on 24 June 'Ike' visited the battlefield looking happy, accompanied by General Omar Bradley. The day before, a second massive attack by Joe Collins's divisions again got nowhere, the 9th in the west and the 4th in the east trying to take Tourlaville and the 79th in the centre trying, with heavy losses to take the La Mare aux Canards strongpoint.

General Bradley had seen at first hand that the huge air force and equally huge artillery bombardment had had relatively little effect on the chain of thick concrete strongpoints. So it was the turn of the Allied navy, with Task Force 129 under Rear Admiral 'Mort' Deyo USN. This comprised three battleships: *Texas* (ten 14-inch guns), *Arkansas* (12 12-inch guns) and *Nevada* (ten 14-inch guns); the four cruisers *Tuscaloosa* (nine 9-inch guns), *Quincy* (nine 8-inch guns), *Glasgow* (12 6-inch guns) and *Enterprise* (six 6-inch guns); with 11 USN screening destroyers and two minesweeping flotillas (one USN, one RN). Sailing from Portland on 21–22 June, this powerful force with enormous fire power arrived some 28,000 yards north of the harbour.

The bombardment on Querqueville and Fermanville coastal defences started at mid-day on the 25th, and went on until 15.40 hours. Some ships went into action at 14,000 yards range. As Admiral Nelson well knew, properly defended shore batteries have the edge on their seaborne attackers. The waterside batteries of Hamburg, Brommy, Yorck and Landemer and many others, such as Fort des Flamands, gave as good as they got. They had 15 guns, 150mm or greater, including three of 280 mm. They had clusters of 75 mm and 88 mm guns firing out to sea. It was a well-documented naval battle. The US ships fired 318× 14-inch shells, 58 × 12-inch, 167 × 8-inch, 429 × 6-inch and 1976 5-inch shells. The *Texas, Barton, Laffey, O'Brien*, and *Glasgow* were all hit. Enemy shore batteries on Cap de la Hague, 12 miles northwest of Cherbourg also gave a good account of themselves.

Admiral Deyo USN admitted afterwards that the attack had stirred up a hornets' nest, and little material damage was done to the forts. Hamburg on a hill six miles to the east of Cherbourg had four 280 mm (11-inch) guns that could fire at a range of 25 miles. Defended by a garrison of 1,000 Kriegs-marines and protected by five inches of reinforced concrete, the complex included 12 anti-aircraft dual-purpose and six 88 mm guns. The destroyer *O'Brien*, battleship *Texas* and RN cruiser *Glasgow* suffered quite heavy casualties. But von Schlieben radioed to Rommel 'Loss of the city shortly is unavoidable. There are now 2,000 wounded without a possibility of being moved. Is the destruction of the remaining troops necessary as part of the general picture in view of the failure of effective counterattacks?'

Eisenhower had told Bradley that he hoped Cherbourg would be taken on the 26th. The Fort du Roule, facing 79th Division south of the town centre, was the most formidable of the Cherbourg fortresses. Built into the face of a rocky promontory on several levels, it housed coastal guns. In the upper levels were mortars, and machine-guns defending the fort from landward attack.

P47 Thunderbolts attacked Fort du Roule at 08.00 hours on 25th and dropped 24 bombs of 500lbs, which all missed. The 314th Infantry Regiment (British brigade strength) under a heavy artillery barrage achieved little. But at 22.00 hours the top level was captured by use of Bangalore torpedoes, and individual human bravery was paramount. Colonel Warren Robinson's force captured a lower level manned by several hundred German defenders. Corporal John Kelly and Lieutenant Carlos Ogden were awarded the Congressional Medal of Honour. The Ninth Division stirred up a tremendous reaction at the old fortress of

Equeurdreville covered by a minefield, and dry moat, sited on top of a hill. Eventually Thunderbolts, mortars, and artillery helped Colonel George Smythe's 47th Infantry Regiment take the small town.

A vivid description of a typical pillbox and its capture follows, as reported by CBS's Larry Lesueur on 25 June 1944:

German pillboxes were still burning from the attack of our flame-throwers. It was so hot within the pillboxes that German ammunition was popping right and left from the intense heat. The yellow scar of a 15 foot deep anti-tank ditch wound its way across the wooded ridges; there were wide vistas of pulverised steel with craters big enough to hold a farmhouse—the result of our air bombardment. The most striking feature of the battlefield, however, was the concrete German fort—the walls six foot thick, they extended thirty feet or more below the earth's surface; apparently the Germans had first dug enormous holes in the ground, built the concrete blockhouses inside, and then they filled in the dirt around the underground fort.

Covered trenches, now badly dented by our air bombardment, led to other underground pilboxes, of which only the round roofs appeared above ground, with apertures facing in every possible direction. These underground bomb-proof forts contained room after room; the only way the Germans could be driven out was for our men to poke explosives into the apertures on long poles, and this is exactly what they did. From one underground fortress alone 300 prisoners were taken, stunned by the explosion and panicked by our flame-throwers. The whole pattern of the German defences on the rear of Cherbourg appeared to be designed like a miniature Maginot Line, but in much greater depth.

While I examined the captured German fort, parties of American engineers arrived by jeep, carrying huge charges of explosive. They placed them deep inside the concrete structures and blew them as wide open as an empty sardine can; that was done just in case the Germans might infiltrate back into the captured territory.

Lieutenant Colonel Woolley reported on the 30th Assault Unit's moves towards Glanville and Cherbourg,

The final assault on the naval base was launched on the morning of 26 June when, against the thunder of the demolition work being carried out in the port by German sappers, American tanks moved into the town without meeting much opposition. The objective of 30th AU was the Villa Meurice, which stood on a hill above the harbour.

With an American infantry company in support, our party advanced on the target which was secured without opposition since all the enemy garrison had retired to the labyrinth of underground workings which had been excavated from the rock. Two American anti-tank self propelled vehicles were brought up, with the one infantry company and the three troops of 30th AU, to deal with the situation.

Blasted by the anti-tank guns firing directly into the mouths of the tunnels, the capitulation of the enemy was soon secured, led by General Karl von Schlieben, commanding the garrison, and Kontra-Admiral Hennecke, the naval officer in charge of the port, both of whom surrendered to Capt Hargreaves-Heap, RM, the liaison officer of 30thAU. In all, 21 German officers and 500 other ranks surrendered and these were handed over to the Americans.

A signal log was captured indicating that, on the afternoon of the day preceding the capture, von Schlieben had appealed to Rommel for assistance but had been brushed off with the reminder that the Führer had ordered him to 'fight to the last round of ammunition', but the General had no stomach for this and the same evening the officer commanding the heavy battle forces was reporting to all concerned that Cherbourg had been lost to the enemy. Actually, resistance was continued for some days by isolated fanatical units and these had to be dealt with individually.

As to the main objective of 30th AU, a search of the tunnels occupied two whole days and brought to light 'a mass of interesting material but little of high grade importance'. This seems hard to credit and makes one question the capability of the men entrusted with the search, although they did take possession of a 'well stocked wine cellar'. The search of all possible targets in the area of the port occupied the whole available strength of the unit for four days with all hands working flat out from dawn to dusk. In line with similar operations in the past, particularly in the Mediterranean Theatre, this proved dirty and dangerous work, because of thickly sown mines and booby traps and occasional fanatical snipers who had to be eliminated.

The Germans had had ample time to compete a comprehensive programme of demolition in the port and this had been carried out with characteristic competence and thoroughness. The U-boat pens had been completely destroyed. As Hugill reports in his book *The Hazard Mesh*, "Great reinforced concrete walls 10 and 15 feet thick had been shattered. Irregular lumps of concrete 100 cubic feet in volume had been blown 100 yards. Enormous girders were lying twisted and torn like paper. The pens themselves were large, cavernous, cathedral-like structures, magnificent in their usefulness and strength and sparse simplicity." Commander Postlethwaite and his crew did, however, find a store for underwater weapons which had escaped destruction and these revealed, amongst other things, a hitherto unrecognized type of mine and a new type of acoustic sweep. Otherwise all torpedo components and relevant confidential books and working drawings had been burnt, sunk or otherwise disposed of. There was thus at least one capture of important material accomplished in this operation.

Von Schlieben radioed to Rommel 'The enemy has split the front. We can hardly withstand an attack. Phosphorous shells have put eight batteries out of action. Losses of unit leaders heavy. Our morale is low.' On the night of the 25th the defenders destroyed the Fort des Flamands, already badly damaged by the navy bombardment. They also blew up the Amcot aircraft works and a train in the Gare Maritime. They used 35 tons of dynamite to blow up more piers and jetties. All the *bassins* were now blocked by sunken ships. Channel water poured through a hole into the inner harbour breakwater. The US 47th Infantry Regiment attacked the town arsenal on whose parapets were emplaced anti-tank, anti-aircraft and machine guns.

On the 26 June elements of 9th, 79th and 4th US divisions in small combat groups started house to house fighting in the city. Eighteen-year-old labour-service lads with bazookas defied them and still the German battlegroups fought on from rooftops, cellars and windows. Colonel Koehn's 739th Grenadier Regiment, Lieutenant Colonel Rohrbach's 729th Regiment, Lieutenant Colonel Kiel's 919th Grenadier Regiment and Colonel Muller's 922nd Grenadiers fought to the end. Their Führer would have been proud of them.

The Fort du Roule was tackled by anti-tank fire from tank destroyers, by lowering demolitions down the side into the emplacements and by final assault by Sergeant Paul Hurst's engineer demolition team. Von

Schlieben's headquarters in Octeville produced 350 prisoners of war. In a hospital in the northwest sector a hospital fell to the 9th Infantry Division yielding 1,200 wounded Germans and 150 US patients. In the large fortress at St Sauveur, at the south end of the harbour, tank destroyers with 39th Regiment under Colonel Flint forced out 842 prisoners of war including the two main prizes—General von Schlieben and Vice Admiral Walter Hennecke. Only hours before, Hitler had awarded Hennecke the Knights Cross to the Iron Cross 'for carrying out an exemplary destruction of the port of Cherbourg.' At 15.00 hours he got off a final message before his capture to the Seventh Army headquarters. 'Documents burned, codes destroyed.' Von Schlieben refused to make a general surrender of the Cherbourg fortress. In the Hotel de Ville 39th Infantry Regiment captured 400 prisoners of war. The second in command Major General Robert Sattler in the Arsenal—a fortress within a fortress with moat, many guns, food and ammunition—surrendered at 08.30 hours on the 27th with a mixed force of 400. Sattler had requested that US Sherman Tanks fire a salvo or two at the Arsenal for 'his' honour. They did and his garrison with cases already packed for captivity, marched out. The 4th Infantry Division had a bitter fight for Maupertus airfield east of the town. Eventually Colonel Foster's 22nd Infantry Regiment over-ran the Batterie Hamburg taking 990 Kriegsmarines prisoner. The indomitable Major Küppers holed up in the powerful Fort Osteck seven miles to the east eventually ran out of ammunition and surrendered to General Barton on the 28th. Barfleur the little port on the northeast of the peninsula was found to be unoccupied.

At 16.00 hours on the 27th a big ceremony attended by most of the surviving 5,000 French civilians took place at the Hotel de Ville. Five American generals attended—Ridgway of the 82nd Airborne, Taylor of 101 Airborne, Eddy with the 9th Division, Wyche of the 79th and Barton of the 4th Division. The VII Corps blue and white flag was hoisted, and General Joe 'Lightning' Lawton Collins with the elderly mayor of Cherbourg, Paul Reynaud took the salute of victory. A great ceremony and much champagne was consumed. But it was not quite over. All the forts along the breakwaters (digues) held out. They were dive-bombed by Thunderbolts. Captain Witt in Fort L'Ouest, the OC Fort du Centre and of Fort du Hamet (where 50 US paratroops were held prisoner) eventually gave up. Still 6,000 Germans under Lieutenant Colonel Kiel held out in the Cap de la Hague in the northwest tip and made the 9th Division pay heavily before they eventually surrendered. Colonel Flint's 39th Infantry Regiment eventually took Auderville on 1 July. It had been a 24-day struggle, but now it was over.

But the second battle remained. Major General Cecil Moore, Chief Engineer SHAEF said that Hennecke had 'knocked hell out of the port'. Colonel Alvin Viney prepared a plan for the rehabilitation of the harbours, 'The demolition of the port was a masterful job, beyond a doubt, the most complete, intensive and best planned demolition in history.' In fact demolition had started as early as 7 June. Navy Group West received a daily account of the progress of demolitions. The US 1056th Engineer Port Construction and Repair Group, 305 men strong under Captain Walsh arrived on 27 June. Two days later Lieutenant Commander Harries RCNVR also examined the wreckage, even though the forts on the breakwater were still active and firing. Commander F.L. de Spon RNR was commanding officer of British naval parties 1571 and 1572 which had arrived on 5th July and started clearance work under Commander Sullivan USN. By then the 'P' parties had commenced diving operations in Bassin à Flot and Avant Port du Commerce with minesweepers operating in Grande Rade. They found many 'Y' and 'P' mines. A methodical search continued of Bassin des Subsistences, the Digne and Quai d'Honnet, Avant Port de l'Arsenal, Bassins des Napoleon and Charles X. On 14 July British Port Party No 1573 (under Lieutenant Commander Irving in surveying ship HMS *Franklin*) arrived to work on Darse Transatlantique. HM ships *Sluga, Domino, Sirra* and MFVs 1024 and 1027 served with USS *Brant*. Working together, American and British clearance parties searched and cleared 1.7 million square feet, with 300 man-hours of diving time.

Ships had been scuttled alongside jetties and in all the dock entrances, with cranes capsized on top of them. Piles of twisted steel lay under water against jetties preventing any craft going alongside. Dozens of railway wagons had been shunted into the harbour. No less than 67 ships and craft up to 12,000 tons weight had been sunk. Twelve lifting 'Camels' were allocated and started work as soon as the 'P' parties had cleared for underwater mines. Commodore T. McKenzie, principal salvage officer on Admiral B. Ramsay's staff worked closely with Commodore Sullivan USN, chief of USN Salvage. Ramsay visited Cherbourg on 6 July and found 'The damage is unbelievable, the place lending itself readily to demolition owing to the peculiar construction of the quays. Dry dock basins undamaged but blocked by sunken ships and crafts.' He reckoned it would take up to three months to clear. By 16 July over 100 mines had been swept for the loss of three minesweepers and seven smaller craft.

By the beginning of August 8,500 tons of oil were being discharged each day and a month later over 12,000 tons daily. But the Pluto operation to pump oil from 'Bambi' on the Isle of Wight had many technical problems. By 3 October both types of pipe (Hamel and Hais) failed, so the Tombola system ship-to-shore continued on the Normandy beaches at Port-en-Bessin.

General Patton and his army engineer, Colonel Conklin, visited the area about 8 July and examined the German defences and Patton reported, 'The whole northern tip of the Peninsula was covered with launching sites for V-2 bombs. [Aimed at Portsmouth] When they were over-run, the Collins assault teams helped save many lives in southern England.'

VII Army Corps had done very well but at a cost from D-Day of 22,119 battle casualties during the Cherbourg-Cotentin campaign. Those killed in action totalled 2,811, wounded 13,564, and 5,665 were missing (some captured but others drowned). The German casualties were assessed at 47,070 killed in action, wounded or prisoners of war, including six generals, an admiral and 826 officers. Apart from the last dramatic week of bombardment from the air, land and sea the defenders had lived a comfortable existence as Larry Lesueur of CBS found when on 30 June he inspected the submarine and E-boat pens, impregnable under a 20-foot thickness of reinforced concrete. He reported on 30 June 1944: 'In their gloomy depths German submarine men could service their U-boats without fear. There seemed to be nothing that the Germans had not provided for the comfort and well-being of the now defeated defenders of Cherbourg—wine, cognac, champagne, were theirs for the asking. They had good food in plenty, and you can see heavy-calibre shells stacked in rows, capable of sinking the entire Allied Navy. Every German barracks was fitted out with running water and electric heating devices. They had plenty of German propaganda books to read, and the walls were plastered with the German version of the pin-up girl, plump Fräuleins in various stages of undress. All that the Germans lacked was the will to win, and from their unmailed letters to Germany you can tell that they were filled with fears of invasion and forebodings of doom, mainly because of the mighty Allied air fleet that thundered overhead incessantly.'

In a Wehrmacht storehouse near the Fort du Roule 80,000 cases of French brandy were found. Alan Moorehead in his book *Eclipse* describes how he visited a prisoner of war cage at Bricquebec. 'In five separate compartments were German officers; German NCOs; German soldiers; a mixture of Russian, Polish and Czech conscripts. In the last cage were the Todt workers in civilian clothes, mostly Italian and Spanish. The

German officers and NCOs sat in taut and rigid little groups, looking over the heads of their guards conveying dignity, pride, contempt, indifference and strength in defeat.'

General von Schlieben's last words to his Führer conveyed that spirit. At 7.32 p.m. on the 25th his message was, 'The final battle for Cherbourg has begun. The General is fighting with his troops. Long live Führer and Germany.' Then came the sign-off prefix and 'Heil the Führer, Heil Germany.' Field Marshal Keitel ordered a court-martial 'in absentia' to examine the negligence and omissions that had apparently weakened the Cherbourg garrison. Then General Friedrick Dollmann, GOC Seventh Army, committed suicide, and Hitler was told it was a heart attack. Field Marshal von Rundstedt was relieved of his command on 2 July, supposedly on the grounds of age and health, and General Geyr GOC Panzer Group West also lost his command. When Rommel heard of it he said, 'I will be next'. Since D-Day he had lost 2,360 officers and over 94,000 men and received only 6,000 replacements. Shortly afterwards he was badly wounded by a British Typhoon strafing near Vimoutiers.

Hitler then put on a brave face and told his generals 'If people now say, "look, the British are in Cherbourg", I reply "to you that is the beginning of their conquest of France, but I look at it differently. After all we already hounded them out of France once, so Cherbourg is just the last ground they still hold. When war broke out it was not we who were in France, but they...."' From the Allied press he read reports that von Schlieben's surrender had been inglorious. 'A braggart', he said to Jodl, 'On 31 July he issued a defiant proclamation, then waits for the others to arrive, whereupon he immediately runs up a white flag.' This was unjust. The Cherbourg garrison had fought well, but within a few weeks by superhuman efforts, the docks were unloading vital supplies for the Allies.

CHAPTER FIVE

Von Aulock's Gallant Defence of St Malo

AT THE CONCLUSION OF THE OVERLORD PLAN IT WAS ASSUMED THAT US forces would push into Brittany and capture the Breton ports of St Malo, Brest, Quiberon Bay, Lorient, St Nazaire and Nantes. After the capture of Cherbourg a month of fierce attritional fighting took place in Normandy around Caen (by British and Canadian forces) and at the southern end of the Cotentin peninsula around St Lo (by the Americans). Field Marshal von Kluge informed Hitler, 'Whether the enemy can still be stopped at this point is questionable. The enemy air superiority is terrific and smothers almost every one of our movements....losses in men and equipment are extraordinary. The morale of our troops has suffered very heavily under constant murderous enemy fire....'

After the bomb explosion at Hitler's headquarters on 20 July the Führer's distrust of his generals reached manic proportions. He now 'directed' the battle himself but used General Walther Warlimont as his personal assistant at von Kluge's headquarters at La Roche Guyon. Rommel had been severely wounded, was incriminated in the plot and was soon 'allowed' to commit suicide.

General Hermann B. Ramcke, in charge of the defence of the Brittany ports, was personally instructed by Hitler to hold out for a minimum of 90 days. Hitler was sure his new weapons V-1, V-2, 'oyster' mines, new ME262 jet fighter, new super tanks, and new Mark XXI submarines would start to take effect. On 23 July he sent a message to all the fortress-port commanders, 'Strong garrisons commanded by officers of proven courage and resourcefulness must be sacrificed to defend the main French ports and deprive the enemy of their use.'

General Omar Bradley on 1 August became GOC of the US Twelfth Army Group, which included the newly arrived Lieutenant General George S. Patton's Third Army. Bradley wrote in his memoirs,

When Patton entered combat, he did so initially with a single corps, Middleton's VIII. The Overlord plan called for Patton's full Third Army to first clear Brittany, seizing the major seaports of St Malo, Brest, Lorient and St Nazaire. By this time, we knew from Ultra that von Kluge had virtually stripped Brittany of its major German divisions to fight the battle of Normandy. Accordingly, I made the decision, in consultation with Ike, Monty and Patton, to greatly reduce our commitment of forces to the Brittany campaign. We would do it with one corps—Middleton's—rather than the full Third Army as called for in the plan. Patton's other corps could thus be made available to throw against the Germans in the east.

Patton blazed through Brittany with armoured divisions and motorised infantry. He conquered a lot of real estate and made big headlines, but the Brittany campaign failed to achieve its primary objectives. The Germans withdrew to the major seaports, organised strong defences and prepared to carry out Hitler's orders to fight to the death. As it developed, none of these ports could be captured without an expensive siege. By the time we wrested them from the Germans—Brest at great cost in US casualties—the war had moved on and we had little use for them.

Some military historians have roundly criticised me for even undertaking the Brittany campaign. They hold that I should have ignored Brittany entirely; that I inflexibly and stubbornly clung to the original Overlord plan merely because it was there; that Middleton's corps, employed in Normandy against the Germans, might have been the decisive extra weight necessary to insure an annihilating victory rather than the outcome that ensued.

There was one overriding reason why I sent Patton and Middleton to Brittany: logistics. This is the dullest subject in the world, and no writer has ever succeeded in glamorising it. The result is that logistics are usually either downplayed or ignored altogether. But logistics were the lifeblood of the Allied armies in France. Without ports and facilities we could not supply our armies. We could not move, shoot, eat, land new troops or evacuate the wounded. One

1 Reich Minister Albert Speer inspects an Atlantic Wall installation in 1943. (IWM)

2 Heavy cannons on the Atlantic Wall in action. (AKG London)

3 An impressive display of Atlantic Wall firepower. (AKG London)

4 A German pillbox outside Cherbourg blown up by advancing Allied troops, 17 June 1944. (IWM)

5 Major General 'Lightning' Joe Collins and staff survey Cherbourg town and harbour, 27 June 1944. Some of the port facilities are ablaze. (IWM)

6 US troops searching German prisoners routed out of a captured fort at Cherbourg, June 1944. (Corbis)

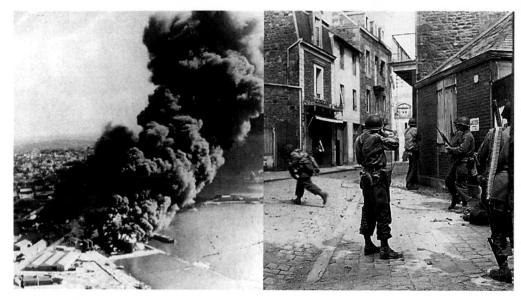

7 Port Facilities at St. Malo burning fiercely. (AKG London)

8 House-to-house fighting as Allied soldiers push into St Malo, 8 August 1944. (Corbis)

9 Brest town wrecked by Allied bombing and German demolitions. (IWM)

10 The wrecked Jan of Arc Bridge at Brest Harbour, 13 September 1944. (Corbis)

12 A Passionate welcome for the liberators of Antwerp, September 1944. (Author's collection)

11 Lieutenant H. G. Stubbs leads C Squadron into Boom, on the outskirts of Antwerp, August 1944. (Authors collection)

13 The attack on Le Havre - Operation Astonia - supported by the 'funnies' of 79th Armoured division. A flail tank and bridge layer are seen here. (IWM)

14 The sunken SS *Paris* in the Harbour at Le Havre, captured 12 September 1944. The construction to the left is a German anti-aerial torpedo net. (IWM)

15 Troops wading ashore for a dawn landing at Flushing. (IWM)

16 Colonel Reinhardt, CO of the 1,019th Regiment, after his capture at Flushing. (IWM)

17 The landing at Walcheren, October 1944. (IWM)

18 The Atlantic Wall finds a new owner: a British soldier. (AKG London)

division in combat required about 700 *tons* of supplies a day. The Allies had thirty-seven divisions on the Continent....

In addition to the single Mulberry harbour at Avranches, Cherbourg and half a dozen minor harbours, the Allies desperately needed additional major ports. St Malo, an auxiliary supply port, was capable of 1,000 tons per day. St Lo, then Coutances, Villedieu and eventually Avranches were the main objectives of Operation Cobra, which started on 25 July backed by four American Army Corps. And now Patton came into his own, as he wrote, 'The passage of [my] Third Army through the corridor of Avranches was an impossible operation. Two roads entered Avranches, only one left it over the bridge. We passed through this corridor two infantry and two armoured divisions in less than 24 hours. There was no plan because it was impossible to make a plan.' Major General Wood's 4th Armoured Division advanced 50 miles in four days bypassing the German garrison in Rennes. Despite wrangles about objectives, the 4th Armoured drove further west and invested Lorient between 6 and 10 August. Montgomery had bet General Patton a modest five pound note that he would not take Brest by August.

Some 40 miles due west of Avranches lies the enchanting medieval seagirt fortress of St Malo. Situated to the northeast of the wide River Rance, the old town known as Intra-Muros, with its huge strong wide ramparts commands a useful port. Across the harbour at the northwest end of the Rance is the smart town resort of Dinard. Twelve miles due south down the wide estuary of the Rance is the attractive small town of Dinan. The whole area was commanded by Colonel Andreas von Aulock. The FFI (French Resistance movement) under Colonel Meon had over 2,500 local members, many of them living in the three towns around the Rance. US intelligence had estimated there were between 3,000 and 6,000 German defenders. The two main Allied formations were 266 Infantry Division plus elements of the 2nd and 3rd Parachute Divisions. The FFI had advised that recent consolidations within the region had brought the garrison's numbers up to 10,000. Actually split 2:1 between St Malo and Dinard there were 12,000 defenders. Von Aulock had vowed to his Führer 'I will defend St Malo to the last man, even if the last man has to be myself.'

General Patton sent Major General R.W. Gerow's 6th Armoured Division towards St Malo and then on to invest Brest, which they reached on 7 August. General Middleton's VIII Corps was now entrusted with the capture of Brittany and of its five ports. Specifically Major General

Robert Macon's 83rd Infantry Division plus a combat team Task Force 'A' were to surround, invest and capture the port of St Malo, which harboured several E-boats and minesweepers. On 1 August the flotilla of patrol boats and another of minesweepers left St Malo harbour, some headed south down the River Rance to help defend Dinan, but the majority fled west along the coast to Brest. Two Allied air bombardments had taken place on 17 July and 1 August. The French population pleaded with Colonel von Aulock to declare historic St Malo—the pearl of Brittany—an open city. The message was passed to Field Marshal von Kluge and thence to Hitler who replied, 'In warfare there is no such thing as an historic city. You will fight to the last man.' OB West regarded St Malo as the most advanced of any fortress in the west. There were major strongpoints at the Fort la Varde (just to the east) and at St Ideuc, east of the suburb of Paramé. Additionally there was the near impregnable citadel a mile south of the old walled city, called Citadel d'Aleth, with a garrison of 410 defenders with six powerful guns in a huge Blockhaus, it commanded all the western approaches to St Malo and Dinard across the mile-wide Rance estuary. Three miles offshore was a powerful defence unit on the small island of Cézembre, with heavy artillery and gunners concealed in rock caves. From the Channel Islands came supplies, usually at night, of water and rations and the returning boats took back German casualties. As the American forces gradually closed around St Malo, many French civilians left on the afternoon of 5 August under white flags. Von Aulock, a veteran of Stalingrad, told OB West at the same time, 'I was placed in command of this fortress. I did not request it. I will execute the orders I have received, and doing my duty as a soldier. I will fight to the last stone.' On the same day, the 5th, General Macon co-ordinated the initial attack on the outer defences, east of St Benoit-des-Ondes, south of Chateauneuf and southwest at Pleurtuit (near Dinard). A battalion of 329th Infantry Regiment crossed the Rance in assault boats to cut the Dinard-Dinan road but met strong resistance and were recalled. On the eastern flank the defenders abandoned St Benoit and the fishing harbour of Cancale occupied by 331st Infantry Regiment the next day. By now the Americans were making use of minor harbours at Isigny, Granville, St Michel-en-Greve and Cancale. To the south Dinan which had been identified as a strongpoint, was heavily bombarded and was surrounded by the FFI.

The FFI informed the American divisional staff that demolitions to the harbour of St Malo took place during the nights of 1 and 2 August. Also the garrison had been reinforced by two combat units of 319th Infantry Division from Guernsey. The artillery on Cézembre Island fired shells on the 6th, which struck and demolished the steeple of the cathedral in the old town of St Malo—a bad omen to the surviving civilians. Fires broke out around the cathedral but the Americans had cut off supplies of water. During the same day General Macon tightened his grip as the three regiments advanced in a semi-circle attack from the Rance in the west, to the sea west of Cancale. Pillboxes, anti-tank ditches, minefields, wire entanglements and steel gates held up the advance. The 121st Infantry Regiment and a medium tank company were sent up to help from 8th Division at Rennes.

The next day Colonel von Aulock ordered a general demolition of the port; breakwaters were dynamited; cranes were toppled into the docks; quays and locks were destroyed; surviving small craft were scuttled. St Malo was by now a complete shambles. A new attack took place on the 7th, but Colonel Robert Foster's 330th Infantry Regiment were held up by a strongpoint on St Joseph's Hill, with guns emplaced in a granite quarry. Repeated artillery barrages had little effect and it took two days of repeated infantry attacks before the garrison of 400 surrendered. Von Aulock received a radio message on the 8th that the Adolf Hitler and Hermann Goering Divisions would counterattack the US forces at Avranches and thus might relieve pressure on the St Malo operation.

General Patton wrote on 8 August, 'I found R C Macon near St Malo. When he saw General Hughes in the car with me, he turned white as he thought he was about to be relieved, but his division was doing well, but not too well, had lost 800 men, taken 1,300 PoW. The fighting had degenerated into a sniping contest. Not much noise but dangerous to stick one's neck out.' Macon, Patton and Hughes were in fact within 40 yards of the front line. 'The 83rd took [part] of St Malo town on 8th, but the islands off St Malo [Cézembre] were still giving trouble firing at our troops on shore with their long range guns. I had no success in persuading the *British* Navy to do anything about it.' Patton hated all the British commanders, and indeed most of the American generals as well. In fact a few days later HMS *Warspite* and HMS *Malaya* arrived to help batter the island defences. 'We decided to ask for air on Dinard because we were having too many casualties trying to avoid bombing towns.'

Colonel York's 331st Infantry Regiment made progress northwards through the suburb of Paramé to the sea, cutting off and bypassing the garrisons of the strongpoints of St Ideuc and La Varde (which held out for another week). On the left flank Colonel Crabill's 329th Infantry Regiment had taken the Fort de Chateauneuf, had surrounded a strongpoint of La Balue and moved through the suburbs of St Servan up to the gates of the citadel. One battalion now invested La Varde. General Macon had deployed 121st Infantry Regiment under Colonel John Jeter to cross the River Rance, accept the surrender of the German garrison cut off in Dinan (who refused to surrender to the FFI) and then move northwards to capture Dinard. Enemy resistance was considerable at Pleslin, with heavily defended roadblocks, underground strongpoints, minefields, small-arms fire as well as *nebelwerfer* mortars. Reinforcements arrived to help the Allies, in the form of the 965th Field Artillery and on the 8th, the 1st Battalion of the 331st Infantry Regiment. The next day Pleurtuit, only four miles from Dinard, was taken, but the 3rd Battalion, 121st Regiment was ambushed in front and attacked by German tanks from behind. Five American planes trying to drop supplies were shot down and the US 908th Artillery Battery suffered heavy losses.

The highly experienced Colonel Rudolf Bacherer, the commanding officer of the German Kampfgruppe, mostly from the 77th Infantry Division, was putting up a determined resistance. He told his men, 'Every house must become a fortress, every stone a hiding place, and for every stone we shall fight.'

General Macon realized he had a serious problem and moved the rest of 331st Regiment across the Rance to reinforce the beleaguered 121st Regiment. There American 4.2-inch mortars fired white phosphorous chemical shells. On 11 August the co-ordinated advance on the west bank of the Rance was still very slow. Macon radioed General Middleton, 'I want "Monarch 6" (code for Middleton) to know that the resistance we are meeting south of Dinard is more determined than I anticipated.' The next day 331st Infantry Regiment broke through near Pleurtuit and made contact with the isolated battalion of 121st Regiment who had lost 31 killed in action, 106 wounded and 11 missing. Five bunkers were over-run with 88 mm anti-tank guns and over 100 prisoners of war were taken. Several awards of the Distinguished Service Cross were made for gallantry. Private Francis Gardner, Headquarters Company, took on an enemy tank with a bazooka, hit its turret and killed the crew. Sergeant Milford Wilson directed enemy fire to himself to cover his squad's withdrawal. Captain Arthur Kaiser led his company though minefields, barbed wire and tank barriers under machine gun and artillery fire. General Macon was much relieved when on the 14th both regiments entered Dinard and its suburbs and, the following day, cleared the town and the villages of St Briac-sur-Mer and St Lunaire to the west. The German Colonel Bacherer and his headquarters were captured with 400 prisoners of war. Hill 42 and Hill 48 at St Briac were strongpoints and their captured German guns were then turned on the island of Cézembre.

The German troops really did call their commanding officer Colonel von Aulock, 'a mad colonel'. Tall, monocled with a Semitic appearance he had a curious sense of humour as this order indicates.

9 August 1944

To all Soldiers of the Garrison ·

From this moment there will be only three types of punishment:

(1) Whoever leaves the corridors of his billets not clean, whoever does not use the WC properly, whoever does not take care of his arms, will receive ten to twenty five strokes on his behind.

(2) Anyone found lacking in interest or showing reluctance in his work, and anyone exhibiting pessimism, will be punished in the following way:

The individual will be chased in broad daylight, without weapons, in the direction of the enemy.

(3) Disobedience and cowardice will be punished by death.

F. AULOCK.

Major General Ferenbaugh, the assistant divisional commander, as Macon was heavily involved in clearing up the Dinard operation, was tackling the two obdurate forts at St Ideuc and La Varde. It took three days from 9 to 12 August to subdue them after artillery and engineers winkled out the various bunkers and pillboxes. Finally 160 prisoners of war were taken at the first and 100 prisoners of war at the second, which fell on the 13th.

The Casino strongpoint was taken on the 11th and the Château de St Malo was battered by 330th Regiment for two days, backed by 3-inch tank-destroyer guns and howitzers. The causeway and minefields delayed its eventual capture. A truce on the afternoon of the 13th allowed 1,000 French civilians and 500 hostages and internees to cross the lines to safety.

The next day 330th Regiment fought their way into the old town (Intra-Muros), street by street, house by house capturing 150 prisoners of war. Two small offshore forts, the National and the Grand Bey were taken on the 16th at low tide, and 329th Regiment took 150 prisoners of war. But the citadel of Aleth still held out. The thick walls could not be breached by artillery fire. Barbed wire, an anti-tank ditch and four lines of steel rails kept the attackers at bay. Inside food, ammunition supplies, a vast reservoir of water plus field guns, mortars and 20 machine guns acted as a strong deterrent.

At critical moments during the fighting, Lee Miller, the photographeer and journalist, climbed up to an observation post in the honeymoon suite of a hotel. In the first draft of an article for *Vogue* she describes an air attack:

> . . . the boy at the phone said, 'They hear airplanes.' We waited, then we heard them swelling the air like I've heard them vibrating over England on some such mission. This time they were bringing their bombs to the crouching stone work 700 yards away. They were on time—bombs away—a sickly death rattle as they straightened themselves out and plunged into the citadel—deadly hit—for a moment I could see where and how—then it was swallowed up in smoke—belching, mushrooming and column-ing—towering up, black and white. Our house shuddered and stuff flew in at the window—more bombs crashing, thundering, flashing—like Vesuvius—the smoke rolling away in a sloping trail. A third lot! The town reeled in the blast—a large breach had been made—and we waited for the next attack.

This was one of the first times the new secret weapon, napalm, was used. When Lee's photographs were processed at *Vogue*, the British censor grabbed the rolls showing the napalm strike and eliminated all the shots that might be revealing.

A horrendous and futile infantry assault stormed up the steep exposed rock faces that girdled the fort.

> The building we were in and all the others which faced the fort were being spat at now—ping, bang—hitting above our window— into the next—breaking on the balcony below—fast queer noise— impact before the gun noise itself—following the same sound pattern—hundreds of rounds—crossing and recrossing where we were.
>
> Machine gun fire belched from the end pillbox—the men fell flat—stumbling and crawling into the shelter of shellholes—some crept on, others sweeping back to the left of the guns' angle, one man reaching the top. He was enormous. A square-shouldered silhouette, black against the sky between the pillbox and the fort.

He raised his arm. The gesture of a cavalry officer with sabre waving the others on. He was waving to death, and he fell with his hand against the fort.

The picturesque town of Saint Malo which had stood securely on its small promontory was turned into rubble by the fire from the citadel guns.

Tall chimneys standing alone gave off smoke from the burning remnants of their buildings at their feet. Stricken lonely cats prowled. A swollen horse had not provided adequate shelter for the dead American behind it—flower pots stood on roomless wondows. Flies and wasps made tours in and out of underground vaults which stank with death and sour misery. Gunfire brought more stone blocks down into the street. I sheltered in a kraut dugout, squatting under the ramparts. My heel ground into a dead detached hand and I cursed the Germans for the sordid ugly destruction they had conjured up in this once beautiful town. I wondered where my friends that I had known here before the war were; how many had been forced into disloyalty and degradation—how many had been shot, starved or what. I picked up the hand and hurled it across the street, and ran back the way I'd come bruising my feet and crashing in the unsteady piles of stone and slipping in blood. Christ, it was awful.

General Macon called in the USAF, initially with fighter bombers who dropped small bombs and two groups of medium bombers who dropped 1,000lb bombs to little effect. Colonel von Aulock sent a radio message to his Führer, 'The enemy is putting German PoW on his tanks so as to get close to our strongpoints', which was an unlikely claim! A loudspeaker van from a Psychological Warfare Service unit tried propaganda 'warfare' with no result. A captured German chaplain was sent into Colonel von Aulock to persuade him to surrender. No deal! Even von Aulock's French lady friend was persuaded to telephone him. His answer was 'I have other things on my mind.' To all messages he replied 'I am a German soldier and a German soldier does not surrender.' He had heard of the massive German counterattack from Mortain to Avranches and hoped it would draw off the attacking forces. For five days the citadel was pounded by artillery, by medium bombers with 500lb general purpose bombs, by 100lb incendiaries and 1,000lb semi-armour piercing bombs. The 329th

Infantry Regiment with three French FFI interpreters, with engineering teams breached the walls with Bangalore torpedoes to clear the barbed wire entanglements and anti-tank obstacles. With flame-throwers 30 men reached the interior court but were cut down by machine-gun fire. Shells from the Cézembre island defenders added to the confusion and the attack failed. Colonel Crabhill formed two special assault teams, each with 96 infantry and specialist engineers, again to no avail. When a white flag went up, it was only to ask for a truce to let more French civilians out. Each day attacks went in until—perhaps rather surprisingly on the 17th, Colonel von Aulock, freshly shaved, in his full-dress uniform, insolent as ever, surrendered the citadel. Despite having plenty of food and water and ammunition, his troops' morale was low and the direct fire of 8-inch guns aimed singly at point-blank range had destroyed most of his larger field guns and his machine gun emplacements. Nevertheless his brave defence had held up the entire four US regiments (brigades by British standards) for two weeks and finally he had totally destroyed the port. With comparatively light casualties 83rd Divison had finally taken 12,773 prisoners of war, many of them Russians. The various battlegroups Jaeger, Moosmann, Behrens, Plessow, Beilshmidt and Captain Strube's Russian troops had fought valiantly—not to the last troop, not to the last stone— but certainly almost up to their absentee Führer's requirements. Colonel von Aulock's final message to his troops on the 17th ended with the words 'Long live the Führer! Long life to our great German country.'

But it was not yet over.

The little island of Cézembre some 4,000 yards offshore from St Malo, opposite the mouth of the Rance was half a mile long, a quarter of a mile wide. Lieutenant Richard Zeuss commanded 232 German troops of the 608th Battalion Naval Artillery, 71 Italians of the 2nd Cézembre Battery and 20 Russians. Zeuss reported to the commandant of the German garrison in Jersey, whose orders were predictably 'Do not surrender.' No ships could get into St Malo without being shelled from Cézembre. From 9 August until 2 September it was battered by heavy bombers, by land artillery, by P-38s dropping napalm, by 8-inch howitzers, by RAF bombers, by IX US Bomber Command. The Royal Navy joined in and HMS *Warspite*'s 15-inch guns turned the island into a desert. Several times American missions tried to persuade Zeuss to give up. His garrison were 'safe' inside turrets dug into rocks and their manned coastal guns still functioned. Their water distillery plant was however destroyed and as an amphibious attack started on 2 September, Zeuss reluctantly hoisted the white flag. Cézembre was an absolute shambles. No less than 19,729 bombs and shells had landed on the small area. Zeuss had but 20 men killed and 24 wounded. Hitler awarded him the Iron Cross at the same time as he promoted von Aulock, who had just surrendered, to be a general!

In the final result, St Malo port was so badly damaged that the Americans decided it was not worthwhile to repair the damage done by von Aulock and his die-hard 980 paratroops and the 1,000 soldiers of 17th SS Panzer Division Grenadiers.

The *Daily Mail* of 23 August had the headline 'Madman of St Malo; monocled 'mad' Colonel von Aulock marches out to ignoble surrender after swearing he would defend St Malo to the last drop of blood. Hitler gave him the Oak Leaves to the Iron Cross. The next day von Aulock surrendered.' A rather jingoistic view of what really happened. It had taken two weeks for the mainland defences and four weeks for the offshore defences to be subdued. And at the end of it all, the small port was rendered useless.

CHAPTER SIX

The Taking of Brest: 'A symbolic value'

AT THE BEGINNING OF AUGUST 1944 WINSTON CHURCHILL TRIED to persuade President Roosevelt to switch the ten-division attack on the south of France, codenamed Anvil/Dragoon to reinforcing success in Overlord. He wrote 'The course of events in Normandy and Brittany and especially the brilliant operations of the United States Army give good prospects that the whole of the Brittany peninsula will be in our hands within a reasonable time....instead of having to force a landing against strong enemy defences [in South of France] we might easily find welcoming American troops at some point or other from St Nazaire north-westward along the Brittany peninsula. I feel that we are fully entitled to use the extraordinary flexibility of sea and air power to move with the moving scene.' And he said to Harry Hopkins, the president's trusted right-hand man 'In my opinion the American Army have to a large extent demoralised the scattered Germans in the Brest peninsula. St Nazaire and Nantes, one of your major disembarkation ports in the last war may be in our hands at any time. Quiberon Bay, Lorient, and Brest will also soon fall into our hands....Bordeaux could be obtained easily, cheaply and swiftly....' Churchill suggested diverting the ten divisions earmarked for Anvil/Dragoon through the straits of Gibraltar to enter France at Bordeaux. Despite intensive lobbying by Eisenhower, Bedell Smith, and Admiral Ramsay, the original plans went ahead. Hopkins answered'....No one knows the condition of the Brittany ports.' Churchill had visited Cherbourg and had seen the terrible damage done to the port facilities. A month

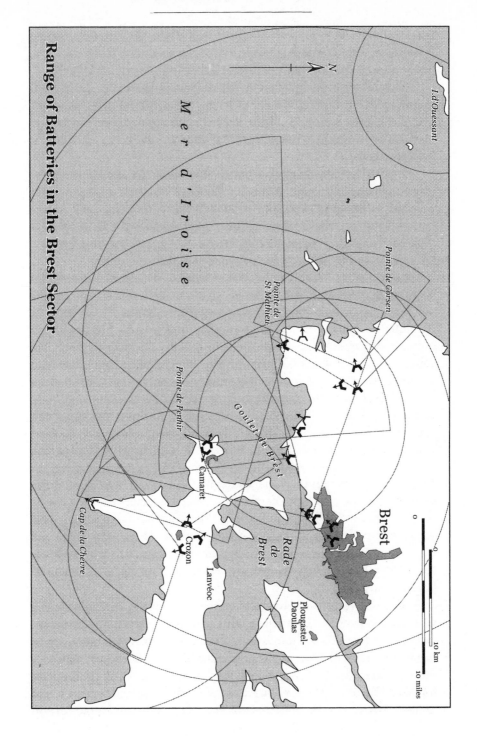

Range of Batteries in the Brest Sector

I.d'Ouessant

Mer d'Iroise

Pointe de Corsen

Pointe de St-Mathieu

Pointe de Penhir

Goulet de Brest

Camaret

Crozon

Lanvéoc

Cap de la Chevre

Brest

Rade de Brest

Plougastel-Daoulas

N

10 km

10 miles

SMASHING THE ATLANTIC WALL

later the port was back in action again. At St Malo, taken in mid-August, the port was considered inoperable. The commandants of Hitler's fortress-ports were defending vigorously and destroying equally vigorously.

General Patton had passed on the responsibility for the £5 bet with Monty to Major General Gerow GOC the 6th Armoured Division. On 1 August Gerow was told, 'Take Brest by Saturday night, by-pass all resistance.' It was 200 miles west of Avranches and he had five days in which to do it.

Brest had been the major port in the First World War for the American forces arriving in Europe. Patton and Bradley were both veterans of that war and so Brest was certainly of symbolic value to them. On 8 August Patton informed Major General Troy Middleton GOC VIII Corps that they had the job of clearing the Brittany peninsula, and securing the ports of St Malo and Brest had priority over the capture of Lorient.

Situated at the mouth of the River Penfeld, the city of Brest, with a wartime population of 80,000, lies north of a magnificent harbour capable of sheltering 500 warships. The roadstead (the expanse of sea within the harbour) is about 14 miles long and four miles wide. The naval port excavated from solid rock extends along both sides of the river. The commercial port has a tidal harbour with wharves and an outer harbour, and then 300,000 cubic metres of cement protected the 15 U-boat shelters.

The Royal Navy had been keeping a watchful eye on Brest and in the period 5–12 August the RAF had sent Halifaxs, Stirlings and Lancasters to help with mine-laying operations. The bomb-proof U-boat pens rendered submarines immune from attack from the air, so early capture was desirable, and on 6 August the RAF dropped two enormous six-ton bombs, a direct hit on the pens. General Hermann B. Ramcke, a tough and skilful soldier with the crack 2nd Parachute Division was, from 12 August, the commandant of the 38,000-strong German garrison. The 343rd Infantry Division consisted of six battalions of infantry, either very young or rather mature, plus two Russian battalions. The port itself was defended by the 24th Regiment Naval Anti-aircraft and the 262nd Batteries of coastal artillery.

The defences of Brest formed a huge circle from Le Conquet (the western headland 24 kilometres northwest from Brest), to Chateaulin (40 kilometres southeast from Brest). Crozon and Camaret on the southern headland across the Rade de Brest were defended by the 343rd Infanterie Division and Admiral Khaler's 3rd Brigade of Marine Flak. In the main town fortress of Brest were a battalion of 898th Infantry Regiment and artillerie HAA 1162. General Fahrmbacher had sited battalions of 852/898 and Artillerie Regiment AR 343 around Le Conquet, Chateaulin and Crozon respectively. The most powerful of the many batteries were the Graf Spee in Lochrist with 280 mm guns, Grand Gouin with 220 mm guns, Rospects at Pointe St Mathieu and the Kerbonn battery at Camaret with 220 and 155 mm guns. There were three key Stutzpunkt (high artillery towers with defences on eight levels) at Portzic (the 8th Festa fortress troops) at Olberg (with 6th Festa) and Marineschule (3rd HAA) in a semi-circle guarding the vital U-boat pens. These were some 340 metres long by 180 metres in depth situated in the main *rade* (harbour). Four naval flotillas were stationed in Brest—the 9th U-Boots, 24th and 40th Minensuch and the 7th Vorpostenboot-Jager. The overall 3rd Sicherungs Division was commanded by Kapitan zur See Bergelt, Kapitan zur See Eugen Richter was Commanding Officer 3rd Brigade of Marine Flak with five groups of mixed heavy and light anti-aircraft guns. Twenty powerful batteries, each with four 105 mm or 88 mm guns, guarded the city, capable of ground fire.

Colonel von der Mosel was chief of staff and Colonel Kroh commanded the 2nd Parachute Division (with the 2nd and 7th Parachute Regiments). Present too were elements of 266th Infantry Division, 9,000 Kriegs-marines, 3,500 artillery personnel and many Todt organization workers. Ramcke, therefore, had over 20,000 troops under command.

General Omar Bradley wrote in his autobiography: 'Under Patton, Middleton's VIII Corps of three divisions had taken St Malo after a stiff fight but the Germans had withdrawn into the ports of Lorient, St Nazaire and Brest prepared for a long and bitter siege. We might have been well advised to give up the good fight and let Brest remain in German hands, contained by our newly arriving green infantry divisions and by the French Forces of the Interior which had ably assisted Patton's run through Brittany. We certainly could have used Middleton's Corps to better advantage in the forthcoming drive towards Germany. But by then Brest had taken on a symbolic value far exceeding its utilitarian value and perhaps imprudently, I was stubbornly determined to capture it.' Patton recorded in his diary: 'Bradley said to me with reference to the Brest operation, "I would not say this to anyone but you and I have given different excuses to my staff and higher echelons, but we must take Brest in order to maintain the illusion of the fact that the US Army cannot be beaten." 'Patton went on, 'More emotion than I thought he [Bradley] had. I fully concur in this view. Anytime we put our heart to a job, we must finish it.'

Martin Blumenson, the US military historian, noted 'that the forces in Brittany had now become step-children.' Hodges First US Army and Patton's Third US Army were driving towards Tours, Orleans and Paris leaving the 'step-children' to clear up the mess behind.

The intrepid British 30th Assault Unit in their heavily armed jeeps were roaming widely through Brittany, as Flight Lieutenant Nutting commanding the part of the unit known as 'Nutforce' recalled,

We waited at Carteret, training the replacements, while the US army fought itself into positions from which it could break out from the bridgehead and cut loose. In the meantime the British and Canadians were holding the bulk of the German armour at Caen. Then came the breakout and things became exquisitely fluid, just as we liked it. We swarmed into the Brest peninsula and across it to Vannes, St Nazaire and Nantes. This was back to the good old days with a vengeance, moving about behind Jerry and unsettling him generally. One place we didn't get into was Brest—Jerry held out there with determination for a couple more months.

The Brest peninsula was also a hunting ground for our old chums in the French section of the SAS. They had got in there before the landings and we gave them what we could spare in the way of food and ammo. We met any number of civilians wearing FFI armbands, French Forces of the Interior, a sort of Maquis or partisan. We were never sure what these chaps had been up to. Some of them were genuine enough, no doubt about that, but many carried German army rifles without their bolts, obviously having picked them up after the Jerries had removed the bolts before throwing their arms away. We helped the genuine ones as best we could.

Most of the Jerries we bumped into were only too glad to surrender to us, rather than submit to whatever the French might do to them. We disarmed them and provided they kept together they'd be safe. Single ones or pairs could be in trouble and generally we gave these a lift until we found a bigger group for them to join. I made them sit on the flat top of my scout car, hanging on to the twin Vickers mount, which they seemed happy to do. They were told to keep on walking to a major road and sit there until collected by the US.

Wherever Germans showed any inclination to stand and fight they got all the fighting they wanted. We had the fire power and we were quite ready to use every bit of it. We encountered no SS troops, the majority of whom were fighting in the British and Canadian sectors.

We had a brief rest and regroup at Mordreuc, on the River Rance south of St Malo, and collected more replacements.

Lieutenant Colonel Woolley, who commanded the 'Woolforce' part of 30th Assault Unit, was tasked with getting into Brest to examine the port facilities and the German 'secret' weapons and 'know-how'. 'My next main targets were in Brest, but most of the German forces were concentrating there and they showed no signs of making entry easy for anybody. Numbers of German convoys were constantly moving towards Brest to join the garrison there, and small parties of parachute troops were at the same time searching for escape routes eastwards. Mostly we avoided contact by dodging round the rear ends of the stronger columns, but we ran into one small convoy at Loc Brevelaire, where with the local FFI we made enough show of force to secure bloodless surrender of sixty-four officers and men and a considerable collection of mixed guns and mortars.'

The Château de Massais was an important German headquarters and 30th Assault Unit were determined to capture it as Wooley wrote:

After a few minutes thought I decided that we were justified in proceeding, and I put into practice my plan for moving in wheeled vehicles ahead of Allied front-line troops. It was a plan which was to prove effective almost everywhere in France and also (more surprisingly) later in Germany. I led the way myself in Fraser's Jeep, and the scout cars followed at 25 yard intervals, on alternate sides of the road where possible.

I preferred the Jeep as leading vehicle, in spite of its lack of protective armour, because we could see clearly in every direction from it and could reverse or manoeuvre very quickly out of trouble, especially with Fraser's ability to drive very fast backwards; also, it was easy to dive into the ditch from the Jeep if needs be. We carried the lightweight semi-automatic .300 US carbines, which were handy and effective weapons at short range. It was the responsibility of the rather heavier gunned and armoured scout cars to cover our withdrawal if we came under fire. The basic idea was extreme mobility, combined with sufficient firepower and *appearance* of strength to make any small groups of enemy think twice before engaging us. Anything like a dug-in anti tank gun or heavy machine gun was a different matter, of course, but even that might not get all of us if we were quick enough in our reactions.

Above all, we depended on constant advice from the civilian population, who could tell us where the nearest German troops were and what they were doing. We learned quickly that one piece of information was vital for us. Were the German soldiers wearing steel helmets? If they were, they were still a fighting force and to be avoided; if steel helmets had been discarded, the German troops were almost certainly no longer intending to fight and they would probably be quite happy to be taken prisoner. German prisoners, when we were lucky enough to get any, also proved to be a reliable source of information—as were German civilians when we moved into Germany in 1945. The Germans had left their 'control' centre and the FFI were in occupation of the Château.

By 7 August the 6th US Armoured Division was probing the outer defences of Brest. General Gerow had divided his command (the Super-Six) into three combat command formations: Brigadier General James Taylor OC of CCA; Colonel George Read OC of CCB; and Colonel Harry Hanson OC of CCR. Lieutenant Colonel William Jesse commanded the divisional artillery and Lieutenant Colonel Albert Harris the 86th Cavalry Reconnaissance Unit.

CCA arrived northeast of Brest via St Thoan and Guipavas. CCB came up on the east via Bourg-Blanc and CCR via Plouvien and Gouesnou. On 8 August heavy guns from Brest caused losses at l'Or-Meau; casualties were 43 killed in action, 179 wounded and 14 missing. The divisional staff officer GSO-2 Lieutenant Colonel Ernest Mitchell took in an ultimatum for the garrison to surrender which was brusquely rejected. The next day CCA's second attack was violently repulsed with much loss. Worse still, most of the German 266th Infantry Division joined Ramcke's defenders by slipping in through the north of the Brest peninsula. They consisted of 896th, 897th and 898th Infantry Regiments under General Spang.

The three combat units were now within four and seven miles from the city centre. General Gerow asked for a heavy air attack on the 9th to support an attack by CCB in the centre and Taylor's CCA on the left, with four artillery batteries supporting both columns. At Lesneven, 15 miles northeast of Brest in confused fighting General Karl Spang, with his headquarters staff of 266th Infantry Division, were captured. General

Gerow cancelled the main attack on Brest and set out to destroy Spang's division. In the next four days 3,500 PoW were gathered in. On the 11th and 12th CCA tried to secure the high ground near the airport at Guipavas but failed. Gerow knew now that he needed heavy artillery support, more infantry, strong engineer forces and fighter and medium bomber support to reduce the inner defences of Brest. Middleton ordered Gerow to contain (but not attack) Brest with CCA and a battalion from the 8th Infantry Division just arrived from Rennes. CCB and CCR were then sent off to Vannes and Lorient respectively to relieve Patton's 4th Armoured Division. In its week 'investing' Brest the 6th Armoured Division had suffered 130 killed in action, 400 wounded and 70 missing, but had taken almost 4,000 prisoners of war. Gerow had done a good job. On 13th a truce was agreed and no less than 25,000 French civilians made their 'exodus' from Brest.

By the middle of August SHAEF was concentrating on the 'High Noon' shoot-out in the Falaise pocket as 20 divisions of the German Seventh Army, the Fifth Panzer Army and Panzer Group Eberbach were trying desperately to escape to the River Seine. Americans, British, Canadians, Poles and French formations fought, squeezed and eventually closed the pocket on the 19th at Chambois. It was a great victory—the culmination of Overlord.

Far to the west 4,000 US troops of CCA/6th Armoured Division 'surrounded' the fortress garrison of Brest, now estimated to number 35,000 troops. On the 13th and again on the 14th, first by 28 Lancasters then by 155 Lancasters, the RAF deluged with bombs the naval harbour of Brest. Their objective was to sink the French battleship *Clémenceau* at its berth to prevent it being deliberately sunk to block the entrance to the port.

Lieutenant Commander Brian Izzard RN, of the British Forward Interrogation Unit, with Lieutenant Thuermer USN visited Brest on Thursday, 17 August, recording that:

> We found General Taylor's HQ just west of Guipavas [3 miles NE of centre of Brest], 1,500 yards from the front line. The Allied line was being held by 2,000 renegade Russian PoW on the right wing, the remnants of 6th Armoured Div Group in the centre and the FFI on the left wing. As about 21,000 Germans were believed to be in the Brest area, General Taylor was reluctant to press hostilities until he received reinforcements and next to no PoW were being taken [for Izzard to interrogate]. Contacted Capitan de Vasseau Lukas and Capitan de Corvette Levasseur attached with other free

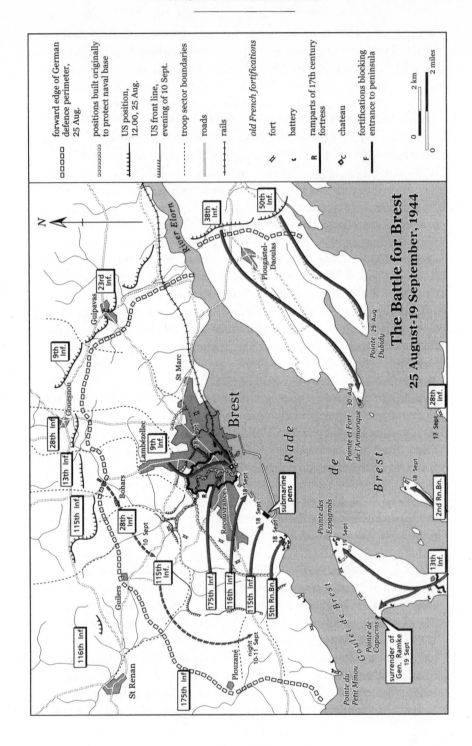

The Battle for Brest
25 August-19 September, 1944

Legend:
- forward edge of German defence perimeter, 25 Aug.
- positions built originally to protect naval base
- US position, 12.00, 25 Aug.
- US front line, evening of 10 Sept.
- troop sector boundaries
- roads
- rails
- old French fortifications
- H fort
- battery
- R ramparts of 17th century fortress
- C chateau
- F fortifications blocking entrance to peninsula

French navy officers, operating a very efficient service on their own. Agents who arrived daily from Brest gave us explicit, detailed information about the port, harbour defences, minefields, demolitions, facilities, movement of craft intended as blockships. Seven hundred German naval PoW were interrogated from the Marine Artillerie, the Marine Flak Artillerie, 6th Sperrbrecher Flotilla [R Boats], 40th Minesweeping Flotilla, 7th Verposten Flotilla and the Hafencommandtur-Brest. The 1st and 9th U-Boat flotillas were co-opted into the Wehrmacht as infantry. The U-Boat 256 was still lying in 3rd pen ready to take Korvetten-Kapitan Lehmann Willenrock and K-K Winter with their staffs and Army HQ command from Brest when their position became untenable. All torpedoes in store had been evacuated; bunkers used as medical dressing stations. Special unit to service Gnat torpedoes had just left Brest.

On 18 August VIII Corps headquarters moved to Lesneven, 15 miles inland from Brest and the bulk of the 8th Infantry Division began to arrive to take over a sector near Gouesnou, four miles due north of the city centre. Meanwhile General Ramcke, the tough dedicated nazi commander, who had fought in the airborne attack on Crete, charged Major General Josef Rauch, the commanding officer of 343 (Static) Division with the defence of the two peninsulas south of Brest, called Daoulas and Crozon. Intelligence and air photographs showed that besides the 12 coastal batteries and the army field artillery, the defence had 18 batteries of navy flak guns (which could be used in a ground role). There were stoutly fortified Vauban forts, with walls 15 feet and 35 feet high, with deep moats, armed with dual-purpose 88 mm anti-aircraft guns and reinforced with guns stripped from naval ships sunk in the harbour by Allied planes. These near-impregnable forts ranged from Le Conquet on the west of the city to forts Montbarey, Keranroux and Bouguer near the centre. General Troy Middleton allocated his task forces (combat groups), 'A' under General Earnest, 'B' under Brigadier General James Van Fleet and 'C' under Colonel Leroy Watson. The latter included 116th Infantry Regiment, the 2nd and 5th Ranger Battalions plus a force of 200 Russian 'renegade' prisoners of war. Their task was to clear the northwest tip of Brittany, between Brest and Le Conquet.

A strong American attack went in on 21 August from Landernau towards Hill 154, south of the Elorn river, but the German 353rd Division had fortified the hill strongpoint with 25 machine gun nests, anti-tank guns and mortars. When 38th Infantry Regiment with tank support finally took the hill, Sergeant P. Casey won the US Medal of Honour for destroying a pillbox with grenades. For the loss of 35 US casualties, the enemy lost 100 KIA and 143 PoW. For the remainder of August fog, rain and wind squalls covered the battlefield. SHAEF realised that in order to use the ports of Quiberon Bay, Lorient, St Nazaire and Nantes it was essential to clear the sea lanes around the northwest tip of Brittany, eliminate the German naval base at Brest and seize the submarine pens. SHAEF estimated the garrisons as 9,500 in Lorient, and 9,500 in St Nazaire. So Bradley now transferred two divisions from the US First Army—the 2nd and 29th Infantry Divisions plus two Ranger battalions to Middleton's VIII Corps, who in turn lost the 4th Armoured Division to XII Corps.

The 2nd Division left for Landernau on 19 August and 29th Division for Lannilis on 23 August. General Troy Middleton requested 8,700 tons of ammunition plus replenishment of 11,600 tons for the first three days of a major bombardment of the city defences starting on 25 August. Since the US Third Army staff estimated the garrison strength at only 16,000 (instead of the actual 35,000), Middleton was allocated only 5,000 tons for the whole operation and only two infantry divisions plus ten artillery battalions. Led by Sherman tanks of 6th Armoured, 29th Division in the west, the 8th in the north, 2nd in the east, the attack commenced. Second Lieutenant Charles Cawthorn was second in command of the anti-tank platoon 'H' Company, 2nd Battalion 116th Infantry Regiment, (the 'Stonewall' Brigade) in 29th Division. H Company was composed of 28 officers, 900 enlisted men armed with 8 heavy machine guns, 6 81 mm mortars and three rifle companies.

Cawthorn described his GOC, Major General Charles Gerhardt as having 'explosive speech, movements and temper. He dominated the division by knowing exactly what he wanted done, discarding those who failed to produce it and rewarding those who did.' His favourite order was '29, Lets Go.' On arrival at their assembly area ten miles northwest of Brest, the newcomers were told by 6th Armoured Division troops 'you are not confronted by a cage of purring pussycats, anxious to please and surrender but by tough soldiers ready to fight, including 2nd Parachute Division intact in the town.' Cawthorn described the defences: 'The lines around Brest were formidable enough; an outer ring of fieldworks dug in among the hedgerows; an inner ring keyed to a series of massive Napoleonic-era forts and finally an ancient stone wall around the inner city. In all three rings were machine guns in concrete and steel emplacements protected by anti-tank ditches, minefields and barbed wire. Three years of air raids had attracted a plentiful supply of AA guns that could bear in any direction and elevations.'

On the night of the 25th, 334 USAF and RAF bombers attacked eight powerful coastal batteries in aid of the land attack by VIII Corps. The battleship HMS *Warspite* had been allocated five targets by the control station ashore. The first was Graf Spee battery at Lochrist, then a 6-inch gun battery at St Mathieu, next Toulbroch Fort, Minou Fort and finally Montbarey. A total of 213 HE and AP 15-inch shells were fired. In turn 11 shells came down around *Warspite* and many splinters hit the ship.

The land attack was unsuccessful, with the 29th on the right and the 8th in the centre. The 2nd Division met parachute troops between Gouesnou and Guipavas and the Military Arsenal at St Nicolas and came under fire from strongpoints at Bourg-Neuf and Kermao. A flak 'fortress' Batterie Domaine commanded the battlefield, and 29th Division on the right flank also made little progress. The *London Daily Sketch* reported the battle: 'Sea Air blitz opens Brest attack. 300 Marauders and Havocs of Ninth Bomber Command assault co-ordinated with Allied sea and land bombardment. Nine separate waves of attacks were made against the stubborn defenders, Arsenal, coastal guns, AA batteries and other strongpoints. Staff Sgt George B Judd, a Marauder gunner, said "Brest is completely hemmed in by huge fires. Battleships outside the harbour and artillery surrounding the city laid down heavy barrages on the port. All the bombers returned, flak was light, no Luftwaffe planes reported."' Possibly by coincidence, all the German U-boats left Brest before 25 August making their way up the Channel, where they caused considerable losses, towards the port of Narvik in northern Norway.

Two task forces, known as TFA and TFB were ordered to clear the southern peninsulas of Crozon and Daoulas to the southwest of Brest city. By the 30th the latter had been cleared and 3,000 prisoners of war taken including Colonel Baumann. Various strongpoints at Hill 105, Hill 154, Hill 90, Hill 63 and the forts at Lesquivit and Kerreraul were taken. Second Lieutenant Cawthorn's unit, the 2nd Battalion of 116th Regiment, 29 Division had a torrid time around the small village of La Trinité, near Plouzane, three miles west of the town centre. In the first three days of the siege they lost 23 and 92 wounded. In the next five days they lost 106 and 361 wounded. 'It was the bloody type of hedgerow fighting that we had hoped had been left behind in Normandy.' Sergeant Wilson Carr helped defeat the usual German counterattack and won the Distinguished Service Cross. 'He saw the crowd of paratroopers and marines coming across the field on the run, firing as they came. He picked them off with his rifle—credited with fifteen—and shouting to his platoon to get up and fight or be killed.' Cawthorn went on describing 'a microcosm of war at all times and levels. It encompassed misconception, chance, rashness, violence, courage, despair, victory and defeat—all monitored by death.'

The main ground attack was resumed on 26 August, to little avail. The next day Fort Pointe de Corson and its radar station were captured and Le Conquet strongpoint and the artillery batteries at Lochrist surrounded. Second Lieutenant Earl Hall, 13th Infantry Regiment won posthumously the DSC in vicious fighting. The combined bombing and shelling started huge fires in Recouvrance, the Kriegsmarine centre near the mouth of the Penfeld estuary. On 29 August the 8th Division had two leading companies captured. Lieutenant Colonel H.K. Wesson of the 9th Infantry Regiment, 2nd Divison led a company reduced to 46 men through hedgerows, destroyed an machine gun nest, took 14 German paratroops prisoners and received a posthumous DSC.

On 31 August Bradley and Patton visited the headquarters of VIII Corps at the northwest end of the Plougastel-Daoulas peninsula, and met there General Troy Middleton. 'He was not sanguine about the capture of Brest and was full of complaint about the lack of daring on the part of the infantry.' He also complained about the lack of ammunition supplies. General Bradley then wrote. 'I had shifted the responsibility for Brest to Bill Simpson's newly arrived 9th Army transferring Middleton's VIII Corps from Patton to Simpson. Three US Infantry Divisions were committed to the final siege, plus thousands of tons of valuable ammunition, scarce air power and transport. Middleton's VIII Corps had suffered 9,381 casualties, killed, wounded and missing. That was far too high a price to pay to maintain illusions of invincibility. If the Germans could hold out so stubbornly in a lost cause like Brest what would happen when we reached her own borders or the Rhine river? The task forces TFA and TFB were stood down as the 6th Armoured Division elements were relieved by Major General H.J. Malony's 94th Infantry Division. It was now a close combat war of nibbling, probing, laboriously destroying pillbox emplacements, winkling out snipers and clearing small minefields. Minor sneak attacks from both sides were made and surprise counterattacks made. Smoke shells were used and the few small handheld flamethrowers used. Middleton launched another co-ordinated attack on 1 September, under a 45-minute barrage from nine Corps artillery battalions and all the divisional artillery. The 8th Divison in the centre gained several hundred yards but lost it all to counterattack. Middleton reported back to General Bradley 'My troops are none too good, ammunition supply poor, replacement troops arrivals behind schedule. The Germans have no intention to fold up right away, having shown no signs of weakening.' Bradley passed this message up to Eisenhower who authorized Major General Hoyt Vandenburg USAAF to utilise maximum aircraft to bomb Brest. The next day the 2nd Division captured Hill 105 southwest of Guipavas, a key feature, one of two key hills overlooking the eastern approaches. 8th Division took another fortified hill position and 29th Division took five days to take Hill 103 strongpoint east of Plouzane. Second Lieutenant Cawthorn of 29th Division wrote, 'The ring around Brest tightened; our artillery, air strikes and naval bombardment steadily reduced the German artillery's power to retaliate... the outer ring penetrated, the constricting lines drew in about the second ring which was based upon the massive forts that German engineers had made more formidable with heavily mined approaches, anti-tank ditches and outworks of steel and concrete MG emplacements. The fort in 166 Regiment's sector was called Montbarey and its glowering bulk dominated the ridge line along which we were advancing.'

In the next few days the 2nd Division reached Hill 92 (approaches), the 8th Division gained Lambezelles (gateway to Brest from the north), and 29th Division on Hill 103 faced the Fort de Mengant, five miles west of the River Penfeld. On 8 September another great effort was made on the whole front with bomber and heavy barrage support. The 2nd Division took Hill 92, the 8th Division pushed two regiments near Lambezelles and Hill 82. Private first class Ernest Prussman led his team gallantly and won the US Medal of Honour. The 29th Division finally took the Kergonant strongpoint north of the Penfeld. During the day 1,000 prisoners were taken with 250 American casualties. That night eight LSTs and two train loads of ammunition arrived to help the American forces.

The American high command had always been lukewarm about the unusual tank-based weapons that the British Army had in their 79th Armoured Division. On D-day they had used DD swimming tanks inefficiently and had spurned the AVRE 'bombards' and Sherman Flail mine-clearance tanks. It may be that their request to borrow a now highly experienced Churchill tank 'Crocodile' flame-thrower squadron resulted from a conference held on 9 September between Bradley and Patton. 'We both felt that the taking of Brest at that time was useless because it was [now] too far away and the harbour was too badly destroyed. On the other hand we agreed that when the American Army had once put its hand to the plan, it should not let go. Therefore it was necessary to take Brest.' Major Nigel Ryles of 'B' Squadron 141 RAC (The Buffs) reached the area by tank transporter late on the 8th. The troops were soon ready for action as they moved to Locmaria, west of Brest in support of the US 29th Division.

General Robertson commanding the 2nd Division called it a 'corporal's war' as, against suicidal defence, his small infantry squads fought their way through the streets. Every building was defended by machine-gun or anti-tank fire. George Scanlon, Staff Sergeant of 121st Regiment won the DSC in a street fighting action. The 8th Division secured Lambezelles and launched two regiments into the city suburbs, and 29th Division took the village of Penfeld. During the day 2,599 German prisoners of war were taken. On 10 September the 8th Division under General Stroh reached Fort Bougen, defended by a 20 foot deep dry moat and thick walls 25–35 feet high, which held out for several days.

General Bradley now assigned Brest (which he had originally hoped would be taken on 1 September) top priority for supply. LSTs beached near Morlaix and train and truck supplies came in from Normandy. The airport at Morlaix was used for emergency supplies and for evacuation of the wounded.

Lieutenant Commander Brian Izzard RN, of Forward Interrogation Unit, noted on the 10th, 'From tip of Plougastel peninsula [3,000 yards due south of estuary opposite the town centre and recently taken by a Task Force], across the [sea] roads, port and harbour are completely pulverised, useless for some time to come. Every mole, every quay have been blown by land mines at 20 yards intervals. A large tanker sunk across the entrance of the harbour. Several other vessels lying submerged in inner harbour. Whole port nothing but mass of rubble and twisted girders. Naval school behind U-boat bunker partially destroyed and burned out. Two large holes visible roof to U-boat bunker. Every part of the town and particularly the harbour is being pounded, when weather permits, by medium bombers, dive bombers, 240 mm and 155 mm shells. The whole place is a shambles beyond description.'

On the 11th and 12th General Charles Gerhardt's 29th Division moved towards Hill 97 with the key tasks of reducing forts Keranroux and Montbarey. When General Middleton sent in an invitation to surrender, Ramcke refused and Middleton told his men 'Take the Germans apart.'

175th Infantry Regiment of 29th Division were given the doubtful honour of capturing Fort Keranroux. Covered by smoke and blasted by bombs and shells, it eventually fell with 350 prisoners of war. Staff Sergeant

Sherwood Hallman took out a machine-gun post with grenades, killed several defenders and took 12 prisoners of war for which he was awarded the US Medal of Honour.

Fort Montbarey was more difficult, casemated with earth-filled masonry, the walls were 25 feet thick and the deep dry moat was 50 feet wide. The covering minefield with 300 naval shells with pressure igniters was covered by 20 mm guns and manned by a determined garrison. Second Lieutenant Cawthorn, 116th Regiment described it as 'A grim devastated landscape in which squatted the huge fort, like some felled monster, its hide frayed and worn by shell fire and bombs but not torn open.' Lieutenant Colonel 'Big Tom' Dallas 1st Battalion, 116th Regiment asked for artillery and self-propelled gunfire to keep the fort defenders' heads down whilst the VIII Corps engineer Colonel Winslow's men tried to clear a path through the minefield covering the fort. During the night of the 13th they had penetrated to within 200 yards before being pinned down. Lieutenant Tony Ward (who subsequently won an American Silver Star award) led Number Eight troop of the Buffs Crocodiles through the minefield. Sergeant Morley's Crocodile hit a naval shell, which killed his driver and wounded the crew, and blocked the column. Ward alone continued through craters, over the anti-tank ditch, up to a sunken road, 'flaming' every target, including two 50 mm anti-tank guns. Out of fuel and ammunition he returned, fell into a ten-foot deep tank trap, and was surrounded by Germans. Using a Bren gun he persuaded 39 defenders to surrender. At dawn on the 16th, under smoke cover, Number Ten and Number Six troops of the Buffs, as Captain Harry Bailey related, 'Terry Conway, Cliff Shone and Roy Moss pounded away with flame and HE in a truly Walt Disney nightmare of flame, smoke, flying metal, sound and fury.' The engineers placed 2,500lbs of explosives around the walls; 105 mm close-support Howitzers battered down the main gates and the garrison gave up. By the end of 17 September only Fort de Portzic and the submarine pens were left in enemy hands, until they surrendered on the 18th. The 2nd Division fought their way through the old city walls and took the railway station strongpoint then reached the inner city almost to the water's edge. 29th Division captured Recouvrance sector together with Colonel von der Mosel, Ramcke's chief of staff. Soon 10,000 German prisoners of war were in the bag. Second Lieutenant Cawthorn wrote, 'Surrender began everywhere, junior officers emerged from bunkers bearing white flags asking to surrender to officers of the same grade or senior...long lines of soldiers, sailors, marines and airmen filing out from their underground shelters carrying full packs and hand luggage. The men Hitler had ordered to defend Brest to the death were well fed clean-shaven and well turned out.' The final action took place on the 19th on the Crozon peninsula, where General Ramcke surrendered at the Pointe des Espagnols to Brigadier General Charles Canham of the 8th Division. In the clearance of the Crozon peninsula 7,639 prisoners of war were taken for 487 US casualties. Finally on the 20th Douarnez was taken with 300 prisoners of war,

The specialist Ranger battalions were prominent in the task force activities. The 2nd Ranger Battalion under Lieutenant Colonel J.E. Rudder, after their desperate mission on Omaha Beach, played a key part in the Le Conquet peninsula action. Under Lieutenant Colonel R. Sullivan, the 5th Ranger Battalion, also heroes of Omaha, fought with distinction in the Brest campaign capturing the forts at Pointe de Petit Minou, Mengant and Dellec.

Brest had a total of 75 defended strongpoints. The American forces suffered 9,831 casualties (2nd Division 2,314, 29th Division 2,650, 8th Division 1,500). Into the prisoner of war camps marched 38,000 prisoners of war (of which 20,000 were combat troops).

Under a deluge of 500,000 artillery shells bombarded by 3,200 bomber sorties, the end of Brest was inevitable. But as at Cherbourg and St Malo the dedicated nazi commandants had wrecked their ports. The parachute general, Hermann Bernhard Ramcke was a capable tactician and his pugnacious face showed the brutal determination to resist at all costs. In the First World War he had won the Pour la Mérite award and for Crete, the Oak Leaves with Swords and Diamonds. Yet when he surrendered he had already packed eight suitcases, a complete set of chinaware, fishing tackle with four rods and an aristocratic setter dog!

On 6 October Lieutenant Colonel Maylin Greaser RE had carried out a detailed survey of the wrecked port, with various possible strategies. His Plan A could handle 12,200 tons of supplies daily, Plan B handle 6,000 tons and Plan C handle 3,000 tons daily. It was not to be. With the startling and dramatic capture of Antwerp at the beginning of September, SHAEF recommended on 3 September not only *to abandon salvage plans* for Brest but also plans to conquer and try to use the ports of Lorient (15,000 garrison), St Nazaire (12,000 garrison), Quiberon Bay and Nantes. This recommendation was accepted on 7 September and on 14th for Brest.

General Bradley wrote in his memoirs, 'Had General Ramcke been ignored he would have caused us no end of trouble. An airtight seal would have required a 100 miles north/south line from Avranches-Rennes-St

Nazaire. To guard against his attacks the line would have had to be manned by at least three divisions. A limited offensive in Brittany against 50,000 German troops was preferable to a long, vulnerable defensive holding operation.'

CHAPTER SEVEN

The Mousetrap War: Containing the Atlantic Fortress-Ports

ADOLF HITLER HAD DECREED THAT LORIENT WAS AN IMPORTANT *Fortress Festung* and Engineer B. Hepp deployed 15,300 Todt workers to construct the defences. Major General Junck was the commander of 265th Infantry Division which was responsible for several hundred kilometres of defences from Douarnenez to Etel. The 895th Infantry Regiment and Number 11 Festa Company plus artillery group HAA 1163 garrisoned Lorient. In the sector along the River Laita, around Lomener port and the town of Ploëmur in the west six more Blockhaus towers were built on the three sandy beaches of Guidel, Loc'H and Fort Bloque. The central sector including Ploemer, Lanester and Riantec was guarded by two battalions of IR 896, a company of Festa, two batteries of field artillery, three marine artillery groups and the 5th Marine Brigade of Flak troops. The submarine base of Keroman was used by the 2nd and 10th Flotillas U-Boote and 14th Unterseeboots-Jager under Admiral Matthiae. The citadel of Port Louis guarded the main entrance to the port opposite the pens of Keroman. Offshore were the heavily fortified islands of Belle Isle and Isle de Groix.

Lorient was a formidable destroyer and U-boat port, although on 16 August Admiral Dönitz had ordered all his submarines based on the isolated Atlantic ports to make for Norway. One 'pack' of eight caused mayhem in the Channel and sank six merchantmen, a Canadian corvette, a minesweeper and an LSI (Landing Ship Infantry). For many weeks the USAF had pounded the naval harbour and done considerable damage.

General Middleton's VIII Corps despatched 4th Armoured Division through Rennes to Vannes and on to Lorient, Quiberon Bay and St Nazaire. Much of the Brittany peninsula outside the towns was now more or less dominated by the French Forces of the Interior (FFI) under Colonel Meon. Colonel Clarke's combat group CCA moved out on 5 August and reached Vannes that night. CCB under Colonel Dager captured Redon and circled north towards Lorient via Maure and Plöermel. The next day CCB moved slowly towards Lorient because of cratered roads and blown bridges. Wood radioed on 7 August, 'Hoped to argue Boche into surrender of Lorient. However he still resists. Am attacking him from two sides. He may fold up. He has considerable fixed fortifications, can resist strongly. Believe infantry division should be sent here at once.' On the 7th at dawn CCB attacked to the northwest across Pont Scorff and met a violent defence in which there were 105 casualties and 35 vehicles destroyed. CCA, led by light tanks, tried to seize the bridge at Hennebont, three miles northeast of the town, found it blown up and established a thin cordon around Lorient. By the 9th it was clear the defences were too strong for the 4th Armoured Division alone to reduce, meeting anti-tank ditches and minefields with interlocking bands of fire. The FFI estimated a total of 500 guns lay in front including anti-tank, anti-aircraft, coastal defence and naval guns. Also the anti-aircraft Flak was so heavy that the combat groups' artillery spotter planes could not get over their targets. The FFI also reported that the Germans had a great supply of provisions, with herds of cattle, and could hold out for a long time. Any attack would need support from the sea so that Quiberon Bay and Belle Isle, 20 miles to the southeast would need to be neutralized. Major General Wood was told by General Middleton to keep his armour at a distance from the fortress of Lorient, 'Do not become involved in a fight for Lorient unless the enemy attacks first. Take secure position and merely watch developments.'

General Wilhelm Farrmbacher the German commanding officer, said afterwards that had a strong tank attack been made and launched between 6 and 9 August, the fortress would probably have fallen as his defences were not yet organized. The garrison of mixed arms including 275th Infantry Division was 25,000 strong and 10,000 French civilians were still ensconced in the town. Farmbacher had 197 guns in the main fortress plus 80 anti-tank pieces and many anti-aircraft guns. On 10 August a massive aerial bombardment of propaganda leaflets was made. The 4th Armoured Division CCB stayed in a containing role until 15 August and were then relieved by the 6th Armoured Division, who in turn stayed until they were relieved in mid-September by 94th Infantry Division.

CCA had left the Orient sector for Vannes then went further southeast on 19 August towards Nantes. The following night, approaching the town having bypassed St Nazaire, loud explosions were heard as the defenders destroyed their installations. With great help from the FFI, CCA 'took' Nantes on the 12th, the defenders having decamped hastily south of the River Loire, having destroyed all the bridges, quays and jetties. On the 14th CCA were relieved by the 2nd Cavalry group.

On 19 January 1944 Adolf Hitler had decreed that St Nazaire would become an official fortress, 'Festung Saint-Nazaire' mainly to guard the 14 submarine pens. The 6th and 7th U-boat flotillas and the 8th and 10th minesweeper flotillas were based at St Nazaire. On 13 April 1944 Rommel inspected the naval base commanded by Major General Hunten. The Todt organization had deployed under Engineer Probst 13,385 workers to try to make St Nazaire impregnable. The IR 984 was stationed near Vannes, IR 983 at La Baule and IR 985 south of the River Loire. Various regiments of Festa XXV, Artillerie regiments, Kriegsmarines and Flak troops formed the town garrison. A network of coastal batteries ran eastwards from Batz-sur-Mer, with a 240 mm gun on railtracks near Kermolsan and the Panzerwerk at Pen-Bron, at Canneve and Fort de Lève.

St Nazaire under their Major General Werner Junck had a substantial garrison of 35,000—part of 275th Infantry Division, the 684th Battery of naval artillery, the 22nd Regiment equipped for naval anti-aircraft defence and a large contingent of Kriegsmarines. St Nazaire was duly contained without undue difficulty and a large garrison was kept out of the war.

Lorient surrendered on 8th May 1945 to US Major General H.F. Kramer at Caudan and St Nazaire three days later at Bouvron. Further south another great naval base of La Rochelle and La Pallice, with ten submarine pens surrendered on 8 May 1945. Lieutenant Colonel P.F. Brine USNR visited the port and found little or no destruction. Apparently the French naval Captain Meyer had negotiated with the German Commander Admiral von Schirlitz over an eight-month period and persuaded him *not* to destroy the facilities on the grounds that doing so at that stage of the war was quite pointless. Soon 8,000 to 10,000 tons of daily supplies were being landed and trucked to the US armies of occupation in Germany.

Winston Churchill was keeping an eagle eye on the situation in Brittany and wrote on 4 August to the First Sea Lord (Mr A.V. Alexander), 'What are the Navy doing on the western flank of the armies? They should be more lively all along the Atlantic shores of the Brest peninsula, driving off all enemy vessels, isolating the Channel Islands from all food, escape of the German garrison, being ready at Quiberon Bay or elsewhere to join hands with the advancing American columns. We shall soon be possessed of harbours or inlets at which bases for E-boats and destroyers could be established, dominating the waters round the Brest peninsula. There are plums to be picked in the Brest peninsula. Admiral Ramsay must not weary of well-doing.' On the 18th Churchill was concerned that captured U-boat and E-boat pens could not be completely destroyed *before* the end of hostilities, 'We must reserve control over all these military installations until they have been completely destroyed, perhaps by civilian contractors.'

A curious 'twilight' war of patrolling by both sides took place outside Lorient almost on a daily basis. The patrols were usually each between 25 and 50 men. The FFI called them Souricières (Mousetraps). Both sides deployed artillery observation officers although American ammunition was rationed.

For instance on 17 August two German patrols, one of 50 men and the other of 25 burned the village of Kerroch and the second patrol had a small pitched battle near Hauntmont. Two days later enemy patrols were very active, 70 men at Keranaré, 60 at Kerdenowtolder, 100 at Le Boulaye and 100 at Kervenou. On the 26th the Americans laid a trap at Kergonnet and killed half of a 50-man patrol armed with five machine guns and 20 80 mm mortars.

Rifleman Leon Standifer, First Platoon, K Company, 301st Infantry Regiment was part of the green 94th (Pilgrim) Infantry Division. They arrived fresh off the beaches, via St Lô, still shelled to rubble, and before arriving at Redéné, a small village west of Quimperlé, were treated on the way as conquering heroes by the French civilians. Their sector (see map) was a two-mile area northwest of Lorient, between Queven and Guidel. On their first day in the line Sergeant Westmoreland told Standifer's squad, 'We are the first company in the division to take up a combat position.' German radio propaganda was heard. 'Midge' (Mildred Gillars, educated in Ohio) was known as 'Axis Sally'. In a strongly accented American voice, each evening she produced 'news'. 'We hear the 90th Division has been refitted and is ready to try again. You tough *hombres* made a good showing last time. Too bad you were fighting a panzer division with three years of combat experience,' and 'The 94th Pilgrim Division ran into some German marines. I'll bet they hope that doesn't happen again.' In fact 'I' Company 301st Infantry Regiment had been badly hit by the Kriegsmarine Infantry. 'Axis Sally' taunted the GIs every day about the draft dodgers back at home sleeping with the fighting soldiers' wives. Standifer mentioned the boredom of their daily rituals: sunrise serenade by the Krauts; 'C' rations with powdered coffee for breakfast heated over a small twig fire; the cleaning of rifles; washing and shaving, although all platoons were allowed to grow beards. Nobody drank the local well water.

'H' Company sent out a strong patrol to meet a group of Germans who apparently wanted to surrender, near Cap Kerdudal. Lieutenant Devonald's 3rd Platoon was ambushed with 44 men lost. The prisoners of war were marched through Groix up to Fort Surville. Colonel Hagerty, the regimental (i.e., Brigade) commander was furious and ashamed of his men.

Standifer noted, 'During October we gradually came to understand that there would be no assault on Lorient. Brest had surrendered after weeks of intense fighting, after the Germans had blown up the entire port area. The same thing would happen at Lorient, but we couldn't just walk off and leave 25,000 German soldiers. We were being shelled and shot at nearly every day. I was First Scout in an Infantry Company playing nursemaid to 25,000 Germans at a lonely submarine base on the Atlantic coast. On line we stayed wet, muddy and smelly. Our feet were always wet and cold. Night guard duty was boredom and misery.' After Christmas 1944, the 94th Infantry Division was replaced by 66th Infantry Division, which had lost 800 men when their ship was torpedoed in the Channel on Christmas Eve.

Field Marshal von Rundstedt never agreed with his Führer about the Atlantic Wall philosophy and his fortress system. He wrote:

Strategically the value of these fortresses was insignificant because of their inability to defend themselves against a land attack. When the Führer's instructions for the defence of the fortresses was sent to me I had the words "defend to the last drop of blood" changed to "defend to the last bullet" before I sent them forward to the troops. We subsequently lost over 120,000 men in these concrete posts. When we withdrew from France I always considered this to be a tragic waste of useful manpower. As for the Atlantic Wall it had to be seen to be believed. It had no depth and little surface. It was sheer humbug. At best it might have proved an obstacle for 24 hours at any one point, but one day's intensive assault by a determined force was all that was needed to break any part of this line. Once through the so-called Wall the rest of these fortifications and fortresses facing the sea were of no use at all against an attack from behind. I reported all this to the Führer 12 October 1943 but it was not favourably received.

By June 1944 von Rundstedt had a nominal command of 60 divisions but only 15 had the equipment or personnel to be classed as fighting divisions. The rest sitting in their bunkers were mainly non-German, convalescents from the Russian front, elderly men equipped with non-German artillery, with horses and bicycles.

CHAPTER EIGHT

Rouen and the
Return to Dieppe

THE AMERICAN OPERATION COBRA HAD BEEN SUCCESSFUL AND
the Hitler-inspired counterattack at Mortain had been seen off. By mid-
August the converging armies—British, American and Canadian forces,
with Polish and French formations—had squeezed the German Seventh
Army and Fifth Panzer Army into the Falaise-Argentan pocket. Hitler
promptly fired Field Marshal von Kluge and on the 16th replaced him
by Field Marshal Walther Model. Within the pocket were 100,000 German
troops, the remnants of 15 divisions. Here the Wehrmacht suffered its
greatest disaster since Stalingrad and Tunis, with the loss of practically
all their tanks, transport, guns and heavy weapons. The American XX
and XV Corps had reached the River Loire, had taken Le Mans and were
advancing towards Paris. By the 20th General Patton's forces had crossed
the Seine near Mantes and, driving northwest down the left bank of the
river, met the British Second Army advancing on Rouen. This valuable
inland port depended entirely on Le Havre, 60 miles to the west, being
cleared. On 26 August Montgomery ordered the First Canadian Army
to take Le Havre, secure the port of Dieppe and destroy all enemy forces
in the coastal belt—at Boulogne, Calais and Dunkirk—on the way to
Ghent. By now there were 36 American, British and Canadian divisions
ashore, with nearly 2 million troops fighting on French soil. Their daily
supply of 25,000 tons of food, ammunition, fuel and replacement transport
was being supplied from the Normandy beaches and the six small harbours

opened in Normandy and Brittany (but not St Malo or Brest). Cherbourg was just starting to unload supplies.

Adolf Hitler had not needed to designate Rouen as a 'defended strongpoint' since Le Havre had been so comprehensively fortified. But it was surprising that Dieppe had not been strengthened.

The 2nd Canadian Infantry Division under Major General Foulkes had suffered heavily in Normandy and more recently in the Forêt de la Londe against German rearguards protecting the loops of the River Seine. First the 7th Brigade and then the 9th crossed the river on 28 August near Elbeuf and pushed downstream to outflank Rouen. Major G.D. Sim led a patrol of the Highland Light Infantry into the town. Sergeant G. Hunter of the North Nova Scotias drove by mistake in a jeep into the town centre, when armed only with a pistol. He and his crew were mobbed by French civilians as 'liberators'. But at noon Hunter's men were sent packing by a long line of Wehrmacht having their lunch by the roadside. The famous BBC journalist Frank Gillard, describes his entry into Rouen on 31 August 1944:

> Outside in the square, our jeep was being used as a grandstand. Twenty-six people had somehow managed to climb up on to it to see what was going on. Standing by there was a young man wearing the FFI armlet. He told me how, yesterday morning, the officers commanding this secret army, which numbered over 11,000 in Rouen, decided that the time had come to take action. The Canadians were at the approaches to the city. So orders went out, and suddenly the Germans making frantic last minute preparations to leave found themselves set upon by armed Frenchmen. There was fierce fighting in the streets. Many Germans were killed; many more were taken prisoner. The rest fled as the Canadians came in. Meanwhile, the City Police were rounding up the worst of the French traitors and the Gestapo. Fourteen members of the Gestapo were killed in the skirmishes which followed, and all the rest were put safely behind bars. This man, who had a close up view of the whole thing, was enthusiastic about our air attacks on the Germans in the last few days just south of Rouen in the loop of the river.
>
> He said that thousands of Germans had been killed in these bombardments. They'd only managed to get the remnants out by running rafts to and fro and laying temporary pontoon bridges— all in the darkness.

Rouen is not extensively damaged. The waterfront is pretty much in ruins; the cathedral, unfortunately, has lost one of its towers and it's in a pretty bad state, and the eastern end of the city has suffered a little, but it's certainly the least damaged town of any size yet entered by the Allies on this part of the front. The people of Rouen were aching for every crumb of news they could get. Since the electricity failed, many of them, so they told me, had made crystal sets, so that they could listen to the BBC. They were almost overwhelmed at the flood of good news that we were able to bring them.

Ross Ellis, battle adjutant of the Calgary Highlanders, wrote home to his wife, 'We came through a town [Rouen] yesterday, that really lifted our spirits. The "Calgary Stampede" had nothing on us. My armoured car looked like the rose festival float by the time we were out of town. The people cheered us, gave us fruit, wine, and flowers and generally went a bit mad.'

Lieutenant Commander Spon RNR, commanding 1571 Royal Naval Port Clearance Team, was responsible for the clearance of Rouen's port facilities. They examined the Quai Richard Waddington, Quai Emile Duchemin, Quai Ferdinand de Lesseps, Quai de Boisquibert, Quai Gaston Boulet, Quai du Havre and Quai de la Bourse. They found no mines in the 11,100 square feet they checked but found wreckage of tugs, lighters, cranes, motor cars and debris. But floating in the river they 'caught' 11 mines and at the base of the quay walls 22 'C' or 'Y' Star mines.

From Rouen it was 40 miles for the Canadian Army to return to Dieppe, where they had had such terrible losses 25 months previously. In December 1943 Hitler boasted that the defences at Dieppe were 'a thousand times stronger than they had been in 1942' at the time of the disastrous one-day raid. At the Führer's conference on 20 December, Hitler told his audience, 'I am constantly thinking out new ways to improve the defences, devising the most diverse devilries.' But now, strangely, Hitler's wireless message to the Dieppe garrison to fight to the last man had been delayed by 24 hours.

At 13.30 hours on 1 September the Royal Hamilton Light Infantry (nicknamed the Rileys) caught their first glimpse of the Channel and, a few minutes later, the rooftops of Dieppe. There were mines ahead, boobytraps, two anti-tank ditches (helpfully bridged by the French Resistance) and tons of barbed wire. But the garrison had gone and the RHLI walked into the town without a fight. The journalist Stewart

MacPherson was there and watched the return of the Canadian Army to Dieppe, reporting on 1 September 1944:

> One of the most important entries in any Canadian war diary is *Dieppe*. At twenty-five minutes past twelve this afternoon, Canadians made another entry in the Dieppe account. This one was 1 September 1944, and completely wiped out the entry of 19 August 1942. They say they never come back. That's a saying long associated with champions, but today from a scout aircraft I watched the 2nd Canadian Division—champions, if I've ever seen any—come back to Dieppe, this time to stay. Flying straight down the main axis of advance, I could see them on the main road from Rouen, through Tôtes, speeding on their way to Dieppe. Even in the air you could almost sense their desire to get as much out of their machines as possible—anything to get them into Dieppe in a hurry. I suppose I noticed that because I was a Canadian. They were all there. The first troops into the town were the Essex Scottish, the Royal Hamilton Light Infantry, and the Royal Regiment of Canada, and speeding up behind them were the Camerons of Winnipeg, the South Saskatchewan Light Infantry, the Fusiliers of Montreal, the Toronto Scottish, the Black Watch—they were all there—all the regiments that were there on that fateful day of 19 August 1942. But today it was their turn.

The 2nd Canadian Division had been given the task of re-taking Dieppe for historical and sentimental reasons. The RHLI in the 1942 raid had lost two-thirds of their battalion killed or captured. The cemetery was nearby, which contained the graves of the men who had fallen. Majors J.M. Pigott and J.B. Halladay, survivors of that terrible day, were now photographed by the graves of those they had known so well. Lieutenant Colonel E.P. Thompson, commander of the Queen's Own Cameron Highlanders, with three pipers, also survivors of 1942, paraded and played at the Canadian cemetery where a total of 800 officers and men are buried. The next day, 2 September, the pipers of the Essex Scottish regiment played 'Retreat' at the Place Nationale. That night there was a dance and reception in the old Town Hall, now the Maison de la Fête. On Sunday, 3 September, memorial services were held under warm, bright skies. All units of the division marched past, six abreast in front of General Crerar, Lieutenant General Guy Simonds, the Mayor and the FFI leaders. Massed pipe bands played as the troops marched past the saluting base in front of cheering Dieppoises. The reporter Frank Gillard was there to see it, reporting on 1 September:

> Many of these troops were the same men who'd made that gallant attack just over two years ago. What a memorable return this was. At one point in the town the people had crowded out in the road, leaving only a very narrow lane for traffic to pass through. We wondered why until we reached the spot, and then we saw. A Nazi flag was spread out on the ground, and you were simply obliged to drive right over the swastika and trample it into the dust.
>
> The people of Dieppe told us that the Germans started to get away yesterday. They blew up their great ammunition dump in the vaults of the castle, in fact explosions were still going on there this morning every few minutes as more and more magazines went off. The Germans fired their oil supplies. Down on the waterfront immense columns of black smoke were coming from the storage tanks, and they demolished and smashed up everything in the harbour area. All the dock installations were blown up, and ships sunk everywhere to block the harbour. They blew the great bridge over the river and then, as a last act before leaving, they destroyed the power station and the town water tower. But Dieppe itself is not greatly damaged. Its streets are just as attractive as ever they were. Today they were bright with flags and bunting and streamers— for it was a real carnival day.
>
> It was about the flying bombs that the people wanted to talk to British people like myself. They reeled off a great list of bomb sites just around Dieppe which are now lost to the enemy. Most of them, they told us, had been blown up by the Germans a few days ago. They described how these robots used to come over the town just after they'd been launched—how any amount of them had crashed into the sea—how some had exploded within a few seconds of being sent off. They were anxious to know how the people of Britain are standing up to these attacks, and how much damage is being done. These people of Dieppe were delighted to feel that the liberation of their town by this amazingly rapid 40-mile advance of the Canadian troops had also brought at least some slight measure of relief, if only comparatively light, to southern England.

The 4th was also a day of rest before the division was off to the war again, northeast along the coast, across the river Somme towards the

Belgian border. The British Royal Naval clearance party Number 1686 and 'P' party Number 1571 had arrived on the 3rd to clear and sweep the harbour for mines. Three blockships and 18 wrecks littered the harbour according to Hitler's instructions. After 11 hours of diving no mines were located. A total of 456,500 square feet was searched around the Quai Henri IV in Avant Port; and around Quai de l'Yser, Quai de Somme and the Gridiron, all in the Arrière Port. They searched on 6 and 7 September, the Bassins du Canada and Paris, the Duquesne and the Forine Radout. The enemy had fled in a great hurry—no heroics here, and had left several uncompleted pillboxes and heavy gun emplacements. The demolitions on the beaches had been done in haste. Within a week of capture the highly experienced teams had repaired the port and from coasters and LSTs, 7000 tons were being unloaded daily. General Crerar was ordered to attend an important commanders' meeting at Field Marshal (with effect from 1 September) Montgomery's headquarters, Crerar asked for a four-hour postponement to attend the Dieppe raid services of remembrance. The meeting was to discuss future co-operation between the Second British and First US armies, so Crerar's presence was not that important. Monty got on his high horse and was furious with Crerar, whose position was 'untenable'. Crerar said he would report the whole conversation back to the Canadian government. Later the field marshal apologized but vindictively sent a message back to London to the CIGS, Alan Brooke, 'Since the crossing of the Seine, First Canadian Army's operations had been badly handled and very *slow*; ie four days at Dieppe.' The Prime Minister of Canada sent General Harry Crerar a message, 'I share your joy upon the entry of Canadian troops into Dieppe today. Nothing has so stirred Canada as the *rapid* series of victories achieved by our forces in recent weeks.' The cost of these victories and the Normandy campaign had been heavy. Crerar was awaiting 1,000 reinforcements at Dieppe to be integrated into the 2nd Canadian Division.

CHAPTER NINE

The Capture of Antwerp: 'A stunning surprise'

ON 4 SEPTEMBER ADOLF HITLER ISSUED A NEW DIRECTIVE: 'BECAUSE of the breakthrough of enemy tank forces toward Antwerp, it has become very important for the further progress of the war to hold the fortresses of Boulogne and Dunkirk, the Calais defence area [inc. Cap Gris-Nez], Walcheren Island with Flushing Harbour, the bridgehead at Antwerp and the Albert Canal position as far as Maastricht. For this purpose the Fifteenth Army is to bring the garrisons of Boulogne and Dunkirk and the Calais defence area up to strength by means of full units. The defensive strength of the fortresses is to be increased by means of additional ammunition supplies, from the supplies of Fifteenth Army, especially anti-tank ammunition by bringing up provisions of all kinds from the country and by evacuating the entire population. The commanders of the Calais defence area and of Walcheren Island receive the same authority as a fortress commander.'

General Gustav von Zangen, commandant of the Fifteenth German Army, had six divisions still under command and by a vital Allied strategical error, managed to follow his Führer's instructions perfectly. The three coastal fortresses were manned and provisioned and in addition 80,000 men, 616 guns and 6,200 vehicles managed to escape to continue the war in Holland, and later in Germany. On Winston Churchill's journey to the Quebec Conference of 10 September he wrote, 'It is difficult to see how 21st Army Group can advance in force to the German frontier until it has cleared up the stubborn resistance at the Channel ports and dealt with the Germans at Walcheren and north of Antwerp.'

By early September three British divisions of VIII Corps were static, because all their transport had been stripped from them. Adolf Hitler and Winston Churchill were unwittingly both agreed on the situation—the logistical supply problem facing the Allies. Lieutenant General Brian Horrocks, General Officer Commanding 30 Corps, had allocated various objectives to his three brilliant armoured divisions. The Guards Armoured had taken Brussels, the 7th Armoured (and 1st Polish) divisions Ghent, and the author's 11th Armoured by a *coup de main* had taken Antwerp. As Churchill noted at the time, 'Without the vast harbours of this city no advance across the lower Rhine and into the plains of Northern Germany was possible.' The potential of Antwerp was enormous. In pre-war days 11,000 seagoing vessels entered it each year with cargoes of 24 million tons. Additionally, 44,000 smaller river craft shipped in a further 12 million tons annually. Admiral Bertram Ramsay sent a signal on 4 September to SHAEF headquarters and 21st Army Group headquarters so that Field Marshal Montgomery *must* have seen it.

> It is essential if Antwerp (and Rotterdam) are to be opened quickly enemy must be prevented from:
> 1. a) Carrying out demolitions and block ports.
>   b) Mining and blocking Scheldt (and new waterway between Rotterdam and the Hook).
> 2. Both Antwerp (and Rotterdam) are highly vulnerable to mining and blocking. If the enemy succeeds in these operations the time it will take to open the ports cannot be estimated.
> 3. It will be necessary for coastal batteries to be captured before approach channels to the river routes can be established.

In his diary the Admiral wrote, 'Antwerp is useless unless the Scheldt Estuary is cleared of the enemy.' Major General 'Pip' Roberts, 11th Armoured Division, the 'Black Bull',[*] had thrust vigorously from the Seine to Beauvais, captured the German General Eberhardt and the headquarters of the 7th Army in Amiens, then Arras, Lens, Vimy Ridge, Tournai, Alost, Malines and into Boom. In this town, ten miles south of Antwerp, Lieutenant Robert Vekemans, a Belgian engineer officer met the advance guard of 11th Armoured. By skill, guile, luck and bravery he led them through Boom's defences. Edouard Pilaet, codenamed 'Francois', a key member of the Resistance, with

---

1 The British army divisions always had a name or nickname derived from their divisional badge or emblem worn on both shoulders.

Vekemans led the Shermans of 3rd Regiment RTR and the half tracks and carriers of 8th Battalion Rifle Brigade into the heart of Antwerp. Hitler had not designated Antwerp a 'fortress' and no proper fortress division was available, but Major General Graf Stolberg-zu-Stolberg arrived from Brittany on 5 June to take command of the Antwerp garrison. A week later the headquarters staff of 136th Infantry Division arrived. The 15,000 to 17,000 defenders consisted of the usual mixture: a security battalion, a 'stomach invalid' battalion*, a Belgian renegade battalion, an OST Russian prisoner of war battalion, Luftwaffe ground crews, anti-aircraft batteries, transport guards, and various Kriegsmarine troops for naval servicing. There were no specialist anti-tank weapons, but all the many 88 mm anti-aircraft guns were now dual purpose. There were two lines of defences of roadblocks, pillboxes at main road junctions, with a line of forts from a bend in the River Scheldt to Fort Ste Marie and Kruisschans village at the far end of the docks. A second line of defence was based on the ancient inner forts which reached as far as Merxem, the northern suburb over the Albert Canal. In the main Central Park Stolberg had his headquarters in three large bunkers.

From June, in accordance with Hitler's instructions, plans had been made for the destruction of the huge docks. Fortunately for the Allies, the Belgian Resistance movement was substantial—with 3,500 men—and well organized.

M. Eugene Colson, codenamed 'Harry', was the chief co-ordinator of the Resistance in the Antwerp port area. Although the Gestapo arrested several key Resistance members on 25 August, Colson's groups captured the port commandant, Captain Mohr and his staff, then took control of the southeast of the port area.

Antwerp at that time had a population of 2.5 million inhabitants. The docks extended for *six* miles along the Scheldt below the city. The whole dock area was criss-crossed by long water barriers with quays, long lines of cranes and warehouses. Colson's Resistance men had locked many of the lock-lifting bridges in the down position, to make road access easier for the British.

Stolberg reported to Field Marshal Model by radio that British tanks were across the River Rupel in Boom, and that the Belgian Resistance in Antwerp was now very active indeed. He was told to withdraw north across the Albert Canal or if that was impossible, to fight or take flight to the southeast of the city. The infantry brigade of 11th Armoured Division supported by tanks at 21.30 hrs captured the Central Park bunkers and the Belgian Resistance

---

2 One of several formations of invalids hauled out of hospital by the desperate German command.

groups captured General Stolberg. By midnight 6,000 German prisoners of war had been locked up in cages and bear pits in the City Zoo!

The vital Kruisschans lock was seized by the Resistance, but the Germans held Merxem in strength and on the 5th blew up Yserbrug Bridge across the Albert Canal. Although the 4th Battalion King's Shropshire Light Infantry gallantly defended a small bridgehead over the canal in the northeast sector they were forced to withdraw on 7 September.

Nevertheless the capture of Antwerp was an amazing success. Nearly 9,000 prisoners of war were taken. Nearly all the vital Antwerp Dock area with its 30 miles of wharves, 632 cranes and hoists, 186 acres of warehouse storage space and its oil storage facilities (for over 100 million gallons) thanks mainly to the brave Resistance movement, were safe. The Sherman tanks and motorized infantry had then cleared the city and the port area. Almost immediately RN Port Clearance team Number 1572 arrived to inspect and repair port damages.

General von Zangen, General Officer Commanding German Fifteenth Army, wrote at the time, 'When we retired from the Somme about 1 September I planned slowly to fight my way [back] to Brussels and Antwerp and then take up a line in Holland. I had no fear that Antwerp would be taken since it was far behind the front line and there was a special staff organized to defend it. When I heard on 4 September that it had been captured it came as a stunning surprise. The reason for the fall of Antwerp was the failure of the High Command to appreciate how badly beaten the Fifth Panzer Army really was. Instead of an army on my left flank there was an empty gap. My own forces were neither strong enough nor fast enough to get back to Antwerp in time to defend it. We were constantly being attacked by armoured columns.' 11th Armoured division had advanced 230 miles in six days and nights and the sheer speed and brutality had 'foxed' the Germans.

On the face of it the British armour had pulled off a magnificent coup, but it could have been very much better if there had been a back-up infantry division available to strengthen the bridgehead over the Albert Canal and force the defenders out of the Merxem suburb. An advance 15 miles northwest of Antwerp would have proved extremely embarrassing to General von Zangen. On hearing the amazing news of the capture of Antwerp, Hitler's immediate command to German Naval Group West was 'mine and obstruct the Scheldt energetically'. And they did just that!

The original six divisions that came under command of General von Zangen, were joined in early September by the remnants of five divisions escaping from the Falaise 'Gap' slaughter in Normandy. He wrote, 'It was only by the greatest of efforts that we succeeded in withdrawing at all. One

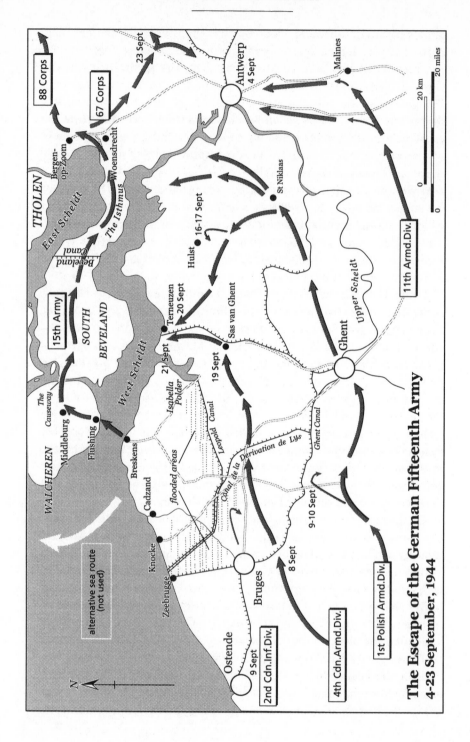

88 Corps

67 Corps

23 Sept

Antwerp
4 Sept

Malines

20 km

20 miles

THOLEN

Bergen-
op-Zoom

Woensdrecht

St Niklaas

15th Army

East Scheldt

The Isthmus

Beveland Canal

SOUTH
BEVELAND

Hulst   16-17 Sept

Upper Scheldt

11th Armd.Div.

The
Causeway

Middleburg

Flushing

Breskens

West Scheldt

Terneuzen
20 Sept

21 Sept

Sas van Ghent

Ghent

WALCHEREN

Cadzand

Isabella
Polder

19 Sept

Leopold Canal

flooded areas

Canal de la Derivation de Lys

Ghent Canal

alternative sea route
(not used)

Knocke

Zeebrugge

9-10 Sept

Bruges

8 Sept

N

Ostende

9 Sept

2nd Cdn.Inf.Div.

4th Cdn.Armd.Div.

1st Polish Armd.Div.

The Escape of the German Fifteenth Army
4-23 September, 1944

of my divisions marched 90 kilometres in one day during this retreat. With Antwerp in enemy hands there remained only two courses of action open to me—evacuation by sea or a breakthrough to the northeast. I decided on the latter course and on 5 September I ordered my troops to assemble in the neighbourhood of Audenarde with the object of attacking in the direction of Brussels. However, before this operation could get properly underway I received word from the Commander-in-Chief West on 6 September to abandon this breakthrough attempt since the enemy line was already much too strong in the area between Brussels and Antwerp. Instead I was told to make preparations for the evacuation of my army across the Scheldt to the islands of Walcheren and South Beveland.'

Field Marshal von Rundstedt, Commander-in-Chief West, ordered the Fifteenth Army to hold out tenaciously in all the fortress-ports of Le Havre, Boulogne, Calais and Dunkirk and, importantly, the new 'fortresses' of Walcheren, Breskens and Flushing to deny maritime access to the port of Antwerp. The main bulk of the Fifteenth Army would be evacuated through Breskens on the south bank of the River Scheldt, to the port of Flushing on the north bank and march across Walcheren Island eastwards to the mainland north of Antwerp. If the British and Canadians sealed the South Beveland route to the mainland then the defences in Holland west of the river Maas were at risk.

General von Zangen now made sure that the fortress commandants of Le Havre, Boulogne, Calais and Dunkirk were reinforced. He brought the 719th Infantry Division from northern Holland to help defend the canal line between Bruges and Ghent and the vital area north of Antwerp. The crucial retreat of the Fifteenth Army across the River Scheldt he entrusted to the unfortunate General Eugen-Felix Schwalbe. Unfortunate not because he was deaf but because he had lost his division trying to stop the Allied forces at the River Seine. 'When I was told what my new job was to be,' said Schwalbe,

I immediately set up my headquarters in Breskens, from where I could control the situation. Gathering about me as many officers as I could find, I sent them along the roads leading to Breskens, where they set up collecting posts for the assembling of the retreating units. They would telephone to me telling me what formation had arrived and was ready to cross, and I would allot it a specific hour when it was to be evacuated. Until that hour it was to remain well-camouflaged and hidden along the roads.

For the task of crossing the Scheldt I had assembled two large Dutch civilian ships, three large rafts capable of holding 18 vehicles each, and 16 small Rhine boats with a capacity of about 250 men each. The trips were made chiefly at night, although since time was pressing, some crossings had to be made during the day. Allied planes constantly harried the ships and a number of them laden with troops, received direct hits. However, in 16 days we managed to evacuate the remnants of nine shattered infantry divisions—59th, 70th, 245th, 331st, 344th, the 17th Luftwaffe Field, the 346th, 711th and 712th. We left one division *in Dunkirk* to defend the approaches to Antwerp. In terms of men and equipment we brought to safety by this operation some 65,000 men, 225 guns, 750 trucks and wagons and 1,000 horses. By 21 September my task was completed and the bulk of the Fifteenth Army had been rescued from encirclement.

I was in constant fear that the Allies would cut off the Beveland Isthmus by an advance north of Antwerp and thereby trap such troops as were in the process of moving out. If this had happened our alternative plan was to evacuate the troops by sea through the Dutch islands to Dordrecht and Rotterdam. But such a journey would have been slow and dangerous. It would have meant a 12-hour voyage by sea rather than the three quarters of an hour needed to cross from Breskens to Flushing. We could not have hoped to rescue anything but the troops themselves had it been necessary to adopt this course.'

Meanwhile the Allied Supreme Commander, General Eisenhower wrote in his report to the combined chiefs-of-staff,

It was our plan to attack north-eastward in the greatest strength possible. This direction had been chosen for a variety of reasons. First, the great bulk of the German army was located there. Secondly, there was the great desirability of capturing the flying-bomb area, not only to remove this menace to England, but also to deny to the enemy the propaganda which he enjoyed on the home front and in the army from the attacks on London and talk of new weapons which would decide the war. A third reason for the north-eastward attack was our imperative need for the large port of Antwerp, absolutely essential to us logistically before any deep penetration in strength could be made in Germany. Fourthly, we wanted the airfields in Belgium. Finally and most important, I felt that during the late summer and early autumn months the lower Rhine offered the best avenue of advance into Germany, and it seemed probable that through rapidity of exploitation both the Siegfried line and the Rhine River might be crossed and strong bridgeheads established before the enemy could recover sufficiently to make a definite stand in the Arnhem area.

CHAPTER TEN

Dunkirk: 'An unknown, undramatic, dirty little war'

THE DAY AFTER THE CAPTURE OF ANTWERP, GENERAL CRERAR'S FIRST Canadian Army was ordered to capture Dunkirk and he in turn entrusted this task to Major General Charles Foulkes's 2nd Canadian Division. Moving north via Montreuil towards St Omer, the 5th Infantry Brigade under Brigadier W.J. Megill was sent to probe the defences of Dunkirk. Its town and harbour were, a fact not known to the Canadians, strongly held with a garrison of about 10,000 to 12,000 men, with a mixture of coastal defence, Kriegsmarines, OST battalions and Flak anti-aircraft artillery. There were strongpoints sited at Mardick (three miles to the west), Loon Plage (four miles to the southwest), Spycker (three miles to the south), Bergues (three miles to the southeast) and Bray Dunes (5 miles east). Much of the area had been flooded and roads and tracks above the level of the muddy fields were targeted by artillery and mortar fire. Air reconnaissance reported the Boulogne, Calais and Dunkirk areas 'deserted'. This may have been because the defenders were deep inside their Todt-built strongpoints, bunkers, pillboxes and casemented coastal batteries.

The 5th Brigade advancing from Dieppe almost immediately ran into determined opposition from the outposts of Dunkirk. Brigadier Megill mistakenly thinking that Bourbourg (five miles southwest of the main town) was undefended, sent in the Régiment de Maisonneuve. Not only were they repulsed, but the Calgary Highlanders following up on 6 September and ordered to take Loon Plage, five miles to the north, were

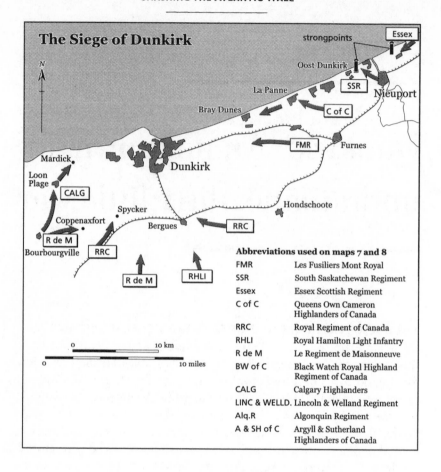

The Siege of Dunkirk

Abbreviations used on maps 7 and 8	
FMR	Les Fusiliers Mont Royal
SSR	South Saskatchewan Regiment
Essex	Essex Scottish Regiment
C of C	Queens Own Cameron Highlanders of Canada
RRC	Royal Regiment of Canada
RHLI	Royal Hamilton Light Infantry
R de M	Le Regiment de Maisonneuve
BW of C	Black Watch Royal Highland Regiment of Canada
CALG	Calgary Highlanders
LINC & WELLD.	Lincoln & Welland Regiment
Alq.R	Algonquin Regiment
A & SH of C	Argyll & Sutherland Highlanders of Canada

abruptly halted on dyke roads and promptly shelled by long-range coastal guns from Dunkirk.

David Bercuson, the Calgary Highlanders' historian wrote, 'So while the British and American armies to the south and east gloried in the liberation of the rest of France and much of Belgium, the Calgary Highlanders and their comrades-in-arms fought an unknown, undramatic dirty little war in water-logged country on the approaches to Dunkirk. Under almost constant shelling fire from the heavy guns in the German held enclave, the Highlanders slugged it out with an enemy determined to follow Hitler's orders to the last man. There were no major assaults and no dramatic victories, and yet this siege, this little war of attrition cost the Highlanders 126 of their number killed or wounded in action.' Having had 700 casualties in Normandy the Calgaries were more than

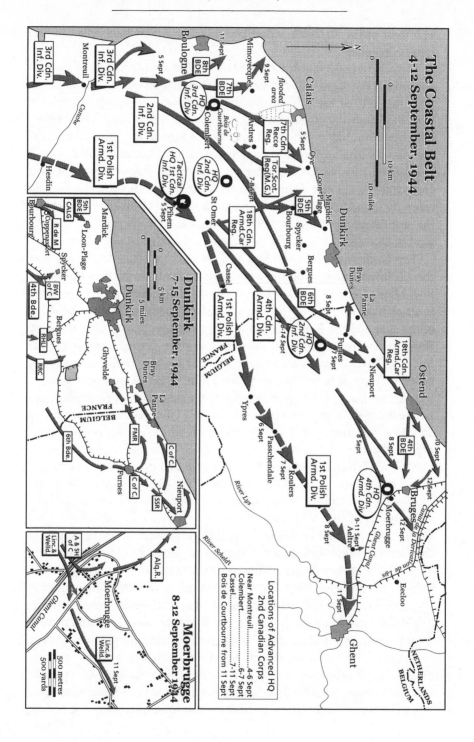

300 men under strength, although on 4 September they received 140 reinforcements.

Brigadier Megill was desperate to secure Bourbourg and fighting went on through the night until the German defenders pulled out before dawn. With the help of the 8th Reconnaissance AFVs and heavy mortar fire from the Toronto Scottish, the Calgaries advanced over flat sodden polderland to within half a mile of Loon Plage. Large-calibre naval guns and German 88 mm and 75 mm guns pounded the Canadians all day on 8 September. Around Les Planches crossroads the three Calgary forward companies could only muster about 30 men *each*. But patrols the next morning found Loon Plage abandoned. Lieutenant Colonel MacLauchlan, the commanding officer of the Calgaries, sent patrols north to the sea, west to Gravelines and as far east towards Dunkirk as was possible.

The Germans were confident and sent out patrols every night, and the 5th Brigade dug in on the west flank on the Loon Plage—Bourboug line. Major General Foulkes now brought his 4th Brigade into the area to attack from due south. The Canadian Black Watch got into the outskirts of Spycker and the Royal Hamilton Light Infantry planned an attack on Bergues. The centuries old fortress with sloping ramparts was defended by an SS lieutenant with 300 men and the night action (subsequently called off) would have been very costly. The Royal Regiment of Canada moved northwards between Bergues and a large area of flooded polder before being held up. But on the 15th the RHLI did put in an unsuccessful attack on the strongpoint at Bergues, from which the enemy withdrew on the next day.

On the eastern flanks the 6th Brigade cleared the coastal villages and towns of Furnes, Nieuport and La Panne. The Queen's Own Camerons of Canada had difficult little battles at La Panne, Bray Dune Plage, and Bray Dunes inland. With the sea on their right, the Camerons attacked through the sand and minefields against the huge concrete forts, part of the German West Wall. Many of the coastal guns could fire inland. But shells and heavy bombing had little or no effect on the concrete casements. Adolf Hitler had earmarked Dunkirk as a possible/probable Allied invasion target and had the Todt organization hard at work on its defence. On 11 September the whole of the Camerons battalion were in action against Bray Dunes. At one stage their 'D' Company, holding a vital crossroads, were cut off for two days, despite 88 mm anti-tank guns firing at them at point blank range. Les Fusiliers Mont Royal were fighting on a parallel line from Furnes west to Ghyvelde and the South Saskatchewans captured Nieuport on 10 September. Temporary reinforcements arrived for the hard-pressed 2nd Canadian Division. Three regiments of 51st Highland Division with 25lb artillery tried their best to help pound the Dunkirk defences. There were no 'Funnies', no tank forces (although flooded ground would have made them useless), not much air bombing and no Royal Naval support.

During the siege the French Red Cross asked for a 48-hour truce, which was extended to 60 hours, during which 8,000 civilians were evacuated to safety. The German commandant stated, 'The preservation of German lives is more important at this moment than the Port of Dunkirk. We shall fight hard, but not to the end.'

The 5th Infantry Brigade held on to their gains on the western flank at Loon Plage and Bourbourg. After eight days under constant and heavy shelling the Calgarys' historian wrote that, 'much of the time was spent digging in enduring heavy and deadly shelling, sending patrols into no-man's land and listening and watching for German patrols. It was like the First World War in microcosm.' One of the other hazards was the French maquis or FFI. They were totally undisciplined, roamed about at will, making such a noise that unwelcome German 'stonks' caused casualties. They shot a Calgary Highlander of 'C' Company when he challenged a group of maquis moving near his position. Lieutenant Colonel MacLauchlan was furious and had the 'guerrillas' involved disarmed and arrested. On the 12th and 13th Brigadier Megill ordered the Calgaries and Camerons north to take the Geerson Farm strongpoint. After a ferocious battle little progress was made, but during the night of 15/16th the Germans moved out of Fort Mardick, just west of the main port.

On the 14th a midnight fighting patrol of Germans approached a Calgary Highlanders' outpost near Mardick. The moon shone brightly and at close quarters Bren guns and grenades did for the patrol. Next morning Privates Field and Macdonald, almost by mistake, captured 22 of the German defenders. Artillery support was now rationed to three rounds per day and supply of heavy mortar bombs to five.

The 2nd Canadian Division now completely encircled Dunkirk, Loon Plage, Bourbourg, Spycker, Bergues, Ghyvelde and Bray Dunes, a ten-mile perimeter of the outer defences, some three miles from the town centre. It was obvious to General Crerar, and to Major General Foulkes that it was a stalemate. It needed the careful considered planning of Operation Astonia, the capture of Le Havre, to repeat the process at Dunkirk. A minimum of two divisions would be needed, massive artillery, RAF bombing and RN support plus the deadly 'Funnies', flails, flame-throwers and AVRES (Armoured Vehicles Royal Engineers).

And on 13th, whilst Dunkirk was being surrounded, Monty again wrote to General Crerar, 'The things that are now very important are:

(a) Capture of Boulogne and Dunkirk and Calais
(b) The setting in action of operations designed to enable us to use the port of Antwerp.

Of these two (b) is probably the most important. We have captured a port which resembles Liverpool in size, but we cannot use it; if we could use it all our maintenance troubles would disappear. *I am very anxious that (a) and (b) should both go on simultaneously* if you can possibly arrange it, as time is of the utmost importance.'

On the 17th Crerar was told to call off the main attacks and 'mask' Dunkirk as the British 4th Special Service Brigade and Czech Armoured Brigade arrived to take over from 2nd Infantry Division. They in turn handed over the perimeter on 26 September to the 51st Highland Division.

On 14 September 48th Royal Marine Commando took over the 10,000-yard front on the landward side of Dunkirk, from the Canadian 8th Reconnaissance Regiment. Digging in the sodden 'polder' countryside was impossible and Lieutenant Colonel J. L. Moulton, the commanding officer, decided to occupy all the farmsteads and buildings as strongpoints even though clearly targeted by the offensive-minded German defenders. 'I picked four localities: on the right Teddy Dunn with 'B' Troop at Hoymille; next Tom Nuttall and 'Z' Troop in Bergues itself. Both troops faced wide stretches of shallow floods. Then 'A' Troop under Dan Flunder at Grande Mille Brugghe and 'Y' Troop at Ferme Le Grand, well out to the left clear of the floods about a mile apart. We had a collection of captured German Spandau machine guns carried in the heavy transport issued to the forward troops. The commando headquarters was at Socx behind Bergues with direct roads to the flanks. The wild and mainly irresponsible FFI Resistance reported for duty.' For 12 days, until the 51st Highland troops took over, the Royal Marine Commandos had frequent small firefights, often defensive actions against the aggressive German occupiers of Dunkirk. General von Trestkow, his 18th Luftwaffen-feld Division and I Festa LXXXII, 1244 Artillery Group, Flak-AA Gruppe and Marine Regiment 618 had put up a ferocious defence.

Dunkirk garrison stayed invested in a stalemate holding operation for another seven months before surrendering—with some dignity, undefeated in May 1945—to the Belgian 'White' Brigade. The troops spent the balance of the war listening to their commandants exhorting them not to desert, reading Allied propaganda on how nice it was to desert, sheltering themselves from constant air and artillery bombardment, carrying out sporadic raids to supplement their dwindling food supply, and apprehensively awaiting a large-scale Allied assault. On the whole, they would have been much happier in a prisoner-of-war camp.

CHAPTER ELEVEN

Ostend and Zeebrugge Cleared

ABOUT 35 MILES NORTHEAST OF DUNKIRK, OSTEND (OOSTENDE) IS a useful port. It had a wartime population of 60,000 and has had a cross-Channel passenger and goods service for many years.

On 8 September Lieutenant Colonel Roberts, Commanding Officer 12th Manitoba Dragoons, then near St Omer was ordered by Lieutenant General Guy Simonds to make for Ostend and, if possible, capture the town and harbour. The armoured-car regiment dashed through Poperinghe, swung north, sensibly avoiding Dunkirk, known to be well garrisoned and swept towards Furnes and Dixmunde. The two troop leaders, Lieutenants Jefferson and Phelps, each with a small Lynx scout car and two Staghound armoured cars, approached a canal south of the town. Ahead the road was obviously mined with large naval shells, noses upright and showing. The ground each side of the road was boggy and using a set of steel tracks (carried on the Staghounds) they made an effective bridge over the naval shells. Each officer then drove the relatively light Lynx gingerly over the mined area! Ahead the bridges were also mined but the charges were removed. Another squadron met the Belgian White Army resistance movement who guided them into the town centre. The main German garrison had just left and only a skeleton group of engineers was left behind, hard at work on dock demolitions. The Belgians gave the Manitoba Dragoons a rousing welcome. Lieutenant Colonel Roberts wrote, 'As evening fell it started to rain heavily but did nothing to dampen the enthusiasm and excitement of the citizens. I ordered 'C' Sqn to dismount their machine guns and to set up guard posts. The poor troopers sat all night behind their guns facing a possible enemy counter-attack, while countless Belgian citizens sat with them, fed and kissed them, asked for cigarettes and generally distracted the attention of the guard posts. Fortunately no one counter-attacked and the wet and dreary night passed. Most of the regiment were given food and beds in hotels and homes and were so well treated that they wished never to leave again.'

The commanding officer had his headquarters in a large, presumably expensive, hotel. During the night he received orders to move north towards Zeebrugge. He was, in the morning, presented with a large bill for himself and his headquarters staff, which he duly signed!

The 4th Canadian Brigade then took over Ostend and cleared the coast from there to Nieuport to the southwest. The Royal Hamilton Light Infantry (Rileys) were asked on 10 September to clear up some heavy sniping reported in the Ostend harbour area near the E-boat pens. Lieutenant A. Parker of 'C' Company took a platoon to investigate, 'It was a lovely day. The operation was just a cross-country jaunt. The sub [sic] pens were deserted and there wasn't a soul around. One mess hall had just been left by Jerry, snowy linen and silver on the tables and cases of liquor all over the place.' Parker was worried about the possibility of poison but allowed his troop to 'rescue' a barrel of brown ale to take back to their billet. 'C' Company also witnessed the unpleasant 'liberation' ritual meted out by Belgian patriots against women accused of collaborating with the Germans.

When the Royal Naval port clearance party Number 1574 inspected the harbour they found 14 wrecks but, rather surprisingly, the E-boat pens were intact and became a useful base for RN flotillas for the Scheldt clearance. By the 25th Ostend's harbour was opened after searching 95,400 square feet of docks with ten hours spent searching for underwater mines. By the end of September 1,000 tons were being discharged daily and by the end of October 5,000 daily. In the month of November 25,000 personnel were landed, 84,254 tons of supplies, 3,481 vehicles and 75,058 tons of POL. Also 2,500 wounded had been evacuated on hospital ships back to England.

The German navy still had a sting in its tail. On 1 November HMT *Colsay* and the tanker *Rio Bravo* were both hit by torpedoes and became total losses just outside Ostend Harbour.

The larger port of Zeebrugge, with a population of 105,000, 15 miles up the coast was taken much later on 3 November. The RN port clearance party spent 113 diving man-hours looking for underwater mines and searched no less than 477,000 square feet of the quays Prins Filipsdok, Vissershaven and the main Haven.

The naval parties were eventually withdrawn on 6 January 1945 as Zeebrugge could not be usefully developed as a discharge port. The German garrison had obeyed Hitler's orders about thorough port demolition. Major General Knut Eberding, 64th Infantry Division, had defended Zeebrugge as the western edge of the Breskens pocket, which was not cleared until 3 November at the end of Operation Switchback.

CHAPTER TWELVE

The Capture of Le Havre: Operation Astonia

THERE WERE MANY REASONS WHY THE ALLIES WANTED TO CAPTURE Le Havre. They knew that when taken and the port facilities repaired, a daily unloading target of 5,000 tons a day of valuable supplies was feasible. Additionally the navy were also anxious to change its ownership. The heavy gun batteries at Le Havre had a most definite nuisance value. Also the E-boat flotillas there were an even greater menace. From Le Havre human torpedoes and explosive motor boats had been making determined attacks on the Royal Naval defence lines in the Channel (Trout line) and against anchorages around Mulberry. Radar showed that exceptionally heavy traffic close inshore was noted towards the end of August, moving reinforcements to the Le Havre garrison from St Valéry-en-Caux (before it was later captured by the 51st Highland Division, to avenge the tragic defeat in 1940).

For a week there were ferocious little sea battles off the French coast between Le Havre, Dieppe and Fécamp. On the one side British Hunt-class destroyers and frigates, motor torpedo boats, US motor torpedo boats and a French destroyer took on German destroyers, submarine-chasers, armed trawlers, R-boats, E-boats, minesweepers and artillery-ferry barges. The British had air superiority against daytime sorties but the Germans often had protection from their coastal batteries. Enemy losses were so heavy that on 29 August their surviving coastal flotillas were withdrawn from Le Havre. Twenty-one boats of various kinds had been sunk and a further 13 badly damaged out of the original strength of four torpedo boats and 41 other vessels. Lieutenant Commander Peter Scott, MBE, DSC and Bar, RNVR, recorded that on 3 September 1944,

> For four fierce nights battles raged off Cap d'Antifer as the enemy ships—coasters, escort vessels, E-boats, and R-boats—crept close under the shore, eastward bound up the Channel. They kept very close into their cliffs so that the heavy guns of their coastal batteries could give them cover, but our forces were not prepared to be kept away. The other night a unit of MTBs fought a gun battle with a party of R-boats at 15 yards range. Of course, that's unusually close, but quite normally the range is only a few hundred yards, with the bright coloured tracers, blinding streaks criss-crossing between the opposing forces and the roll and thunder of automatic guns.
>
> Through smoke screens, and the tall pillars of shell splashes and under the glare of bright white starshells, our MTBs have had to carry out their torpedo and gun attacks against a wide-awake and desperate enemy who was less than half a mile from his own cliffs, so close that our own starshells often burst in the fields on the cliff top. Still they were sometimes able to get in unobserved. It's a lot easier to take careful aim along a torpedo sight *before* the tracer bullets start to fly, but often it had to be done afterwards when the air was already alive with the nasty things, singing overhead and popping and crumping all around. That needs a lot of concentration. And then at last the levers are pulled, the torpedoes leap out with a 'whoosh' and a splash and speed off towards the enemy. Less than a minute later if the aim was true comes the red glow, the column of water, and the thud of the explosion. These were the sort of battles being fought last week. These battles are still going on as the remnant of the enemy shipping streams eastward.

Le Havre had been receiving dire treatment from the RAF. On 14 June a daylight raid by mainly 222 Lancasters with Pathfinders dropped 1,230 tons on E-boat pens and the motor torpedo boats in the harbour. Some 22 12,000 lb Tallboy bombs were dropped, one at least penetrating a pen. Further heavy raids followed on 31 July, and 2, 5, 6, 8, 9, 10 and 11 September. For instance, on 10 September 992 craft bombed eight strongpoints marked by Pathfinders. During the raid of 14 June the German torpedo boats *Falke*, *Jaguar* and *Moewe*, ten E-boats, two R-boats, 15 minesweepers and patrol vessels were sunk. Admiral Kranke, the

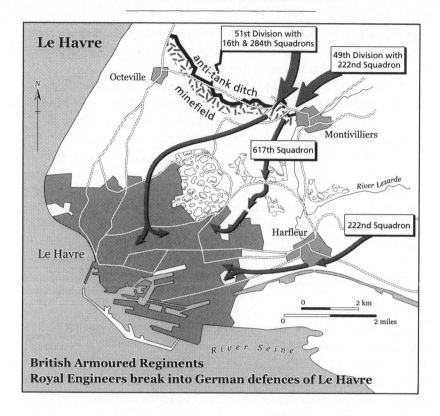

Le Havre

51st Division with
16th & 284th Squadrons

49th Division with
222nd Squadron

Octeville

anti-tank ditch

minefield

N

Montivilliers

617th Squadron

River Lezarde

222nd Squadron

Harfleur

Le Havre

0   2 km

0   2 miles

River Seine

**British Armoured Regiments
Royal Engineers break into German defences of Le Havre**

German naval commander wrote, 'The attack on Havre is a catastrophe. Losses are extremely heavy. The loss of the torpedo boats and the H7Bs is especially bitter. Naval situation in Seine Bay has completely altered since yesterday's attack...'

The task of capturing Le Havre was given to the First Canadian Army. In effect this was the First British Corps under Lieutenant General Crocker with 49th (Polar Bear) Division (who would invest the port from the southeast and east) and 51st Highland Division (who would attack from the northwest and north). In addition to huge artillery support, both British divisions would receive vital support from the 'Funnies' of 79th Armoured Division—flail tanks, AVRE bombards mounted on Churchills, flame-throwers and bridge layers. Unlike the dedicated nazi fanatics commanding the garrisons of Cherbourg, St Malo and Brest, Colonel Eberhardt Wildermuth was an extraordinary choice. He had been a banker by profession, not a nazi, and at the time of the siege—Operation Astonia— was described as being 55, tall, skeletal and balding! He had seen heavy fighting in 1940 in France, then Russia and Italy and was given a peaceful coastal sector near Venice to defend. Out of the blue he was appointed on 14 August, commandant of the bastion of Le Havre.

Wildermuth had nearly 14,000 troops under command, the usual mix of Wehrmacht, coastal defence, Luftwaffe ground and anti-aircraft troops, Kriegsmarines, OST battalions and naval maintenance staff for the E-boat flotillas. Besides several powerful batteries of heavy coastal-defence guns, Wildermuth had over 115 guns of all kinds but few anti-tank weapons. The 15 miles of inland defences were interspersed with minefields, anti-tank ditches, barbed-wire entanglements and many substantial and deep strongpoints impervious to RAF bombing. The risk to civilians was obvious, and the original population of 164,000 had had many opportunities to leave. Leaflets in French had been dropped before the siege commenced. By the end of Astonia, 5,000 French civilians were dead, mainly killed by the bombing. Front line loudspeaker vans exhorted them to leave but in vain. Hitler's order to Wildermuth on 31 July said, 'Take no account of the fate of the civilians in the city.'

Le Havre ranks, with inland Rouen, among the leading ports of France, and consists of a series of dock basins excavated in the broad belt of silt, which runs along the north shore. As a deep-water port it needs continuous dredging. Prewar, to allow the great French liner *Normandie* to berth, the harbour entrance was widened to 820 feet and the Passe du Nord Ouest dredged to a depth of 35 feet.

Inside the entrance is the Avant Port, beyond that the Arrière Port leading east to the 'wet' docks, which are linked to each other by dock gates, locks and passages. Southeast of the Avant Port lies the Bassin Theophile-Ducroq (which can accommodate very large vessels). The Tancarville Canal links the Bassin de L'Eure to the River Seine at Tancarville, which links with Rouen 70 miles upstream and inland.

In the town of Le Havre were two forts and many road blocks, pillboxes and fortified houses together with anti-aircraft and some anti-tank guns. In theory Le Havre was impregnable although the calibre and morale of the garrison troops were doubtful. It was known afterwards that ammunition was plentiful and sufficient food was available to feed the garrison of 14,000 for three months.

It took ten days of very careful co-ordination and planning to get two infantry divisions, the mass of artillery support and 'Funny' tank support into place. The atttack began at 17.45 hours on 10 September. The RAF on 10th and 11th dropped 11,000 tons of bombs mainly on the eight key strongpoints (out of the 400 concrete bunkers in the area). HMS *Warspite*, and the monitor *Erebus* escorted by the destroyers *Grenville* and *Ulysses* reached their bombardment position 15 miles from Cap de la Hève. HMS *Warspite* fired 353 15-inch shells at four coastal batteries throughout the 10th. Spotting aircraft observed and corrected aim. One German defensive coast battery had four 16-inch guns and another three 11-inch guns. Once they straddled *Warspite* and forced her back to a 31,000 yard range.

Major Roland Ward of 617th Assault Squadron, Royal Engineers, wrote an account of the plan, 'The attack was to be in four stages— first the attack by the 56th Infantry Bde [Polar Bears], their objective being the Ardennes plateau which overlooks Le Havre from the north. On this front eight gaps were to be attempted [through the minefields] but only the three middle ones were to cross the [anti-tank] ditch which lay beyond the minefield. The second stage was to be a night attack further to the right [north] by the 51st Highland Division. The third stage was an attack the following morning [11th] through Harfleur by 146th Brigade [Polar Bears]. The fourth stage would be penetration and exploitation into the heart of the city on the second and third days. The obstacles and defences at Le Havre were remarkably similar to those we had been practising on in Suffolk. A total of 11 gaps had to be made through the deep minefields, six of them to cross the wide anti-tank ditch.' Excellent overprinted maps and air photographs were provided which showed two places in the northeast near Montivilliers where the anti-tank ditch had not been completed. The corps commander Lieutenant General John Crocker decided to put battalion attacks through those gaps.

The sheer volume of bombardment from the air, from the sea and from 18 regiments of artillery had certainly softened up the defences before the combined infantry and tank attacks that followed. Crab flail tanks on boggy ground cleared paths through the minefields, AVRE Churchill tanks laid large fascines in the anti-tank ditch south of the Montivilliers-Octeville line. AVRE bombards threw petards at close range at the pillboxes and Crocodiles, also at short range, flamed defence points. But it was the six brigades of infantry (Gordons, Argylls, Black Watch and Seaforth) in the north, and in the south and east, (Gloucesters, South Wales Borderers, Essex, Leicesters, Royal Scots Fusiliers, King's Own Yorkshire Light Infantry, Hallams and Lincolns) who steadfastly winkled out the defenders. Although the German defenders concentrated their fire on the lanes (Mary, Hazel, Laura, etc.) flailed through the minefields, the issue was never in doubt. Later the Place de la Liberté was reached and the Fort de Tourneville taken. The KOYLI took objectives codenamed

Eggs, Ham, Sausage, Bacon, Kidney and Marmalade. German envoys came out to treat with Major General 'Bubbles' Barker, GOC 49th Polar Bears Division. They told the general that Hitler had personally ordered defence of Le Havre to the last man and the last round. The general answered, 'I wish you good luck and a Merry Christmas'. The FFI were helpful with information about defence positions and guarded prisoners. Harfleur in the southeast was taken and the 51st Highlanders captured Octeville, La Hève and Fort Ste Addresse.

The Gloucesters stormed the main fortress and found the garrison well prepared for surrender, including packed suitcases. In one day they captured 1,500 prisoners of war including the naval admiral and his staff, 30 Algerians, 30 Italians, half a dozen French 'comfort' girls and a fine cellar. The Hallamshires cleared the docks and the main Mole—a strip of land, a mile long and 100 yards wide, studded with large concrete pillboxes. They took in 1,005 prisoners of war, three Dornier flying boats and a submarine! Colonel Wildermuth told his captors, 'In my opinion it was futile to fight tanks with bare hands. As early as 9 September I had given orders to all my officers that Allied infantry attacks were to be opposed everywhere even with side arms only. But in the event of an attack by tanks, resistance nests which no longer had any anti-tank weapons were then at liberty to surrender.' There was much evidence that the sight of the fearsome Sherman Crabs flailing noisily away *through* the German minefields broke morale. Over 11,300 prisoners of war were gathered in against British losses of 388 killed in action and 250 wounded. Liddell Hart considered the assault the best planned and the most efficient of all sieges and assaults on the fortress-ports.

Brigade Major Paul Crook, 49th Division recalled, 'And what a night [10th]. There were flail tanks flashing away detonating some mines and missing others. Armoured assault engineer vehicles were chuntering around and tanks following up. There were the noises and effects of our own supporting fire from a variety of weapons, finally of course there was the din of battle, organised chaos and danger.'

The British Assault Unit 30 led by Captain Huntington-Whiteley were given maps showing that their main target was a bank in the square on the seafront—an important information and communications centre. On their way into the city centre in their scout cars they captured two groups of German sailors, leaving only one team of four to continue. Shortly afterwards this team's scout car was ambushed. The captain and Marine Shaw were killed and Marines Feeley and Livingstone captured. The German admiral used Livingstone as an intermediary to negotiate a surrender. Feeley then signed the Allied leaflets advocating 'Surrender' dropped by the RAF for the German garrison to give up. The young entrepreneur charged 100 francs for each signed 'pass'. One assumes he did not sign the leaflets 'Eisenhower' or 'Montgomery'. When members of AU30 went on leave to Paris shortly afterwards their pockets were bulging with French francs!

After the final surrender Major General 'Bubbles' Barker wrote in his diary for 12/13 September, 'We have taken some 6–7,000 PoW and the Jocks [51st Highland Division] a good many also but old 49 has really done the job. I feel I put the chaps into battle with a good plan and they had been able to do justice to their efforts and their high morale and courage. The show went through like clockwork in spite of the very strong defences. Casualties are remarkably light. My tanks of all sorts co-operated superbly and the gunners were quite excellent. The real cause of the success was that the Boche went down into their deep shelters for the bombing and our artillery, and did not get to their positions till too late. We got into them too quick. We had to outflank every strongpoint before they gave in.'

Royal Navy port clearance team Number 1571 came up from Dieppe to inspect Le Havre, with Commander Walsh USN and Lieutenant Commander Freemantle RN. With them was the same US Navy mine disposal party who had operated at Cherbourg in July. They found a new demolition mine, RMK, in a wooden case four feet square. Inside it had an 'o' mine in a unit chamber adapted for electrical firing, suspended from the quayside, resting on the bottom of the seabed. They found 25 surface mines but no mines within the *bassins* or alongside the quays. Three days later the port was declared free of mines but 165 wrecks, wrecked bridges, cranes, etc blocked the waterways. It became a valuable base for Allied coastal forces which had been beating up the German E-boats for the last month. The port was open for traffic and cargo on 9 October and 3,650 tons per day were unloaded, rising to 5,000 in November onwards.

CHAPTER THIRTEEN

The Capture of Boulogne: Operation Wellhit

ON THE EVENING OF 4 SEPTEMBER LIEUTENANT GENERAL GUY Simonds, commanding II Canadian Corps gave out his orders. The 2nd Canadian Infantry Division would clear the coast from Dunkirk to the Dutch border and Major General Dan Spry's 3rd Division was to clear the coast from Dieppe, capture Boulogne, the coastal batteries at Cap Gris-Nez and then Calais. Simmonds's two armoured divisions, plus the 1st Polish and 4th Canadian were directed towards Ghent and Bruges. No one knew whether the Channel ports would be defended or not. Dieppe was not, but Le Havre certainly was.

The headline news of the capture of Brussels and Antwerp now made General Crerar's First Canadian Army the Cinderella of the Allies. His six divisions were strung out over a 200-mile front and were expected to perform miracles. It soon became clear that Boulogne, Calais and Dunkirk were well defended with garrisons of a similar size to Wildemuth's at Le Havre. It was unlikely that this Cinderella Army could count on (a) smashing RAF bombing attacks (b) heavy Royal Navy assaults on their coastal batteries (c) medium artillery (d) APC (armoured personnel carriers) and (e) the manpower needed to subdue these individual fortress-ports. Le Havre was attacked by *two* infantry divisions plus all the supporting arms listed above. Spry's 3rd Division had three major battles and sieges ahead of it without as much support. Led by the 7th Canadian Reconnaissance Regiment, the 3rd Canadian Division covered over 70 miles but eventually ran

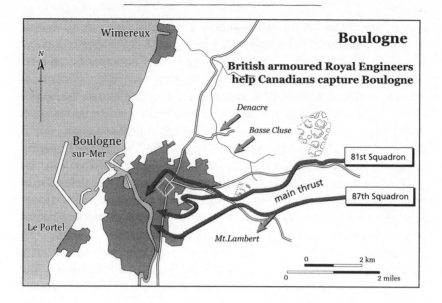

into fire from St Etienne-au-Mont just south of Boulogne, and Herquelingue.

Lieutenant General Ferdinand Heim, aged 50, looked according to the German General Warlimont 'with his thin pinched face and prominent blue eyes a larger version of Goebbels.' Heim had been a first class staff officer and had led a panzer division on the Russian front, and was promoted to command 48th Panzer Corps besieging Stalingrad. Heim had the misfortune to have two Romanian divisions under him who were overrun. Hitler never forgave him and had Heim arrested in January 1943 and sent to prison for five months! Suddenly released, he was sent to Ulm and rather surprisingly in August 1944 to command the fortress garrison of Boulogne, on the usual terms, 'defend to the last man and bullet.' The 64th Infantry Division included engineers and artillery, many low-grade fortress troops, some OST battalions and many Kriegsmarines in a total of about 10,000 men. General Model had ordered a defensive zone to a depth of six miles built around the town, all bridges to be blown and minefields laid. On 2 September every officer of the garrison had to sign this pledge: 'I undertake in the presence of Lieutenant General Heim, commander of the fortress of Boulogne, to hold and defend the strongpoint or sector under my command to the end of my life and that of the last man under me.

Boulogne, which then had a population of 45,000, is a natural fortress completely surrounded by high hills, which guard all the approaches and roads into the town which lies on lower ground. The defences ran from the coast to the west side of the town through the hills of Ecault, St Etienne-au-Mont to Mont-de-Thune and then north through the heavily defended Mont Lambert. On all the hills were sited either coastal guns or Flak anti-aircraft batteries or both. The main artillery group was at Herquelingue, a hill behind Mont de Thune. The FFI met the Canadian advanced forces and reported that La Trésorie (East of Wimereux, the northern suburb) had a battery of six heavy guns and was defended by 500 German marines. At Rupembert there was a garrison of 600 troops with anti-tank guns, three miles northeast of the town centre. At Château Ripots there were 20 blockhouses and many hundreds of troops.

The harbour lies at the entrance of the River Liane, with from west to east, Darse Sarraz-Bourne, Bassin Loubet (near the Gare Maritime), and in the river are two quays, Gambetta and Chanzy, and the large Bassin Napoleon. A heavy RAF air attack on 15/16 July had sunk eight R-boats, three depot ships and 20 miscellaneous coastal craft and tugs. In the first ten days of Overlord 74 vessels had been sunk in Boulogne and a further 47 badly damaged.

The importance of Boulogne was that when it was eventually opened to incoming cargo on 12 October, no less than 11,000 tons daily would be unloaded. It was also the port scheduled to receive petrol, oil and lubricants (POL) via the pipe line under the ocean (PLUTO).

Operation Wellhit was the codename for the capture of Boulogne. Three things now held up the attack; evidence that the garrison was double the size of the attacking force: the need for special assault equipment from 79th Armoured Division (successful at Le Havre—flails, Crocodiles and AVRE bombards) and finally liaison with RAF bomber command. Major General Spry had only two infantry brigades at his disposal, the 8th to assault the adjacent strongpoints and the 9th to attack the town itself. His third brigade was 'containing' the batteries at Cap Gris-Nez and the Calais garrison. Frank Gillard, BBC journalist, wrote, 'Just a couple of miles from Boulogne we found the Germans making a stand, not intending to give up the port very easily. They'd guns on each side of the road—firing on everything that came in sight. A fierce encounter was going on between them and the advancing Canadians.' Gillard met the local FFI leader in a farmhouse who told him the Germans planned to build 600 V-bomb sites in the area. They went to a lot of trouble to make the sites *non* magnetic but the French site workers inserted scraps of iron and metal into the concrete when the Germans had their backs turned!

General Warlimont quoted extracts from a German officer's diary: '*7 Sept* Encircled in Boulogne. For days I knew that there was no getting out of it for us. If Fate is favourable I may become a prisoner of war. *9 Sept* Yesterday late in the afternoon enemy bombers attacked the forward defensive positions. My God, how long will it be until the town itself will be the target? Can anyone survive after a carpet of bombs has fallen? It seems as if all fighting is useless and all sacrifices in vain. *11 Sept* All day long artillery fire on our outlying strongpoints, in between attacks by fighter bombers. The outskirts are being evacuated by the French. The morale of the troops is bad, mostly old married men and the situation is hopeless. *13 Sept* This afternoon more heavy air attacks on the outer defences. Most of the civilians have wandered off. What a tragic spectacle. *15 Sept* No mail from home for six weeks. That is the hardest of all to take....' Allied aircraft dropped leaflets advising French civilians to leave as soon as possible. Major General Spry planned to attack from the east with the 8th and 9th Brigades, each respectively north and south of the main N41 road from St Omer into Boulogne. They would advance in parallel to the River Liane running through the town. Then the 8th would head north to Wimereux and Wimille two miles north, and the 9th would cross the river to take the western part of the town and port, including suburbs of Le Portel, Capécure and Outreau. The main defensive position of Mont Lambert to the east would be pounded by the RAF while artillery neutralized the gun positions. Spry formed a dummy brigade with his machine-gun battalion, divisional engineers, anti-aircraft and anti-tank regiments to threaten from the south. Brigadier G.S. Knight commanded the strong contingent of 'Funnies' to support the Canadians; 141st RAC (the Buffs) with two squadrons of Crocodile flame-throwers; the Lothians Sherman flails with two squadrons, plus the 81st and the 87th Assault Squadrons RE with their versatile Churchill AVRES.

Early on the 17th 370 heavy bombers, mainly Lancasters, dropped 1,463 tons of explosives partly on the port area sinking 31 R-boats and other craft; but also 351 Halifaxes and 41 Mosquitoes dropped the same amount of bombs on the Mont Lambert defences. By 10.00 hours the last bomb fell. Sherman tanks of the Fort Garry Horse, and infantry of the North Nova Scotia Highlanders in Kangaroos plus AVRES of 87th Assault Squadron RE advanced to the attack. Included in the artillery support were three regiments of 25 pounders from 51st Highland Division helping out after the capture of Le Havre. Two AGRAs were available to the Canadian division in their attack. The Novas under Lieutenant Colonel Forbes fought gallantly in the several attacks on Mont Lambert and during the six-day battle had two officers, 28 other ranks killed in action and three officers and 64 other ranks wounded. Halfway up the slope mines and bomb craters halted the attack and they had to fight their way through a labyrinth of trenches, and pillboxes with machine guns in concrete emplacements. The flail tanks were held up by deep craters. But Crocodiles of Lieutenant Ken Macksey's troop, 141st RAC, were most effective using not only flame (FTF squirts or napalm) but also 75 mm rounds and belts of BESA. The Novas had to clear 20 separate strongpoints and by nightfall most of Mont Lambert was in their hands. The rest of Brigadier Rockingham's brigade, Stormont, Dundas and Glengarry Highlanders followed by the Highland Light Infantry of Canada in turretless 'Priests' behind a barrage, had quickly captured the area between La Caucherie and St Martin on the northern slopes of Mont Lambert.

Major General Spry then advanced two mixed armoured columns, with bulldozers, flails, crocodiles, AVRES, together with infantry in Kangaroos to try to seize the two key bridges over the River Liane in the centre of Boulogne. At 15.20 hours the 'A' column set off into the suburbs but were completely baulked by bomb craters and rubble. 'B' column managed to bypass 'A' in the indescribable confusion of mortar and shellfire in the gathering dark, although damaged and knocked out vehicles were blocking the tracks and side streets. There were enormous bomb craters into which vehicles slid and stuck. Eventually eight tanks got through to reach the citadel in the town. The defenders had of course blown the main river bridges, but by the morning of the 18th 'A' column had blasted down the gates of the citadel. The historian of the Glens (the Stormont, Dundas and Glengarry Highlanders) wrote, 'D Company and the battalion command group headed for the Citadel, now entirely surrounded like a castle by a high wall, and under cover of smoke got into position.' Major Stothart took a platoon and followed a FFI man who 'knew a secret entrance into the heart of the Citadel.' Then 'the Churchill tanks rumbled up, raking the ramparts with fire and the Engineers in their AVRES placed petards against the portcullis and the gate was blown in. Scores of dirty white "flags" immediately fluttered from the walls....200 prisoners including 16 officers were captured all delighted to be out of the war.'

The battle for Mont Lambert continued on the 18th. Captain Storrar of 'A' Squadron of the Buffs wrote, 'With Lt Andrews and his Crocs, we scrambled to the top of the hill to clear some pillboxes with some help from the AVRES of 87 A/Sqn. It was a very pleasant party with the AVRES blowing holes in the pillboxes and the Crocs shooting their flame into the holes. Many PoW and other oddments were picked up.' The Novas sent Major Clennett's 'D' Company to attack a position at the rear of Mont Lambert defended by several pillboxes and 88 mm guns. Under a 12-minute intensive barrage they had savage close-quarter fighting and took six strongpoints, four gun positions and a large storeroom full of liquor, plus 311 prisoners of war. 'C' Company, the Novas' historian wrote, 'went in with AVRES, flame-throwers and tanks in a final direct drive on Mt Lambert. There was no stopping them and the flame-throwers did brilliant work. Soon the entire fortress surrendered and out came 1,800 prisoners. Inside the big fortress were huge concrete pillboxes with guns on automatic hoists and food and drink, stores enough to last for months.'

By noon on 18 September the 9th Brigade had done well—both Mont Lambert fortress and the citadel had fallen and the Novas were pushing towards Herquelingue. On the right-hand flank of attack by the 8th Brigade, Le Régiment de la Chaudière and the Queen's Own Cameron Rifles battled their way into the northern outskirts of the town. The North Shore Regiment attacked the heavily fortified positions around La Trésorie. The German marines behind minefields, barbed-wire barricades and concrete walls, enormously thick, caused the North Shore troops heavy casualties.

Bangalore torpedoes blew up the wire but anti-personnel mines hidden in the muddy fields caused many casualties. Armour-piercing shells stopped the Lothians' flails and the Buffs' Crocodiles, but a troop of M-10 tank destroyers posted shells through the 20 mm Flak pillboxes. 'B' Company captured three strongpoints. In one of them the German commandant strapped himself and his second in command into the firing seats of their cross-Channel gun, put demolition charges into the barrels and blew themselves up. La Trésorie caused a lot of trouble but eventually 450 marines surrendered. Food there was in plenty, including live pigs. Each casement contained an electric plant, a diesel engine and a well-equipped hospital. On the evening of the 18th the Queen's Own Rifles fought their way to the harbour and the mouth of the River Liane on the north side of town. The troops of Le Régiment de la Chaudière captured the fortified area about the Colonne de la Grande Armée and patrolled towards Fort de la Crèche. Wimille was taken by the North Shores on the 20th with 140 prisoners of war, and Lieutenant Colonel Anderson on the right started an attack on Wimereux. It was part of the Atlantic Wall and heavily defended against attack from the sea, and also from a landward assault. The German garrison had refused to let the French civilians leave and Anderson was reluctant to use the AGRAs at his disposal. Their historian wrote, 'Darkness came and the companies consolidated their gains and made ready to continue the attack in the morning. Before dawn Crocodiles, AVRES and armoured cars came up to assist. We were glad to see them. We had had a rough time.' Over 500 prisoners of war were taken and hundreds of Germans killed. Three underground storage rooms were found, one full of tobacco, one full of hundreds of cases of liquor and the third full of canned goods. Fort de la Crèche was taken by Queens' Own, with tanks and anti-tank guns, yielding 500 prisoners of war.

Meanwhile in the 9th Brigade attack on the southern flank, the HLI of Canada under Lieutenant Colonel Kingsmill had the task of crossing the River Liane, clearing the built-up area west of the river, the dock area and then on into the forts of Le Portel and Cap d'Alprech. The North Novas after taking Herquelingue would push to the river and capture the suburbs of Outreau, St Etienne and Ecault, heading for the sea.

On the morning of the 20th Le Portel was occupied but the forts held out until the 22nd when Fort d'Alprech was taken. General Heim was captured. He said, 'When I decided that the situation was hopeless from a military standpoint, I felt I could lay down my charge with a clear conscience. It is difficult for us western people to sacrifice our lives when the situation is hopeless and that is the main reason for my troops surrendering rather than dying in their bunkers. The farther East you go the less important death becomes. The Japanese have no fear of death at all and the Russians have almost none. In England and America life is very precious and everything is done in wartime to preserve it and prevent its needless waste. We Germans stand in the middle.'

Mopping up went on for several days in the dock area, and around the many forts with underground cellars. Eventually 9,500 prisoners of war were counted into the cages. The Canadians had suffered 634 casualties. Montgomery and Eisenhower's staff criticised the Canadian capture of Boulogne, comparing it with Le Havre as being too deliberate and methodical. This was completely unfair, as General Crerar had only two brigades (not six), no naval gun fire, far less artillery ammunition and fewer bombers. This was symptomatic of the Cinderella War. Eisenhower only once visited the Canadian Army in northwest Europe and Montgomery made it clear that he had little praise for them.

On 23 September a parade was held and Major General D.C. Spry congratulated his troops (and their British supporters of the 79th

Armoured Division) on their fine performance. Lieutenant Commander Brian Izzard RNVR, with Lieutenant Connell arrived on 25 September to interrogate prisoners of war. Feldweber Preuss, a German naval pilot and Korvette-Kapitan Margen were helpful to the RN Forward Interrogation Unit. There were 30 controlled electrical mines lying across the beaches, 16 mines in the port area and 50 torpedo warheads lying in the sand on the shore. The quays in Bassin Loubet had been blown up by 20 torpedo warheads. 'T' mines, every 20 yards had destroyed Quai Gambetta and Quai d'Echouage. The two German PoWs confirmed that on 16 June the RAF had bombed and sunk 55 craft in the harbour including three 'M' class minesweepers, three S-Boats and one R-Boat. A mobile RN reconnaissance unit under Lieutenant Commander Hickey RNVR spent 5–17 September assessing the German naval wireless and telegraph station at Rupembert.

Number 1574 Port Clearance Unit RN moved into Boulogne on its capture and found 25 wrecks fouling the harbour and 26 blockships had closed its entrance, which remained blocked until on 18 November the *Guernsey Queen* was raised. Captain Eagle RNR of Force Pluto also arrived and by 13–15 October, using the US 'Tombola' moorings, so successful on the Normandy beaches, got the oil pipeline PLUTO discharging.

Operation Wellhit was well planned and carried out efficiently by the Canadian and British forces. Montgomery and Eisenhower should have been well pleased.

CHAPTER FOURTEEN

The Capture of Calais and Cap Gris-Nez: Operation Undergo

JUST BEFORE MARKET GARDEN STARTED IN MID-SEPTEMBER UNDER instruction from Field Marshal Montgomery, Lieutenant Colonel Dawnay wrote up Monty's official log for his tactical headquarters. 'From a purely British point of view, Antwerp had never been a vital necessity. The Pas de Calais ports provided all that we required [only Le Havre, badly damaged, plus Dieppe had so far been captured]. But to the Americans it had become vital and for the British armies it would be very convenient and would save a long haul over bad roads. American maintenance difficulties were responsible for creating the urgency to open the port of Antwerp.' At that time the American armies were rationed to a meagre 7,000 tons of supplies per day. However on 13 September Montgomery, at Eisenhower's urging, woke up to the supply problem and sent to General Crerar General Officer Commanding First Canadian Army an order that 'priority be given to setting in motion operations designed to enable us to use the port of Antwerp', and added later that same day, 'Early use of Antwerp so urgent that I am prepared to give up operations against Calais and Dunkirk and be content with Boulogne.' In *Eclipse* Alan Moorehead wrote,

> It was a most dangerous period of delay. Every hour, every day, the German morale was hardening. As the broken remnants of the Fifteenth and Seventh Armies struggled back to the Reich they were regrouped into new formations. Anything and everything

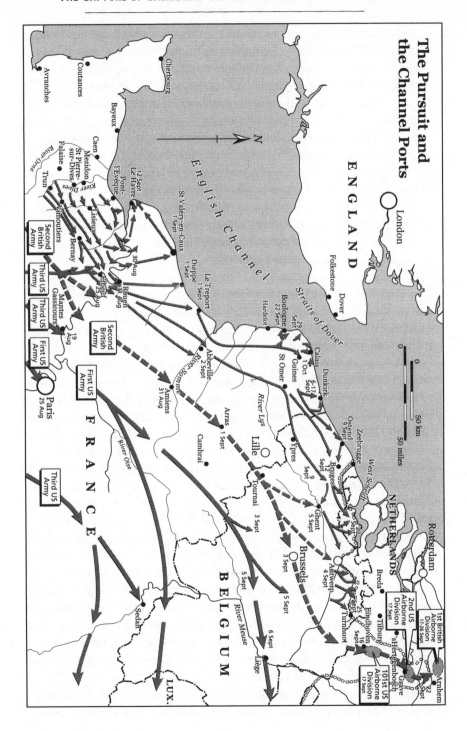

The Pursuit and the Channel Ports

served at this desperate moment. Submarine crews were put into the line as infantry, the German water-police were mobilised; there was a brigade of deaf men who presumably received their orders in deaf and dumb language.... Throughout the Reich every officer and man on leave was summoned back to his post. We began to collect extraordinary prisoners—near-sighted clerks who had left their city offices three weeks before; men with half-healed wounds, even cripples and children of fifteen or sixteen. It was a makeshift, hotch-potch army, an emergency army put in simply to hold the gap, simply to fight for time while the German generals re-organised on a sounder basis...it was useless now to regret that we had headed straight for the Dutch border in early September instead of cleaning up the approaches to Antwerp. Along the city docksides everything was intact but the cranes stood idle.

Crerar's 3rd Canadian Division was now preparing to move north along the coast road from Boulogne, via Wimereux and via a small detour to the west, to capture Cap Gris-Nez. Thence along the coast northeast via Wissant and Cap Blanc-Nez into the southern suburbs of Calais. Since 1940 the ten substantial coastal batteries, with four guns each usually of 38 cm calibre, completely enclosed in huge concrete casements had been harassing convoys passing through the Straits of Dover. Each had gun crews usually 175 strong. Many guns had a 120° traverse but some had all-round traverse. On the inland side there were minefields, barbed-wire entanglements and pillboxes. Adolf Hitler had taken a personal interest in the design of these Channel heavy guns and their protective defences. The Pas de Calais since June 1944 had been raining down on southeast England, initially noisy V-1 rockets, then deadly silent V-2 rockets, another excellent reason for the Canadian/British forces to clear the area.

The considerable number of batteries were arranged as follows: Todt (four 380 mm guns) at Waringzelles, one mile south of Cap Gris-Nez; Grosser Kurfurst (four 280 mm guns) at Floringzelle, half a mile southeast of Cap Gris-Nez; and Batterie Gris-Nez on the cape itself. There was another battery at Wissant, three miles east of the cape; another (Lindemann with 406 mm guns) at Noires Mottes near Sangatte, east of Cap Blanc-Nez, one at Fort Lapin in the western suburb of Calais and finally three in the eastern suburbs of Calais. They included the massive Oldenburg with two 240 mm guns.

The German commandant of the Calais garrison was Lieutenant Colonel Ludwig Schroeder, described thus by General Warlimont, 'At 43,

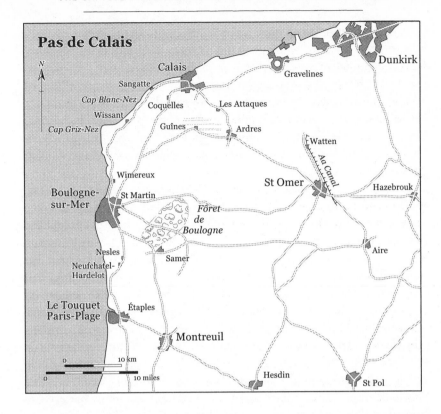

his rather large, long-jawed face was both tired and resigned. After an unimpressive military career on the Eastern front he was posted to 59th Infantry Division, which on 30 August had left the area.' Schroeder had a garrison of 9,000 troops, including second-grade coastal units, many Kriegsmarines, an OST battalion and Luftwaffe Flak units. Half of them were guarding the ten coastal batteries and the many strongpoints including Noires Mottes, Belle Vue Ridge, Coquelles and Vieux Coquelles.

Major General Spry knew that large areas of marshland and floods east and south of Calais meant that the only practical mixed-arms assault must come from the western coast roads, assaulting and capturing the huge well-defended batteries on the way. Major General Spry directed the 9th Brigade initially on the three batteries clustered round Cap Gris-Nez, with Seventh and Eighth given all the coastal objectives leading into Calais from the west and southwest. He would be allocated RAF bombing support and substantial help from the 'Funnies' of the British 79th Armoured Division (the same units that had helped capture Boulogne).

A curious little battle took place on the 13th. Major D.R.R. Pocock, Officer Commanding 'A' Sqadron the Lothians was leading his Sherman flails and gun-tanks southwards to join in the Boulogne battle. 'En passant' they spied the Onglevert strongpoint guarding the inland area of Batterie Todt at Haringzelles. In ten minutes his squadron fired 550 rounds of HE indirectly at 5,000 yards range into the concrete position harbouring two 75 mm guns. These they destroyed, plus several machine-gun nests, blew up an ammunition supply dump and helped the Canadians collect 25 prisoners of war.

Calais had been 'masked' as early as 6 September and four days later the Toronto Scottish of the 2nd Canadian Division had formed a screen around the town. On the 16th two battalions of the 7th Brigade tried and failed to capture the three Cap Gris-Nez batteries. The 3rd Medium Regiment RCA engaged nine of the individual guns and for two days had a duel with the enemy's 16-inch guns. One gun mounted on a 'disappearing carriage' received a direct hit, otherwise the contest was reckoned to be a noisy draw. Major General Spry's bombing help started on the 20th, when 646 aircraft of Bomber Command with 430 Lancasters, 169 Halifaxs and 47 Mosquitoes dropped over 3,000 tons of bombs on the Calais defences, and targets along the coast. The *Daily Mail* ran an article, 'The Dover guns "Winnie" and "Pooh" each 14" and 15" fired alternatively and at 20 miles range knocked out two enemy batteries in the Calais-Cap Gris-Nez area. An AOP with a British FOO directed fire near Calais as one-ton armour-piercing shells crashed into the concrete emplacements.'

The bombers appeared again on the 24th with 188 aircraft: 101 Lancasters, 62 Halifaxs and 25 Mosquitoes. Due to low cloud at 2,000 feet only 126 craft bombed using OBOE armed skymarkers. Light Flak shot down eight planes. On the next day 872 craft appeared but only 287 bombed through breaks in the clouds.

At this stage in the northwest Europe campaign the Canadian Army was extremely efficient at pre-battle planning. Major Bryant and Captain Bristow, of the Buffs flame-throwers found the mass of maps, defence overprints and aerial photographs showered on them, very impressive. They appeared to prove that the German defences were impregnable!

Major General Spry's plan was for 8th Brigade to attack on the 25th and capture the five strongpoints and villages between Cap Blanc-Nez and Sangatte approximately five miles west of Calais. The Fort Garry Horse Shermans guarded the left flank. The de la Chaudières captured Escalles and then Cap Blanc-Nez where the 200 prisoners of war were found to be very drunk indeed. The next morning the North Shore regiment took Noires Mottes strongpoint and then the huge battery at Sangatte. The ground was very heavily cratered and difficult for tank movement, but the Funnies gave excellent support, with 'C' Squadron of the Lothians' flails, 'C' Squadron the Buffs Crocodiles and AVRES of 284th Assault Squadron RE. Beforehand Lieutenant Colonel Anderson Commanding Officer of the North Shores had constructed a sand model of the objectives as infantry, tank crews and Funnies studied their objectives.

Lieutenant Harry Hamley's platoon with a Lothians' flail, 'Broke through the defensive crust and got to grips with the enemy. As the armoured monsters beat a path through the minefields and the Crocodiles unleashed their flame, the Conger's flung out their explosive-filled hose which exploded with terrific violence, further demoralising the enemy. The North Shores rushed the dug-outs and the enemy on the hill [Noires Mottes] were over-run,' wrote Will R. Bird, the North Shores' historian. But ahead on the seaward side, half a mile north was the battery with three 405 mm guns able to fire their 2,000 lb shells at Folkestone. The Sangatte defenders had machine-gun and anti-tank gun positions and the bomb craters made life very difficult. Captain March RE led 3rd Troop, 284 'A' Squadron RE and fired a Conger into the protecting minefield, which was successfully blown. Continuing down the steep slope his AVRE fell over the edge of a German blockhouse. At dusk Major Corbett of the North Shores led a platoon with three Buffs Crocodiles 300 yards down the slope. After dark Corbett and Major Parker of 'B' Company talked to a German prisoner of war, who came from New York. Sergeant Jennings took the prisoners into the labyrinth of German bunkers and sent an ultimatum to surrender to the Sangatte commander. Eventually seven officers and 278 other ranks were persuaded to surrender the three large gun positions, well stocked with ammunition, fresh meat and Danish butter!

Attacking in parallel just to the east were the 7th Brigade, charged with the clearance of the western approaches to Calais. The 1st Canadian Scottish Regiment bypassed Belle Vue Ridge, reached the coast just east of Sangatte and moved rapidly along the coast road towards Fort Lapin. The Regina Rifles tackled Vieux Coquelles and Royal Winnipeg Rifles, took on Coquelles supported by 1st Hussars tanks and met fierce resistance. The Buffs Crocodiles fired HE at the dug-in anti-tank guns and mortars. There was fierce house-to-house fighting and in the afternoon Lieutenant Saunders led four Buffs Crocodiles into a point-blank flame attack 'weaving in and out of the hillocks spouting flame at all and sundry. How they managed to get out of the maze of precipes, bomb holes and pill-boxes is a mystery that will never be explained' wrote the Buffs historian.

On the 26th the RAF sent 722 aircraft, 531 to bomb Cap Gris Nez and 191 to bomb three strongpoints near Calais. On the 27th 341 craft bombed and on the 28th 494 craft pulverized the Calais defences. Bomber Command certainly pulled out all the stops to support the Canadian advance.

Protecting the western flank of Calais were three key strongpoints— Fort Lapin with heavy guns and flame-throwers protected by anti-tank ditches and minefields; Bastion II on the coast road and Fort Nieulay a mile inland.

Captain J.L.Hall 'A' Sqn the Buffs with their Crocodiles belching flame helped the 1st Canadian Scottish take Ferme Tournant, Ferme Oyez, Ferme Trouville and finally Fort Lapin. On their way through a maze of naval shells along the Sangatte seaside road. 'Hall got out of his tank with 250 mm shells raining down, guiding the column on foot through minefields in between craters, prodding, searching, ducking and signalling to his driver regardless of the risk of his tank hitting a mine and blowing him to Kingdom come',wrote the Buffs historian.

During the night of the 27th the 1st Canadian Scottish crossed over the old water defences at the western edge of Calais port, then south of Bastion II but were then cut off by strong machine gun fire from the Citadel and Bastion II. On their right the Winnipeg Rifles helped subdue Coquelles and Fort Nieulay and the Reginas moved over the marshes into the southern factory suburbs. After the heavy bomber attack on the 28th, Lieutenant Colonel Schroeder asked for a truce to evacuate French citizens from the centre of Calais. The machine gun regiment, Cameron Highlanders of Ottawa and the Queen's Own Rifles worked their way round to the eastern flank and by the 30th, Calais was being assaulted from three sides. The truce expired at noon on the 30th. Schroeder surrendered that evening and all fighting in Calais ceased at 09.00 hours on the 31st.

Lieutenant Colonel Schroeder said after his capture, 'Although it was probably understood that I was to resist to the last man, I never actually saw a written order to this effect. I admit that my action in surrendering the port after having suffered so few casualties would likely have rendered me liable to a court martial for disobeying orders. But I had little ammunition with which to continue firing my guns and the standard of my troops was too low to have maintained any prolonged resistance.' One of his corporals wrote home earlier on 4 September, 'I am still alive; we are in the port of Calais and expect to be encircled very soon. The ring will soon be getting smaller. How we shall all end I don't know—death or imprisonment. Our strong points have been left in a panic. Demolitions are going on day and night and the town looks like Stalingrad—Yes! The Atlantic Wall is no more. The average soldier is not to blame for this mess.'

In the main defences of Calais 7,130 prisoners of war, including 130 officers, were captured. The defenders, well dug-in, only had 60 killed in action and 130 wounded. The German Kriegsmarines wanted to keep on fighting but the others had no heart for it. The French civilian casualties were about 250.

For the capture of the three Cap Gris-Nez batteries the 9th Canadian Brigade had the support of 'B' and 'C' Squadrons of the Lothians' flails, half of 'C' Squadron the Buffs Crocodiles and the AVRES of 284th Assault Squadron RE. The plan was for the North Novas to capture the Battery Todt at Haringzelles and move north to Cran-aux-Oeufs. On the right flank shielded by a huge smoke screen west of Wissant, the HLI of Canada would first subdue the Grosser Kürfurst batterie at Floringzelle (Framzelle) before taking on the Batterie Gris-Nez on the cape itself—aided by Lothians' flails, Buffs Crocodiles and AVRE support. Lieutenant Colonel Forbes, the Novas CO, and Lieutenant Colonel Kingsmill, CO the HLI, had thoroughly reconnoitred the ground. At 06.45 hours on 29 September under a creeping barrage by 18 regiments of artillery both attacks, in parallel, but two miles apart, commenced. The HLI helped by Crocodiles soon took the lighthouse and control tower area a mile or so inland. On the way the AVRES failed to get through a covering minefield but the Buffs' Crocodiles took a chance that the RAF bombs had exploded most of the mines and plunged down a hill to deal with the casements in the forts and pillboxes. Lieutenant Andrew Wilson wrote, 'The machine guns started firing. At the bottom of the valley the column stopped. The [HLI] infantry had suddenly gone to ground. A pillbox on the far slope was firing and everyone had their guns trained on it. The armour started moving again firing at the pillbox. Still no mines, but a flail nosed into a small stream [River Noirde] and got stuck. An AVRE with a Fascine lumbered up. The bundle of brushwood spread out and eventually flails and Crocs went over the stream, a section of HLI crept up to the pillbox with sticky bombs and grenades. There was a lot of mortaring and a couple of explosions.' Wilson saw three disabled Shermans and an AVRE trying to put a Conger into position. Later Captain Pattenden's sappers fixed a large Beehive explosive charge to a closed concrete blockhouse before blowing it in. Lieutenant E. McLeish HLI won the Military Cross for using a grenade to damage the mechanism of a 16-inch gun with a 360 degree traverse and putting it out of action.

The German commandant, Colonel Schilling, was captured and the Cap Gris batteries surrendered with 1,300 prisoners of war. The HLI sent the commandant's sword and the fortress flag to the mayor of Dover as tribute to that town's steadfastness under fire for so many years.

The left flank was equally successful. The North Novas had as their objectives the control station at Cran-aux-Oeufs and Battery Todt at Haringzelles both surrounded by minefields and wire. The River Noirde and two streams were additional hazards. Lothian flail tanks led to 'flog' or clear of mines two lanes towards the battery and then one towards the control station. Fascines were laid by AVRES in the water obstacles and two excellent lanes 1,000 yards long and 24 feet across were flailed right up into the forts themselves. Under a heavy barrage the Novas and the Buffs' Crocs forced their way in, and at the last minute AVRES petarded the bunker entrances. The Novas threw grenades down air vents and window slits and the garrison of the three huge 38 cm guns surrendered. In the afternoon many Lothian flails were blown up clearing minefields. Captain Winhold led 'C' Company down a long valley and up a small hill where the control tower stood. The pillbox forming part of the control tower was blown up by the Germans just before they surrendered and another 300 prisoners of war were taken. Lieutenant Andrew Wilson of the Buffs took his troop of Crocodiles into the valley and up, firing 75 mm shells into every target and airburst over the 'ships bridge' shape of the tower. Amongst those who surrendered to the Buffs was a 50-year-old Kapitan-Leutnant whose batman produced a tray, a bottle of Benedictine and two glasses. In the gloom of the smoke filled bunker, Wilson and the K-L solemnly drank each other's health. The Nova infantry arrived. It started to rain—a cold, fine sea rain.

Pioneers and sappers had a busy and dangerous time clearing the area round the batteries. But in Calais Harbour things were much worse. Its port installations had been systematically demolished. Number 1574 Port Clearance Group arrived from Boulogne and it took until 20 November before the port was cleared. Then it was used to capacity as the main personnel arrival and departure port for the British and Canadian armies, many brought ashore by LST craft.

CHAPTER FIFTEEN

Scheldt Operation:
'It lacked glamour'

WINSTON CHURCHILL WROTE IN HIS MEMOIRS, 'THE 2ND CANADIAN Corps had forced the enemy back from the line Antwerp-Ghent-Bruges into the restricted Breskens "island", bounded on the south by the Leopold Canal. East of Antwerp, the 1st Corps under Canadian Army command had reached and crossed the Antwerp-Turnhout canal. The problem was threefold; the capture of the Breskens 'island'; the occupation of the peninsula of South Beveland; finally the capture of Walcheren Island by attacks from east, south and west.'

Six German divisions, nearly 85,000 men of the Fifteenth German Army with their equipment were falling back on the Scheldt, to try to cross to Walcheren Island and then move eastward. But Adolf Hitler had recently designated Walcheren Island and Flushing north of Antwerp as 'fortresses'.

Lieutenant General Wilhelm Daser was the commandant of Walcheren and was described by Major General Walther Warlimont, one of Hitler's trusted staff: 'Daser was mild looking, elderly (60). His small, peaked nose, his horn-rimmed glasses and his pink, bald head effectively hid his military identity. Only a firm, loud voice accustomed to giving orders betrayed it. His last field command had been in 1941. Since then he had been a military administrator of civilians in occupied territory.' Nevertheless, the oath he had taken to his Führer in February 1944 was, 'I am pledged to hold this fortified sector to the last, even to sacrifice my own life. Even if the enemy should already have broken through on my

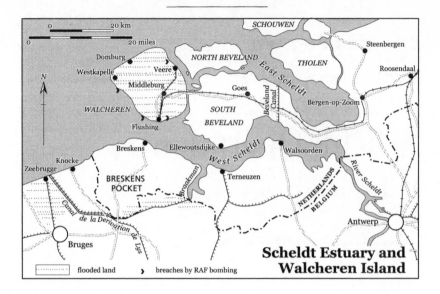

Scheldt Estuary and Walcheren Island

flooded land   ❯ breaches by RAF bombing

right and left, I am not empowered to give up this sector or to negotiate with the enemy.'

On the day after the First Canadian Army started the Herculean task of clearing the defences to the Scheldt Estuary, General von Zangen, GOC Fifteenth German Army, sent out this message to all his troops:

Commander-in-Chief Fifteenth Army. Army Headquarters

7 October 1944

ORDERS

The defence of the approaches to Antwerp represents a task which is decisive for the further conduct of the war. Therefore, every last man in the fortification is to know why he must devote himself to this task with the utmost strength. I have confirmed that so-called 'experts' among the local population are attempting to confuse the German soldiers in this battle task ordered by the Führer.

Whether know-it-alls in some headquarters are participating in such nonsense, which then quickly reaches the troops, I do not know. This I have reason, however, to fear. Therefore, I order commanders, as well as the National Socialist indoctrination officers, to instruct the troops in the clearest and most factual manner on the following points: Next to Hamburg, Antwerp is the largest port in Europe...

After overrunning the Scheldt fortifications, the English would finally be in a position to land great masses of material in a large and completely protected harbour. With this material they might deliver a death blow to the north German plateau and to Berlin before the onset of winter.

In order to pretend that the battle of Antwerp is unimportant and to shake the morale of its defenders, enemy propaganda maintains that the Anglo-American forces already possess sufficient ports which are intact, with the result that they are not at all dependent on Antwerp. That is a known lie. In particular, the port of Ostend, of which the enemy radio speaks frequently, is completely destroyed. Current delays in the enemy's conduct of the war are attributable in great measure to the fact that he still must bring all his supplies through the improvised facilities of Cherbourg. As a result, he has even had to lay a temporary oil pipeline from these to the interior of France....

In his last speech, Churchill said again, 'before the storms of winter we must bring in the harvest in Europe.' The enemy knows that he must assault the European fortress as speedily as possible before its inner lines of resistance are built up and occupied by new divisions. For this reason he needs the Antwerp harbour. And for this reason, we must hold the Scheldt fortifications to the end. The German people are watching us. In this hour, the fortifications along the Scheldt occupy a role which is decisive for the future of our people. Each additional day that you deny the port of Antwerp to the enemy and to the resources that he has at his disposal, will be vital.

(signed) *Von Zangen*

General of the Infantry

Von Zangen had left behind two unusual divisions to obey Hitler's orders to delay the Allied clearance of the Scheldt Estuary. On Walcheren Island the curious 70th Infantry Division (with 1018th, 1019th and 1020th Regiments), together with the usual Luftwaffe Flak anti-aircraft weaponry, 89th Fortress Regiment and Kriegsmarines formed the garrison. The 10,000 men of the 'White Bread' Division of special stomach (Magen) battalions all suffered from stomach ailments of one form or another. After five years of war, bad food, hard living conditions and above all nervous tension, the Wehrmacht was swamped with soldiers complaining of internal gastric trouble. Most of them were genuine sufferers, but others were malingerers. Occupying the polderland bunkers of the island defences were soldiers with acute ulcers, dyspeptic and inflamed stomachs but also those veterans suffering from wounded stomachs. The food in Holland was ideal, with fresh vegetables, eggs and milk, fish and, in particular, white bread available—hence the divisional nickname. But behind Spandau, Schmeisser, bazookas, *nebelwerfers*, 88 mm dual-purpose and coastal guns, they were just as potentially dangerous as any of the Wehrmacht troops.

The historian of the Canadian Calgaries regiment wrote on 6 September of the difficult battle terrain:

> The next day dawned cold and wet and the Highlanders had their first good look at the sodden land they had arrived in as they marched to St Folquin. They were in a 15 to 20 kilometre wide band of polderland that stretched south from the Channel coast. Over the centuries this area had been claimed from the North Sea by farmers building dykes and drainage ditches, which were usually linked to larger navigation canals. The Germans had destroyed many of the dykes and caused water to seep across the fields and soak the farmland. The depth of the water varied from a few centimetres to a metre or more. It was not high enough to allow the Canadians to move by barge or assault boat but it was more than high enough to make walking over the fields very difficult and passage by tracked or wheeled vehicle almost impossible. Dykes ran along the borders of the fields and the larger ones had paths or even narrow roads on them. Sometimes the dykes were mined, but even when they were not German machine guns or 88s made walking atop them certain death. Thus virtually every advance during daylight hours was carried out through the hip-deep water in the drainage ditches, where there was at least some cover. It was an awful place to fight in.

On the south side of the Scheldt ('Scheldt Fortress South') Major-General Knut Eberding was a tough, efficient and ruthless commander of the newly constituted 65th Infantry Division. Its nickname was the 'Leave' Division, because it had been recently and hastily formed in

Germany and rushed up to help stem the Allied advance into the Low Countries. Almost all soldiers on leave in Germany in late July 1944 from the Russian, Italian and even the Norwegian fronts were cobbled together into battlegroups. For a formal traditional army the Germans in the autumn of 1944 showed amazing skill in assembling a diverse collection of soldiery and rapidly reshaping them into competent military formations. For the most part, Eberding's 65th Infantry division were fit, reliable and determined fighters, with the flooded terrain in their favour. With Kriegsmarines and Luftwaffe personnel, Eberding commanded 14,000 troops, backed by 500 machine guns and mortars, 200 anti-tank and anti-aircraft guns and 76 larger guns. On 26 September General Crerar, suffering from dysentery, was flown back to England for treatment and was replaced by Lieutenant General Guy Simonds (who Montgomery thought was the ablest of the Canadian commanders). Major General C. Foulkes moved up from GOC the 2nd Canadian Infantry Division to command II Canadian Corps. Brigadier R.H. Keefler, the CRA was promoted to command the 2nd Canadian Division.

After the capture of Calais and the withdrawal from the investment of Dunkirk, the First Canadian Army had various tasks in and around Antwerp. The 4th Canadian Infantry Brigade of the RHLI, the Essex Scottish and the Royal Regiment of Canada held Antwerp harbour and docks, in what they called the 'Streetcar War'. From 16 September their 5,000 men relieved 53rd Welsh Division. Ordinary urban life went on in Antwerp much as in peacetime. The trams continued to run, nightclubs remained open and the shops sold a good assortment of goods. The Belgian Secret Army dock force patrolled the harbour area. Patrols from both sides clashed in the No Man's Land villages of Oorderen, Wimarsdonck, Eekeren and Merxem. Major Louis Froggett commanded the RHLI 'Lock Force' to guard the bridges and locks that controlled the water level in the whole of the Antwerp harbour—particularly the vital Kruisschans Lock.

The 4th Canadian Armoured Division under Major General Foster had suffered a bloody nose on the way from Moerbrugge to Maldegem and Breskens. At the Leopold Canal and Canal de Derivation de la Lys, the Algonquins lost 148 casualties in 14 hours in attempts to cross.

Alan Moorehead wrote in *Eclipse*, 'Arnhem had failed. The Germans had got the necessary breathing space with which to throw up a new Siegfried line.....There was very little we could do through the rest of September and October to prevent them. All hope of a quick end of the war in 1944 had gone. The Allies had to prepare for a winter campaign, the hardest campaign of them all—and possibly for more battles inside Germany in the following spring and summer. The immediate essential for all this was the opening up of Antwerp. Both British armies were now turned to that task. The bitter freezing battles for the banks of the Scheldt were begun.'

Realizing belatedly the importance of clearing the 'Fortress South', known as the Breskens pocket and then the island of Walcheren, Field Marshal Montgomery pulled the stops out. The RAF, Royal Navy Marine Commandos and Major General Percy Hobart's 'Funnies' were now to participate together in a ferocious five-week series of battles.

Walcheren was bombed by the RAF (Second TAF) on 18, 19 and 23 September by between 50 and 74 aircraft, with their main target the formidable Domburg coastal batteries. On 3 October the tempo was stepped up. 252 Lancasters with seven Oboe Mosquitoes, led by a master bomber, bombed in eight consecutive waves, each of 30 Lancasters, dropping 500, 1,000 and some 4,000 lb bombs. Their objective was to flood the island of reclaimed polder *below* sea level. It was hoped that the flooding would submerge the gun batteries by destroying the sea walls. A breach was made, waves widened the gap until the seas poured into the 100-yard hole. Despite warning leaflets being dropped on 2 October, advising Dutch civilians to evacuate—quickly—nearly 200 were killed by the bombing.

The Walcheren 202nd Naval Artillery Battalion was responsible for the eight largest coastal batteries. These consisted of: W-7 (four 5.9-inch guns) just west of Flushing; W-11 (four 5.9-inch guns) in dunes between Flushing, and Zoutelande; W-13 (four 5.9-inch and two 3-inch guns) plus three 20mm Flak in dunes between Zoutelande and Westkappelle; W-15 (four ex-British 3.7-inch plus two 3-inch for close defence) mounted on sea walls immediately north of Westkappelle; W-17 (four 8.7-inch and one 2.5-inch guns) west of Domburg; W-19 (five ex-British 3.7-inch guns) in dunes near Oostburg on the northern tip, and two further batteries of four British 5.9-inch guns at Schouwen and Renesse.

All the guns were enclosed in thick concrete casements, defended by anti-aircraft Flak guns and guided by radar from four separate stations. In addition the 810th Naval Flak Regiment had no less than 21 defensive gun positions, some along the sand dunes and some guarding the Flushing dock area. There were also seven heavy anti-aircraft batteries on the island. The German defenders had been hard at work since 16 May 1944 laying mines in the sea at the mouth of the Scheldt, the Deverloo and Wielingen channels. By mid-October nearly 2,400 mines had been laid. A flotilla of explosive motor boats was held in Flushing for attacks on shipping in the Scheldt.

On the south side 'Scheldt Fortress South' the 203rd Naval Artillery Battalion had installed two batteries at Zeebrugge, and others at Heyst, Knokke, Cadzand, Nieuwe Sluis and two at Fort Frederik Hendrik. The 702nd Railway Artillery Battalion had three 20.3 cm railway guns sited near Knocke. Walcheren Island and the Breskens pocket were destined to be bombed again and again—on 7th (123 planes), 12th (96 planes), 17th (49 planes), 21st (75 planes), 23rd (112 planes), 28th (277 planes), 29th (358 planes) and 30th (110 planes). Targets varied from Flushing, Fort Frederik Hendrik at Breskens, Veere, Westkappelle and gun batteries and seawalls.

The high command was in some disarray after the relative failure of Market Garden. Brigadier Bill Williams, head of intelligence on Field Marshal Montgomery's staff told the author Richard Lamb that Monty was reluctant to start the Battle of the Scheldt. Antwerp was 55 miles away.... 'To him it was not an interesting military operation.... *It lacked glamour from his point of view and so did not appeal to his vanity.'* It would be a battle of attrition with very heavy casualties. In his memoirs Montgomery wrote, 'I admit a bad mistake. I underestimated the difficulties of opening up the approaches to Antwerp. I reckoned the Canadian Army could do it while we were going for the Ruhr. I was wrong.' Eisenhower too was guilty of complacency. He hoped things were going well with 21st Army Group and it took him several weeks to realise that the Canadians might not be able to launch their main attack on the Scheldt until 1 November because of a shortage of ammunition. On 9 October 'Ike' sent 'Monty' a very strong *order*. This was most unusual, almost unique. '*Unless we have Antwerp producing by the middle of November our entire operations will come to a standstill.* I must emphasise that of all our operations on the *entire front* from Switzerland to the Channel, I consider Antwerp of *first importance* and I believe that the operations designed to clear up the entrance require *your personal* attention.' Monty of course bridled and bluffed a bit, denied there was a shortage of ammunition for the Canadian Army (which there was) but eventually after several brisk exchanges sent a directive (M532) on 16 October.

21 Army Group

GENERAL OPERATIONAL SITUATION AND DIRECTIVE

1. The free use of the port of Antwerp is vital to the Allied cause, and we must be able to use the port soon.

2. Operations designed to open the port will therefore be given *complete priority* over all other offensive operations in 21 Army Group *without any qualification whatsoever.*

3. The immediate task of opening up the approaches to the port of Antwerp is already being undertaken by Canadian Army and good progress has been made. The whole of the available offensive power of Second Army will now be brought to bear also.

So the bitter attritional battles of Operations Angus, Switchback, Vitality I and Vitality II, Infatuate 1 and 2 started. At long last it was recognised by Montgomery and Eisenhower that the 'Cinderella War' was of immense importance to the success of the Allies.

CHAPTER SIXTEEN

Operation Angus: Clearing South Beveland Isthmus

THE ULTRA DECODERS AT BLETCHLEY HAD PROVIDED INVALUABLE information to SHAEF and 21st Army Group. Just after Antwerp was captured, intercepts were decoded that showed the enemy's strength and plans. Hitler's orders were for the Scheldt fortresses to be defended *at all costs* and that *both* sides and banks of the estuary must be held. The Breskens pocket was to be obstinately defended. Substantial amounts of the German Fifteenth Army were being ferried by day and by night across the estuary to Walcheren Island and South Beveland and escape to Germany. Ultra revealed the daily performance of the Breskens ferries from Terneuzen to Flushing. By 17 September 25,000 men and 550 vehicles had crossed and by the end of Market Garden, with all the Allied leaders focussed on the drama at Arnhem, Ultra signals showed that 82,000 men, 530 guns and thousands of vehicles had escaped the potential trap. Soon Holland was swarming with German troops. Hitler had ordered General Kurt Student, to create a new army—'First Parachute Army'— which was soon in action along the Albert Canal in Belgium. The successful escape of Fifteenth Army was a real triumph, almost a German 'Dunkirk'.

The First Canadian Army now received an unusual reinforcement. Major General Hakewill-Smith was GOC 52nd (Lowland) Division, just right for Dutch polder clearance one might think. These Scottish troops had been trained specifically for *mountain* warfare. The 155th Brigade was composed of 7th and 9th Royal Scots, 4th King's Own Scottish Borderers and the 6th Highland Light Infantry. 156th Brigade consisted

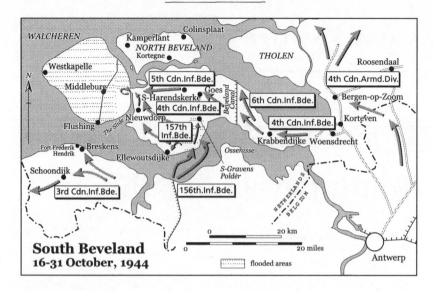

South Beveland
16-31 October, 1944

of 4th and 5th Royal Scots Fusiliers, 6th Cameronians, 1st Glasgow Highlanders, and 157th Brigade of the 5th KOSB, the 7th Cameronians and the 5th HLI. They had their own 52nd Reconnaissance Regiment, five regiments of artillery plus the 7th Manchester Regiment's Machine-gun formation. Their first brigade arrived from the UK at Ostend on 13 October. The opening of the Scheldt Estuary was destined to involve four divisions in a series of most unpleasant operations. From west to east, 3rd Canadian Division would clear the 'Breskens' pocket, including Breskens itself, Knokke and Zeebrugge. The newly arrived 52nd Lowland Division would cross the five-mile estuary by amphibious vehicles, crewed by British 79th Armoured Division and capture the South Beveland Island. The next stage would be to meet up with the 2nd Canadian Division. They would advance northwards from Antwerp to Woensdrecht, cut the three mile isthmus and drive west and northwest towards Goes and North Beveland Island. On the eastern flank the 4th Canadian Armoured Division, working on 'terra firma', would advance northwest some 17 miles to Bergen op Zoom and East Scheldt.

The main attack on Walcheren Island had already started with the brutal RAF bombing. Soon a RN seaborne attack carrying the 4th Special Services Brigade, with selected 'Funnies' to help, would be launched on Westkappelle and Flushing.

❖

Operation Angus the clearance of the South Beveland isthmus started on 2 October.

The German Lieutenant General Kurt Chill, a brilliant soldier, had been ordered, initially to form a battle group to defend the line of the Albert Canal. He quickly gathered in the remnants of the 84th, 85th and 89th Wehrmacht infantry divisions, part of the Hermann Goering Luftwaffe Training Regiment and, best of all, the crack 6th Parachute Regiment. One of Battle Group Chill's responsibilities was to stop the Canadian threat to the South Beveland Isthmus where still elements of General von Zangen's Fifteenth Army were making their devious escape, and secondly to obey his Führer's order to protect the eastern flank of the German defenders on South Beveland and North Beveland.

On 5 October General Student had ordered Colonel von der Heydte's force of 4,000 troops from Alphen: 'Student gave me three reasons for this: first, to secure Fifteenth Army retreat: then to hold open communication from Walcheren through the neck of South Beveland and through to Germany. Finally the Germans expected after the Arnhem experience the Allies would attack up the coast in a pincer movement through Rotterdam and east to Germany. This had to be stopped. It was of extreme importance that we defend Woensdrecht.'

It all went well to start with. On 2 October the 6th Canadian Brigade took Lochtenburg, Camp de Brasschaet and on the 4th, Capellen. The Fourth Canadian Brigade, starting from Antwerp docks with excellent help from the Belgian resistance, cleared the suburb of Merxem and moved six miles north. On the 5th the Essex Scottish, with heavy casualties, took the village of Putte on the Dutch-Belgian border, and Ossendrecht and Sandvliet on the 6th. Each village had been defended, one stronghold being in a sanatorium. Booby traps and the dreaded wooden Schu mine were prevalent. (Schu were German mines. They were metal balls in wood casing (more or less indetectable) which, when tripped, 'jumped' up about nine inches and wounded the legs.) At Sandvliet Les Fusiliers Mont-Royal were bombarded by the Germans with leaflets in French and English reminding the Canadians of the Dieppe disaster; 'Here you are again after those nasty hours at Dieppe where out of 5,000 brave lads of the Royal Regt, the Essex Scottish, the Mount Royal Fusiliers, the Camerons, the South Sasks, the Black Watch and the tank gunners of the Calgary Regt only 1,500 escaped death or capture...' The two key defensive strong-

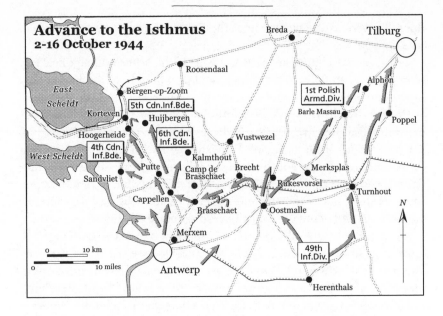

Advance to the Isthmus
2-16 October 1944

points just to the east of the narrow isthmus were the villages of Woensdrecht, and Hoogerheide three-quarters of a mile to the east. Battle Group Chill had their best troops defending the narrow isthmus defences. Colonel von der Heydte's 6th Parachute Regiment had just given 1st Polish Armoured Division by the Albert Canal a bloody nose and were now urgently directed westwards 'To re-occupy Hoogerheide and then pushing southwards to Ossendrecht.' The Maisonneuves and the Calgaries had been directed into the two villages by Brigadier Bill Megill. By the 8th the RHLI and Canadian Black Watch had captured Hoogerheide. The Reconnaissance Regiment had crossed the flooded polders and by the 10th had reached the main road and railway which ran through the isthmus to South Beveland.

The determined counterattack by the German paratroops and Hermann Goering Regiment—2,000 well-trained young soldiers with eight tanks and SPs with 88 mm artillery and mortar support—came in on the 8th, mainly against the Calgary Highlanders. The German official report (battle group MS.B798) says 'In the following days attack and counterattack alternated. Three times the Vanguard unit, Combat Group von der Heydte succeeded in thrusting through the southern edge of Hoogerheide. Every time the position gained had to be given up again for lack of force against the enemy counterattack. In a vigorous attack the paratroop groups succeeded in spite of stubborn resistance of Canadian troops in pushing to the edge of Hoogerheide. On 9 October several enemy armoured vehicles [Fort Garry Horse Shermans] driving up on the embankment, pushed onto the Woensdrecht-Flushing railway line. They were beaten back. The connection with the [German] 70th Infantry Division along the railway embankment continued to exist.' The German 225th Assault Gun Brigade and 70th Artillery Regiment backed von der Heydte's parachute troops. Lieutenant Colonel von der Heydte wrote, 'Chill's battle group had done its job in the first weeks of September. It was gradually replaced by normal divisions although he still commanded the 85th Division. But the army decided to keep the name alive, to intimidate the enemy. Battle Group Chill was merely a camouflage name to disguise the strength and location. My real task was to move quickly from one trouble spot to the next. [General Kurt] Student called me his 'Feurwehr' or Fire Brigade. I had only to attack—and I got everything I wished. If I said, I can't attack without this and this, the next day, I got it. To attack is more interesting, and it is not so difficult as to defend. Our poor infantry had to come in after me to defend the position that we had taken, and I would be sent to another trouble spot.' By now the whole of the 2nd Canadian Infantry Division was hard pressed on a 60-mile front from Hoogerheide to St Leonard. On Friday 13th, 'Black Friday', the Canadian Black Watch lost 56 killed in action, 11 wounded and 36 missing. Brigadier Fred Cabeldu, OC 5th Brigade, produced a very complicated attack on Hoogerheide in which the Black Watch suffered on the 13th. Lieutenant Colonel Ritchie, the Black Watch CO said, 'It was a funny sort of battle plan—crazy. We were instructed to take four [strong] posts, four areas roughly in the form of a square with a 1,000 yard side. The dawn attack was supported by tanks, completely useless due to the flooding and heavy ground fog. We were pinned down by heavy machine gun fire right from the beginning. Our forward troops had to fight their way to the start line. We were devastated by fire from the many strongpoints.' The Black Watch like all the other Canadian battalions had suffered many casualties since D-Day. Their young leaders were all casualties and all the reinforcements were green and untrained in an infantry role. Major William Ewing's company tried to cross 1,200 yards of beet fields with no cover. He started with a strength of 90; at the end, there were only four left unwounded.

The Royal Hamilton Light Infantry hung on grimly in Woensdrecht for five days with 167 casualties. Their CO, Lieutenant Colonel Whitaker wrote, 'The Hun is battling most bitterly and seems to have no shortage of weapons. It is close, hand-to-hand fighting—the enemy is not giving up here the way he has in the past.' On the 16th Field Marshal von

Rundstedt realized he could keep open the land connection with Walcheren and ordered the flooding of South Beveland. Fighting continued and by 24 October the Calgary Highlanders reached the northern sea dyke. Behind, the Canadian 4th Brigade moved west into Beveland towards Walcheren Island. The Canadian artillery and the 2nd TAF Spitfires and Typhoons contributed to this success. As early as 7 September, OB West/OKW had ordered, Fifteenth Army is to ensure that everything is done to put Northern Belgium under water by blowing locks and dykes as soon as the bulk of our forces have been withdrawn behind the sector to be flooded.' It was ironical that the RAF had succeeded in flooding most of Walcheren Island by breaching the sea dykes. Everywhere that autumn there was mud and water, rain, fog, grey skies, cold food and clothing almost permanently wet. Some war diaries noted, 'Mud, mud, mud—relentless rain, water everywhere.'

The polder country reclaimed from the sea was heavily weighted on the side of the defender who could dig in troops and machine-gun sites along the sides of the dykes. These ran dead straight, ten or twelve feet in height and 30 feet across above the flooded fields. At their intersections with roads or tracks, a machine-gun crossfire or *nebelwerfer* salvo would target the attackers. Struggling through flooded fields up to six feet deep in water, and vulnerable to enemy fire made for near impossible conditions. Cold, driving rain, little hope of a change of dry clothes or a warm place to sleep, it was a new form of hell: the polder war.

CHAPTER SEVENTEEN

Hitler's Scheldt Fortress South: Operation Switchback

AFTER THE CAPTURE OF CALAIS MAJOR GENERAL SPRY'S 3RD Canadian Division moved 90 miles east to take part in Operation Switchback. The Breskens pocket held by the 64th German Infantry Division measured 25 miles from Zeebrugge, east to Terneuzen, and about 20 miles from the North Sea of the Scheldt Estuary south to the Leopold Canal. There was a large flooded triangle from Zeebrugge south almost to Bruges and a large semi-circle just north of the Leopold Canal. The 7th Canadian Infantry Brigade arrived at Maldegem with orders to destroy or capture enemy in the area of Moershoofd, Ardenburg, Oostburg andSchoondijke. First they had to assault and force a crossing of the Leopold Canal and enlarge a bridgehead. The canal, 90 feet across and contained between dykes, was raised above the level of the floods. The enemy in considerable force had already seen off the 4th Armoured Division's preliminary attacks, and were firmly dug-in on the reverse bank of the canal dyke. Despite support from 317 field guns, 27 WASP flame-throwers mounted on Bren-gun carriers and incessant Typhoon air support, it took a week of intense fighting before the initial two small bridgeheads were linked. Lieutenant Colonel Siegfried Enfirth, CO German 1039th Grenadier Regiment wrote, 'We really anticipated that the water would be our greatest defence. The Canadians would therefore be forced to advance on the surfaced roads at the top of the dykes, a very difficult

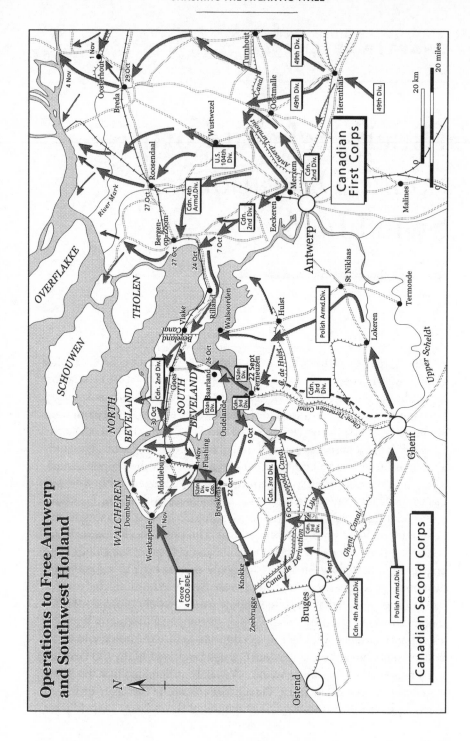

Operations to Free Antwerp
and Southwest Holland

thing to do. We felt that you would try to cross the Leopold Canal. We had you cold as far as the Canal was concerned as we had it heavily defended. Every potential attack point was defended and we had our artillery sited to bring fire to bear on every position there. We could drop shells on you wherever you were.'

During the night of 13 October the divisional engineers bridged the Deliverance de la Lys and the Leopold Canals at their apex at Strooiburg and tanks of the British Columbia Regiment moved across. The *Regina War Diary* noted, 'Past few days have seen some of the fiercest fighting since D-Day. Lobbing grenades at enemy 10 yards away and continued attempts at infiltration have kept everyone on the jump. Ammunition has been used up with unbelievable quantities, men throwing as many as 25 grenades each a night. Artillery laid 2,000 shells on our front alone in 90 minutes on 10 October and our own Mortar platoon expended 1,084 rounds of HE in 3 hours.' In one day 84 Group RAF made 200 fighter-bomber sorties. The German defence was superb, aided by heavy fire from the Cadzand and other batteries which had all-round fire. The ground was waterlogged so that slit trenches could only be a foot or two down. R.W. Thompson wrote in *The 85 Days*, 'Once over the canal, the bombs from heavy mortars and machine guns weaving in a cross-fire made progress impossible. The enemy defences were as tight as a drum and it was suicide to attempt to advance over the open coverless ground. Men strove to inch forward through the water of the dykes only to find that every narrow channel was covered by rifle Spandau or machine gun.' The Dutch themselves say of their polder countryside, 'God did not have a hand in it.'

Lieutenant Colonel Siegfried Enfirth, CO of the German 1039th Grenadier Regiment described the Leopold Canal battle as 'extremely violent'. His regiment had lost half its strength including two company commanders. He agreed a 20-minute truce on 9 October for each side to pick up its dead and wounded. 'I was well aware of the Führer's orders according to which it was forbidden to make any such arrangements with the enemy.... Friend and foe together carried their wounded and dead from the battlefield. Afterwards both sides took up their former positions again—about eighty metres apart—and resumed fierce fighting.'

In the week-long battle the three battalions: the Regina's, Winnipeg's and Canadian Scottish Rifles had 533 casualties.

❖

Major General Knut Eberding, commanding the 64th Infantry Regiment, plus Kriegsmarines and Luftwaffe Flak troops was a highly experienced soldier. He was however surprised by the next of the Allied moves. The Canadian 7th Brigade was relieved by the 157th Infantry Brigade of the newly arrived 52nd Lowland Division on 18 October. The next day Lowlanders occupied Aardenburg and Middelburg. But the next key break-in to the Breskens pocket was made by 9th Canadian Brigade's attack from the Scheldt.

Brigadier Rockingham's troops now 'married' up with the British 5th Assault Regiment RE. Two months ago they had been equipped with amphibious beasts called 'Buffaloes' (Landing Vehicles Tracked) with a land speed of up to 25mph and a water speed of five knots, a Buffalo could hold a platoon of 30 men. The MkIV version had a movable ramp at the stern and could carry small vehicles such as scout cars, carriers, jeeps or a 25 pdr field gun. In the darkness they looked like small turretless tanks and carried a Browning or Lewis machine gun. After two days of training, a daring waterborne assault took place at midnight on 9 October: From Terneuzen the Buffaloes 'swam' 20 miles down the Ghent-Terneuzen Canal, entered the River Scheldt, turned left across the mouth of the River Braakman inlet. They took the Germans by surprise on the northeast corner of the Breskens 'island'. The five AVRE assault squadrons with 100 Buffaloes carried the North Nova Scotia Highlanders to 'Green Beach', two miles east of Hoofdplaat, and the HLI of Canada on the left, to 'Amber Beach' closer to the Braakman inlet. Captain R.T. Forde RN led the flotillas in a motor boat at a speed of three knots to cover a distance of 5.5 miles. Naval and Royal Marine frogmen and divers were working all along the shores of the estuary clearing the small jetties and inlets as they were won. There were all types of mines and underwater devices including Element C, which they knew all about. But this was clearance in the treacherous mud and silt of the Scheldt, in darkness and a Low Countries winter. At 02:11 hours the first assault troops of the North Novas were ashore, up and over the first dyke onto 'terra firma'.

Within eight hours the 'Funnies' of the 79th Armoured Division returned in their Buffaloes and at 08:00 hours they carried Stormont, Dundas and Glengarry Highlanders, plus heavy machine guns and mortars of the Cameron Highlanders of Canada. The whole brigade was landed without enemy action, although at daybreak General Eberding reacted quickly. A small force sailed across from 70th Division on Walcheren to reinforce the 64th Division, and the heavy guns of Breskens and Flushing were soon in action. Hoofdplaat fell to the SDG Highlanders on the 10th, and HLI took Biervliet the next day. General Spry changed his plans and 8th Brigade followed up behind Rockingham's 9th, and landed on the 12th. As the entire 3rd Canadian Division advanced on land through the polders criss-crossed by dykes, the battle turned into a series of platoon scraps. Each MG and rifleman had to be 'taken out' painfully. By 18 October, the 9th Brigade was two miles from Breskens and the 8th Brigade six miles from Oostburg, at the centre of Scheldt Fortress South.

Major General Dan Spry wrote, 'The troops were always soaked and really exhausted. If we'd had fresh warm dry men to put in there, we could have done the job faster. As it was, we finally had to pull some out, send them through the mobile baths, give them clean, dry uniforms and socks, serve them a decent meal and a few tots of rum. Then we'd leapfrog them back into the fight and pull some other poor Water Rats out.

The 9th Brigade was now helped by 42 Terrapins of the British 6th Assault Regiment RE. These were the British made equivalent of a DUKW, with a load capacity of three tons, powered by two engines, two propellers and rudders for water warfare. They briskly ferried urgent supplies of food, drink and ammunition across floods and polder up to the front line. During Switchback, Buffaloes carried 880 loads and, besides their infantry 'cargo', carried 680 vehicles and guns. The Terrapins lifted 800 tons of ammunition, petrol and supplies. Both Buffaloes and Terrapins also took back to relative safety the Dutch civilians caught in the crossfire. They also carried back the many Canadian wounded and large batches of German prisoners of war.

Whilst the Canadians were dying in the Dutch polders, the generals were still arguing. On Black Friday, 13 October the Black Watch were being torn to pieces on the outskirts of Woendsdrecht, the HLI of Canada were being bombed by the RAF at St Pieter's Polder near Biervliet, and the coastal guns of most of the German batteries were raining shells down on the SD&G Highlanders advancing cautiously along the coast road to Hoofdplaat. General Eisenhower wrote to Field Marshal Montgomery on the same day, 'I do not know the exact state of your supply but I do know *in what a woeful state it is throughout the American and French forces* extending all the way from your southern boundary to Switzerland. By comparison you are rich!.....I keep reverting again and again to the matter of getting Antwerp into a workable condition.'

R.W. Thompson in *The 85 Days* describes some of the strange armoured help now available, 'Through the landward route gap the Fascines, Bobbins, Flails, Ploughs, Petards and SBGs, a whole lumbering ark of armoured monsters of 79th Armoured Division, were moving steadily. All of these armoured vehicles could fight and shoot as well as perform their numerous roles. The fascines carried huge bundles of faggots to tip forward into anti-tank ditches or dykes, or to lay down mattresses to give armour a grip. The SBGs dropped their own bridges down in front of them. The Petards were huge mortars to blast concrete strongpoints at point-blank range, lumbering up into the enemy, staring up the vast spouts of those weapons, tried to scream his way out of his concrete trap like an animal. In their way the Petards were as hideous as the flame-throwing Crocodiles, to the men facing death through the weapon slits of their strongpoints.'

The 9th Canadian Brigade was given the difficult task of capturing the three key strongpoints of Scheldt Fortress South. The SD&G Highlanders would take the port of Breskens, the HLI of Canada, Schoondijke, the key to the new German defence line, and the North Novas the formidable Fort Frederik Hendrik, whose guns controlled the Scheldt Estuary opposite Walcheren.

Breskens was surrounded by a 20 foot anti-tank ditch full of water, 12 feet deep, plus minefields and belts of wire. Major General Eberding knew that the game was almost up and now issued an order to all the defenders, 'In cases where the names of deserters are ascertained these will be made known to the civilian population at home and their next of kin will be looked upon as enemies of the German people.' The enemy had plenty of nasty surprises, such as Schu mines made of wood and more or less undetectable and they sometimes booby-trapped their own dead. The Queen's Own Cameron Highlanders had the CO of their 108th Anti-tank Platoon captured by a German patrol dressed in *Canadian* uniforms.

On the 20th the 284th Assault Squadron RE with their AVRES assembled at a farm near Ijzendijke, southeast of Schoondijke. An explosion of nitro-liquid fuel (perhaps for a Conger) caused 138 casualties (RE and army service corps of the HLI of Canada), and destroyed ten AVRES. 617th Assault Squadron RE, Crocodiles of 'B' Squadron, the Buffs and the flail tanks of 'B' Squadron, 22nd Dragoons were soon to be deployed, although roads were now impassable.

The SD&G Highlanders (the Glens) attacked Breskens at 10.00 hours on the 21st, crossed the deep anti-tank ditch and advanced into the town. From 9 to 11 October, 15 Glengarries were killed in action and 46 wounded. Lieutenant Colonel Roger Rowley, their CO said, 'Finally the Novas came along to protect our left flank and we moved on. I though it was endless. You'd get to Hoofdplaat and somebody would say "Take out Driewegen", and then somebody would say "Take out Hoogeweg"...."take out Roodenhoek".' Then on 21 October he was told '"take out Breskens", a fortified city, completely surrounded by an anti-tank ditch, mine fields, wire and every other conceivable defence....what we did was to go in on a one-man front. We went along the seawall and used Kapok bridging equipment which got us over the anti-tank ditch into Breskens. The Germans never believed that anybody would be so foolish as to put in an attack from there, so we got in with very few casualties. We were on top of them....and took 150 prisoners of war.' A heavy gun duel then took place between the Walcheren batteries three miles north and Canadian 9-inch heavy artillery guns followed by rocket-firing Typhoons. By noon the harbour area was clear and soon the Buffs' Crocodiles were helping by flaming pillboxes along the mole. Lieutenant Harry Barrow and Sergeant Brandi squirted flame at blockhouses and spandau nests encouraging 50 prisoners of war to come in. By midnight Breskens were captured, so badly battered by RAF bombs and artillery shells as to be unrecognizable as a town. Patrols then pushed westwards towards Fort Frederik Hendrik.

Schoondijke, three miles south was then attacked by the HLI of Canada, and despite fierce resistance was taken on the 25th. Fort Frederik Hendrik, a mile west of Breskens was an ancient ruin surrounded by two moats. Inside the Germans had built modern concrete defence works, which had been deluged with RAF bombs. The North Novas attacked on the 22nd but mortar, machine-gun and rifle fire drove them back. Brigadier Rockingham ordered a withdrawal under a smokescreen and a substantial new attack was planned for the 25th at 02.00 hours. A deserter came out to tell Colonel Rowley of the Glens that the 50 survivors of the garrison wished to surrender—and they did just that.

Major General Spry then withdrew the 9th Brigade for three days' rest and sent the 7th Brigade clearing the defences westward along the coast towards Cadzand, Retranchement, Knokke and finally Zeebrugge. The 8th Brigade were operating further south around Oostburg taken on the 26th, Waterland Oudeman and Zuidzande on the 29th. For nearly a week the Régiment de la Chaudière were surrounded, counterattacked and partially over-run. Finally on the 28th they were rescued by support from the Funnies. Two minutes of flame petards, BESA, 75 mm shells and smoke caused the enemy to surrender. Near Sluis Lieutenant Scaife DCM fired rounds of Petard at extreme range at enemy dug into dykes, plus a couple of belts of BESA, which brought in 40 prisoners of war.

The 7th Brigade were brought back into action on the 30th, and reached the fortified coastal batteries and then spent three days capturing them.

On 1 November at the Zoute golf course, near Knocke, General Eberding was captured. Two days later 7th Reconnaissance Regiment entered Zeebrugge. Zoute and the fortress area of Heyst, marked on the enemy maps as 'little Tobruk' were captured by the HLI of Canada.

Operation Switchback, the capture by 3rd Canadian Division of the Breskens pocket had taken four weeks to accomplish. In the process the division lost 2,077 casualties, including 314 killed in action, 231 missing and 1,535 wounded. They captured 12,707 PoW out of General Eberding's original 14,000 troops. A few escaped north by sea to Walcheren but many hundreds lay under the rubble or in the flooded fields and dykes. The historian of the Buffs Crocodiles wrote, 'After Breskens for the next five days Crocs, Crabs and AVRES fired at every possible target westwards towards Knocke, 75s, BESAS, flame and petards when required. It was heady stuff. On 29th all spare crews were sent up to help the Canadians march back the amazing column of some 3,000 PoWs that now came down the road. It was a motley crowd—old men, young men, Mongols, Russians, Germans, Poles, French, the long and the short and the tall.' But the Canadian infantry were the real heroes, as Lieutenant Colonel Barnard, CO Queen's Own Rifles put it, 'The fighting was marked by the utter misery of the conditions and the great courage to do the simplest things. Attacks had to go along dykes swept by enemy fire. To go through the polders meant wading, without possibility of concealment, in water at times up to the chest. Mortar fire, at which the Germans were masters crashed into every rallying point. Spandaus sent their whining reverberations across the marshes. It was a rifleman's fight, there were no great decisive battles, just a steady continuous struggle.' General Eberding had brought his Führer four weeks of precious time defending Scheldt Fortress South.

CHAPTER EIGHTEEN

Operation Vitality I:
'Felt increasingly forgotten'

AFTER THE TERRIBLE FIGHT WITH BATTLEGRUPPE CHILL AROUND Hoogerheide, Woensdrecht and Korteven at the east end of the South Beveland Isthmus, 2nd Canadian Division were now tasked with the clearance of the whole 'island'. Operation Vitality I started at first light on 24 October. The 'island' was 25 miles west to east, sliced through after ten miles by a five-mile long north-south canal for ships and at the very western end by a causeway—The Slide—between South Beveland and Walcheren. Lieutenant General Wilhelm Daser the German commander of the Walcheren garrison sent Colonel Reinhardt, CO of 1,019th Regiment to defend the southern half of the South Beveland and 1,020th Regiment, with the 70th Artillery Division, to defend the line of the Beveland Canal. Daser set up his HQ at 'sHarendskerke, realizing that the Canadian capture of Breskens was now a major threat to South Beveland and Walcheren. The Breskens pocket, 30 miles to the west had just been cleared and Lieutenant General Guy Simonds now planned a three-brigade attack by the 2nd Canadian Division. Two would leapfrog each other through the two-mile wide initial 'neck' of the island and the 5th Brigade would land on the south side in an amphibious operation.

The Royal Regiment of Canada followed by two mixed columns of armour and infantry of the Essex Scottish in 15 cwt trucks led through half-flooded polders. The railway and main road from the mainland running east-west ran long a wide dyke, cratered and mined. The RHLI

(Rileys) followed up and occupied the villages of Bath and Rilland into the Krabbendijke area. On the 26th, the 6th Canadian Infantry Brigade took over and reached the Beveland Canal early on the 27th. Casualties had been so heavy since leaving Antwerp that many new reinforcements were apparently ignorant of basic infantry tactics according to the *War Diary* of the RHLI. One company commander noted, 'After a while we tried *not* to get to know the men too well, or even to get to know them at all. It seemed about this time that we didn't have any of them with us long enough.' Lieutenant Colonel Whitaker, however, spoke to the new men in each company, explained the basic principles of infantry tactics, about fire and movement and that their object was to close (and kill or capture) with the enemy.

The Beveland Canal varies in width from 190 to 290 feet and is a formidable obstacle as its banks are raised well above the countryside. Drainage canals alongside make additional obstacles. There are locks at each end, and two roads and the railway cross over by swing bridges.

Several attempts by the Camerons to cross were beaten back, but the Saskatchewans scrambled across the broken spans of the bridges and made a small bridgehead. Next morning Les Fusiliers Mont-Royal got across at the locks at the southern end, called Hansweerd and took 120 prisoners of war. By noon on the 27th a bridge was completed and the 4th and 5th Brigades began advancing through the 6th Brigade. Lieutenant General Guy Simonds had decided that the southern amphibious landing should be carried out by 52nd Lowland Division in Operation Vitality II (see Chapter Nineteen).

The RHLI led the 4th Brigade across (in five small boats, as the bridge had been destroyed) all under heavy shellfire. Soon they had taken the village of Biezelinge, and the Royals took over and met the 156th Scottish Brigade near 's-Gravenpolder. The acting GOC of the 2nd Canadian Division Brigadier R.H. Keefler had encouraged a race between 5th and 6th Brigades. The first to reach the Walcheren Causeway would hold the rear (eastern) end whilst the 'losing' brigade would have the very doubtful honour of advancing 1,200 yards over cratered flat land, exposed in every way to the defenders' fire. The defenders of the Beveland Canal were eventually outflanked and the RHLI advancing in moonlight, clearing mines as they went, moved to Nisse and by the 30th, Heinkenzand to a fine welcome by the Dutch villagers. The 5th Brigade liberated Goes, the main town, and the Black Watch and the Régiment de Maisonneuve made good progress towards the causeway. Major Dick Porteous led 'A' Squadron of the 8th Reconnaissance Regiment along the north coast.

With a company of heavy mortars and machine guns of the Toronto Scottish he commandeered boats and barges and crossed the Zand Kreek to tackle the 'island' of North Beveland. Porteous' CO asked for air support and 18 Typhoons hurtled overhead at 50 feet and a scared garrison of 250 soon surrendered at Colinsplaat and 350 at Kamperlant.

The unfortunate 5th Brigade were given the appalling job of crossing the 1,200 yard long road and rail Walcheren causeway, dead straight, 20 yards high and 40 yards across. Brigadier W.J. Megill decided there was not enough water in the tidal flats to float assault boats and too much mud for wheeled or tracked vehicles. The Germans had turned the causeway into a death-trap with bunkers and firing trenches in the side of the dykes, railway track and barbed-wire hazards, several 88 mm, heavy mortars and machine guns. Troops of the 70th 'stomach' Division and survivors of 64th 'leave' Division from the Breskens pocket, were dug in and ready. In the centre of the causeway was a huge crater almost cutting it in two. It was the Black Watch of Canada who made the first attack. In four months of fighting they had suffered 1,400 casualties, slightly more than the Calgary Highlanders. Their CO, Lieutenant Colonel Bruce Ritchie wrote, 'Battle morale is definitely not good. Inadequately trained men sent into action ignorant of their own strength. After their first mortaring overwhelmingly convinced of the enemy's strength.' At mid-day on the 31st, Captain Lamb led 'C' company into a storm of fire including shells from the Domburg Battery heavy guns but held a position near the far end. Brigadier Megill then sent the Calgary Highlanders, then the Régiment de Maisonneuve along the causeway in a three-day battle. Counterattacks and heavy shelling ensured that no bridgehead was established and 135 casualties incurred. All this despite close air support and six regiments of field and medium artillery raining down shells.

Major General Edmund Hakewill-Smith, GOC 52nd Lowland (Scottish) Division, who was due to command all the land operations on Walcheren, after the causeway battle, had been watching the Canadians' ordeal. He was ordered on 1 November to take over and continue the causeway attack. He refused and said that he would find another way across—and he did! The history of the 52nd Division describes the scene: 'The Germans had the Causeway completely taped and plastered. The smoke of continual explosions eddied always over the embankments. The noise and incessant shocks tried the stoutest of nerves. The whole of the dam, sides and surface was pockmarked with craters. To move a foot in daylight was nearly impossible, to advance a yard in the darkness was an adventurous success.' Brigadier J.D. Russell's 157th Brigade sent two intrepid Sappers, Lieutenant F. Turner and Sergeant Humphrey to reconnoitre, during the night of 1 November, a way though the mud flats of the Slooe Channel, about two miles south of the causeway. A day later before dawn the 7th Battalion Cameronians crossed in single file and despite violent shelling and counterattacks established a new bridgehead. Soon the 5th HLI followed over and broke through the German ring. They then linked up with the 1st Glasgow Highlanders, who had taken over at the causeway. Full credit to Hakewell-Smith, Russell and his gallant sappers, Vitality I ended with the capture of South Beveland and North Beveland and the establishment of bridgeheads across the causeway.

In the clearing of the eastern sector of the Scheldt battle, 2nd Canadian Division had lost 207 officers and 2,443 other ranks. They had captured over 5,000 prisoners and killed almost as many of the enemy.

R.W. Thompson in his *The 85 Days* wrote, 'A peculiar sense of isolation had been growing in the Canadians up from the Seine. They had felt that the main stream of war had turned away and *they were increasingly forgotten*. They heard the triumphant echoes of the armoured thrusts, the tears, laughter, flowers and champagne of the liberations of Brussels, Paris—even Antwerp....after all they were fighting a war not making headlines...and they came to believe they were fighting it alone, fighting it in this God-forsaken corner, this flat and flooded patch.'

CHAPTER NINETEEN

Operation Vitality II:
Lowland Division in Action

THE 52ND (LOWLAND) DIVISION HAD IN 1942 BEEN ORGANIZED AS A mountain formation and had trained as such for 18 months. Then it was 'reorganized' as an infantry division for airborne operations but including a seaborne echelon using part of its 157th Brigade. On 21 October 1944 the 156th Brigade under Brigadier C.N. Barclay was briefed for an assault landing on South Beveland to link up with the 2nd Canadian Division advancing westwards from the isthmus and the Beveland Canal. Following feverish planning Vitality II started on the night of the 25th. The original objective was to seize the small, well-defended port of Ellewoutsdijke on the southern central tip of the island. Barclay reminded his Canadian masters that the frontal attack on Dieppe had been a disaster and the assault landing point was changed to three miles east of the little port with 'Amber Beach' on the left, 'Green Beach' on the right.

Major General Hobart's Funnies of 'DD' swimming tanks, Buffaloes and Terrapins, would carry and supply the operation across. The first wave on 'Green Beach' would be the 4th and 5th Royal Scots Fusiliers, carried by 78 Buffaloes of 5th Assault Regiment RE; and on 'Amber Beach' the 6th Cameronians would cross in 59 Buffaloes of 11th RTR. In the second wave would come on 'Amber' 18 DD Shermans of 'B' Squadron, Staffordshire Yeomanry, leading 37 Buffaloes of 11th RTR, carrying 7th Cameronians, plus 27 Terrapins of the 5th Assault Regiment RE and 25 LCA (Landing Craft Artillery).

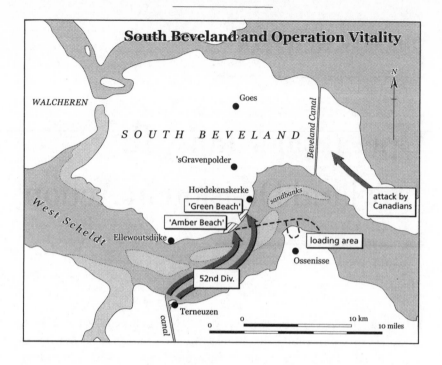

All over the Ossenisse Peninsula the Lowlanders, infantry and artillery were concentrating and having their first sight of the Buffaloes and Terrapins. At 02.45 hours on the 26th the fleet set off from Terneuzen on a dark clear night for their eight-mile journey. Commander Franks RN was the key navigating officer, who had led the flotilla in the Breskens assault, 'At 04.30 the supporting artillery opened fire. It was most accurate and heartening. We were very close, not more than 200 yards away and we could smell the explosive, but no shells fell short and I felt quite safe although the noise was a bit disturbing. There was still no opposition and the LVTs roared in ashore but had great difficulty in negotiating the steep dyke.' By 06.30 hours the beachheads were joined up and by nightfall the 156th Brigade was a mile inland with a three-mile perimeter, having taken 200 prisoners of war for the loss of 60 casualties. Elleswoutsdijke was taken on the morning of the 28th and in Heerenhoek the Glasgow Highlanders from Scotland met the Essex Scottish from Canada. The 9th AGRA from south of the Scheldt pounded any enemy resistance and the 157th Brigade, having crossed over on the 28th and 29th, then joined the 5th Canadian Brigade on the western edge of the island, not far from the dreaded causeway. Altogether 600 German prisoners of war were taken. But mines, mud, wire, water, sniping and mortars had given the Lowlanders their first induction to battle. The combined operations involving the Funnies' amphibious transport had again been very successful. Over 700 Buffalo and Terrapin loads were carried across. 11th RTR took back Scottish wounded, many civilian refugees and, of course, 600 German prisoners of war. Operation Vitality II went to plan, but the next two operations would be more demanding.

CHAPTER TWENTY

Operation Infatuate I: 'It was very nasty'

OF ALL ADOLF HITLER'S FORTRESSES THERE WAS LITTLE DOUBT that Walcheren Island—the main bastion of Fortress Scheldt—was the most powerful of them all. The island had over 30 powerful gun batteries in heavy concrete casements trained on the sea approaches. And on the southern bank—facing the Breskens pocket—another 35 were in place based at Zeebrugge, Heyst, Knokke, Cadzand, Nieuve Sluis and Fort Frederik Hendrik. Operations Switchback and Vitality had eventually knocked out the latter, but the River Scheldt clearance for entry into Antwerp could not begin until Walcheren Island was captured.

After the bombing of the sea walls (30 feet high, 300 feet wide) and consequent flooding the island now resembled a round soup bowl adrift in sea water. Middelburg, the main town, was in the centre and the town and port of Flushing was five miles due south. Flushing and Middelburg were linked to Veere, six miles northeast of the latter by a substantial canal. At the time of Infatuate I and II over 80 per cent of the island was under water, flooding a few of the minor batteries and causing the garrisons severe problems of supply and reinforcement. Most of the island was below sea level and the ferocious bombing by the RAF on the formidable coastal batteries, at Westkappelle and Flushing did little damage, but had satisfactorily breached with four gaps the sea walls. Nearly 2,200 aircraft sorties had dropped 10,219 tons of bombs between 3 and 30 October.

Lieutenant General Guy Simonds, now acting commander of the First Canadian Army in Crerar's absence in the UK, had asked for an airborne drop, either by parachute or glider. Lieutenant General Brereton, the US commander of the First Allied Airborne Army advised Eisenhower against such a drop. However, the Royal Navy had been planning with great care their highly complicated and dangerous role in the capture of the island. 'Infatuate I' was the codename for the first combined operations attack from Breskens across the Scheldt to take the port and batteries of Flushing. 'Infatuate II' was the codename for the amphibious attack on Westkappelle, which would take place either between 1 and 4 November or between 14 and 17 November, depending on the weather. The Naval Force T, entrusted with the attacks by sea, had calculated that in winter major landing craft could operate off Westkappelle an average of two days a week and minor landing craft only on one day.

After the loss of South Beveland, Lieutenant General Daser set up his command headquarters in Middelburg; his 1019th Regiment held the northwest and southwest coasts, the 1020th the northern dunes and coastline, and the 89th Fortress Regiment held Veere on the northeast coast, the eastern causeway and the eastern area above the floods. The 202nd and 810th Coastal Artillery Regiments manned the batteries.

Two of the sea wall breaches were situated one mile northwest of Flushing and another two miles east. The incoming rush of sea water had flooded some of the batteries and had isolated the enemy. A double anti-tank ditch was part of the Flushing perimeter defence. Many of the streets of the town (which then had a population of 21,000), now resembled canals, with water lying up to three or four feet in depth. To the east of the town the beaches were flooded and impassable, but just southeast a small beach used as a rubbish dump was selected for the initial landing codenamed 'Uncle'. It had a gradient of one in six, with groynes, rows of stakes and minefields and it was covered by mortars and many machine guns. The three Flushing batteries were W1, W6 and W33. Naval Force T, commanded by Captain A.F. Pugsley RN had been training for the two assaults with Brigadier Leicester's 4th Special Service Brigade at Ostend. The 52nd Flotilla sailed safely into Breskens from Ostend. The small harbour was full of craft, 40 LCAs, 20 LVTs (Buffaloes) of 11th RTR and 26 Weasels. The Flushing assault was masterminded by 52nd Lowland Division with the 4th Commandos, RN small craft and the amphibious craft of Hobart's Funnies under command. Under a 284-gun artillery barrage controlled by Brigadier Bruce Mathews, the opening assault would be made by the 4th Commandos, a small section of Dutch troops from 10th (Inter-Allied) Commando and one RN 'Tarbrush' party (RN MTB for beach reconnaissance). They would sail across the three miles of sea towards Uncle Beach, seize a bridgehead and then clear Flushing to a depth of half a mile. The 4th Battalion King's Own Scottish Borderers in the remaining 20 LCAs would then pass through the bridgehead and clear north of Flushing. The 7/9th Royal Scots and the 5th KOSB with Brigade headquarters (Brigadier J.F.S. McLaren) would follow and land the next day. The LVTs and Weasels would provide a non-stop ferry service across the Scheldt. H-Hour was 05.45 hours on 1 November and the RAF bombing support was cancelled due to indifferent weather. By 09.00 hours the 4th Commandos supported by the 4th KOSB had captured half the town, with help from French and Dutch commandos and Poppe's Dutch resistance group. The planners had given codenames to objectives, the harbour south of the locks was 'Falmouth'; the three main docks were 'Haymarket', 'Strand' and 'Piccadilly'. Two heavily defended barracks were 'Worthing' and 'Hove'. But the next morning Colonel Rheinhardt's 7,000 defenders fought back with a vengeance. Before 08.00 hours a terrible close-quarter battle took place in the 'Old Town' although the 'Arsenal' and 'Winchester' barracks had been captured. The last flight of the 4th KOSB arrived on Uncle Beach at 07.30 hours, but when the 5th Battalion tried to cross the Scheldt at noon, Commander R.D. Franks RN said, 'We ran into such a curtain of fire that the leader turned back and I was not sorry. We also put up a mine which shook us up. It was good to get back to land [Breskens] though the harbour was then shelled. It was very nasty.' Typhoons then temporarily quietened the batteries with their rockets. Landing on Uncle, five LCAs at a time, the two following Lowland battalions arrived and then hurried into the town. During the first night of the street fighting, under cover of a white flag, several hundred Dutch civilians were evacuated to safety.

Fighting in Flushing continued throughout 2 November under heavy barrages from the 284-gun support south of the Scheldt. The waterfront barracks, most of the docks, and the Goosjebusken straat strongpoint were captured. Brigadier McLaren was tasked with reaching either the town of Middelburg, a few miles to the north, or heading eastwards to link up with 157th Lowland Brigade at their Causeway Bridgehead.

But McLaren had one more vital clearance task in Flushing. The ironically named Hotel Britannia on the northwest seafront contained 1019th Infantry Regiment Headquarters and turned out to be heavily defended. Lieutenant Colonel M.E. Melville commanding the 7/9th

Royal Scots was ordered to capture the hotel early on the 3rd. Under a barrage from two medium RA regiments on the Scheldt south bank, the Royal Scots in single file waded through flooded streets between three and five feet deep in water. Five Weasels accompanied the attack and by 07.30 hours the hotel was burning. After savage hand-to-hand fighting the Britannia was captured by noon. Lieutenant Colonel Melville was badly wounded and two company commanders, Majors Thompson and Chater shot dead. The Royal Scots lost 20 killed in action and 40 were wounded in the siege. Inside the network of bunkers were 50 dead Germans; 130 prisoners of war were gathered in including Colonel Rheinhardt. Early on the 5th, aided by a barrage and rocket-firing Typhoons, the 5th Battalion KOSB took control of the Walcheren Canal and cleared the eastern dock area, taking 100 prisoners of War. The 4th KOSB sent a company north up the canal towards Middelburg, but half-way there, were held up by pillboxes and Schu mines. The Commandos, the Lowlanders and supporting gunners and 'Funny' teams had carried out a classic victory in Infatuate I.

Colonel Gustav Rheinhardt's defence, the efforts of RAF bombers and the three-day artillery duel over the Scheldt had extensively damaged the port of Flushing. By 12 December the Dutch 'P' NP 3006 port clearance party had cleared 311,000 square feet of docks and in 81 hours of underwater clearance found 43 mines and 45 depth charges.

CHAPTER TWENTY-ONE

Infatuate II: 'All hell was let loose'

THE ALLIED OPERATION TO CAPTURE WESTKAPPELLE, THE HEAVILY defended western corner of Walcheren Island was as difficult as Overlord but in miniature. For a start the weather—based on a 1 November launch (a few hours later than Infatuate I) was a gamble. Rough seas would make the beach landing assault impossible. Bad weather, fog or low cloud would deter the planned heavy bombing support that was deemed necessary. In the event a high-powered team consisting of Admiral Ramsay, Lieutenent General Guy Simonds, Major General Foulkes, Captain Pugsley RN and Brigadier Leicester RM had to make up their minds on the morning of 31 October. Pugsley was the naval force commander and Leicester, the military force commander.

Excellent air photographs of the Westkappelle defences showed exactly where the main gap in the protecting dyke was—and its width. Lieutenant General Wilhelm Daser's 70th Division had given a spirited defence to the South Beveland campaign. His coastal defence artillery in his 30 or so batteries had kept up incessant shellings of the Bresken pocket and could be counted on to do the same from Westkappelle batteries (W17, W15, W13, W287 and W11).

The orders for the assault were as follows:

(1) T Force will assault Island of Walcheren.
(2) Clear area from inclusive Westkappelle to Flushing and destroy all batteries therein.
(3) Clear area from inclusive Westkappelle to Breezand and destroy all batteries therein.

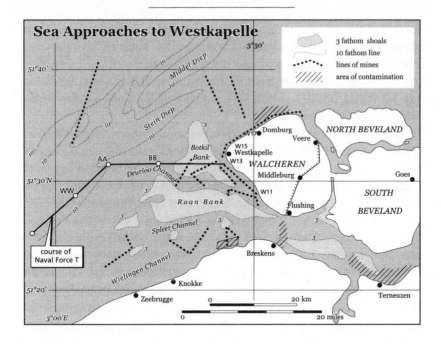

Sea Approaches to Westkapelle

3 fathom shoals
10 fathom line
lines of mines
area of contamination

[Part of T Force was SSEF, Support Squadron Eastern Flank, with 25 ships containing 500 Royal Marines and 600 Royal Navy personnel]. Codeword Tare was given to the three beaches selected for the landing. Tare Red was north of the Westkappelle 'gap', extending half a mile; Tare White, the 380 yards 'gap' itself; and Tare Green, about a quarter of a mile south of the town of Westkappelle, extending for 350 yards. Green was the maintenance beach, and Red and White were the assault beaches. For an island that was now 80 per cent flooded, an armoured presence was perhaps surprising. Four LCTs (Landing Craft Tanks) would land in close support on Red Beach. Under command of Lieutenant Colonel Dallmeyer, CO Lothians and Border Horse, a team of ten Sherman flail tanks, two Sherman gun tanks and eight AVRES of 87th Assault Squadron RE (with fascines and bridges) would immediately land and push forward behind three troops of 41st Commando with RN beach signals and seize the left shoulder of the 'gap'. The 41st Commandos would then capture Westkappelle and neutralize the powerful W-15 six-gun battery. Five minutes after H-Hour, 48th Commandos in three LCTs would pass *through* the 'gap', seize a footing on the dunes to the south and capture battery W13. Follow up waves of 41st and 47th Commandos would land on Tare White at H+25 and H+60. Two field companies RE provided a platoon for each of the three commando troops to deal with mines, gun emplacements, clearance and beach areas. The 'Funnies' also provided four armoured bulldozers of 149th Assault Park Sqn RE. No less than 104 Buffaloes and 80 Weasels of the 5th Assault Squadron RE, 82nd Assault Squadron RE and 11th RTR would land the Commandos on the beaches from the larger LCTs.

Saturation bombing of the coastal batteries was planned to take place just before the assault but due to bad weather none did take place on 31 October. But 12 Typhoons of 183rd Squadron rocket-bombed the beach defences 20 minutes before the landings, and remained as a circular 'cab-rank' for the assault. The Royal Navy joined in the battle by providing the 30-year-old HMS *Warspite* (about to fire her 15-inch guns for the last time) and the two monitors *Erebus* and *Roberts*. *Warspite* fired 353 shells, which neutralized the smaller batteries (W5 and W18) in the Domburg area (four miles northeast of Westkappelle), and for a time silenced the main battery (W17). The *Roberts* and the *Erebus* took it in turns to attack the Westkappelle battery W15, near Tare Red Beach. After much discussion aboard HMS *Kingsmill*, the headquarters ship for 'Infatuate II', H-hour went ahead at 09.45 hours, four hours later than 'Infatuate I', the attack on Flushing. The German battery W15 opened the battle at 08.09 hours, answered by HMS *Warspite* at 08.20 hours from 26,000 yards away directed on W17 and by *Roberts* on W15. Later it was discovered that *Roberts* (and Typhoon rockets) had destroyed two of the four W15 guns. Ever since the capture of Cherbourg at the end of June, then St Malo, Brest, Boulogne, Calais and Le Havre, it was tacitly recognized that even heavy bombers and battleships at sea were not only in the main, inaccurate, but even on target they did little damage to the casemented batteries (and for that matter U-boat and E-boat pens). Ten, 12 or 20 feet of reinforced concrete would keep out any shell and any bomb, except the six-ton 'Tallboy' with a direct hit. For the record the RAF did its very best, dropping on

Boulogne	3,232 tons of bombs
Calais	3,600 tons of bombs
Cap Gris-Nez	6,000 tons of bombs
Le Havre	5,800 tons of bombs
Walcheren	10,329 tons of bombs

When the various Cap Gris-Nez batteries were eventually taken by stealth and bravery from inland they were found to be almost free of damage and all in good working order. In an attack such as the Allied one on Walcheren, Adolf Hitler would probably have ordered Ostbf die W SS Otto Skorzeny's Kommandos (as in Crete, the rescue of Mussolini,

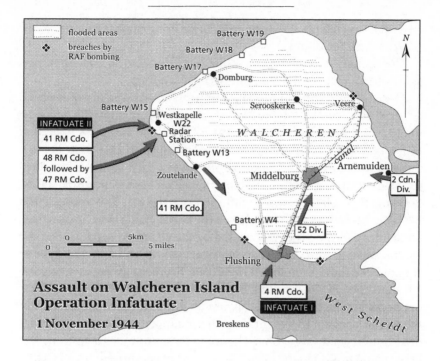

and later in the Ardennes) to drop by parachute or glider *on top of the* casemented batteries. But the Allied airborne commanders thought that it would be too risky in the case of Walcheren.

The leading waves of landing craft beached at the following times:

LCI(s)	three troops of 41 Commando	09.58 hours
Group I(g)	two troops of 41 Commando	10.05 hours
LCT	three troops of 48 Commando	10.05 hours
Group 1(h)	one troop of 41 Commando	10.15 hours
LCT	two troops 10 1-A Commando	10.15–30 hours
LCT	two troops of 48 Commando	1015–30 hours

By 12.30 hours all the Royal Marine Commandos were ashore with light casualties of five killed in action and 28 wounded, but 14 of their craft had been destroyed (11 by gunfire, three by mines) and many others damaged. Only 11 craft were fit for action (of which four were damaged). During Infatuate II the Royal Marine Commandos lost 172 killed in action and 200 wounded. Most of them were serving with the support squadron, which with its array of rockets, Oerlikons, mortars and machine guns attracted the bulk of the fire from the defenders. By 12.30 hours only

seven of its 27 craft (including three fitted for firing smoke only), remained completely fit for action.

The scenes on Amber and White beaches were as bad—perhaps worse—than most of the Normandy D-day landings.

The landing rocket ships opened up with broadsides, many of which fell short in the midst of the support craft. A LCF (Flak ship) with 200,000 rounds of Oerlikon ammunition was hit, exploded and sank. A second LCF was ablaze from our own rockets. The Hospital LCT blew up on a mine. 48th Commandos landing on White beach south of the 'gap' suffered—two craft on fire, another trapped on underwater iron stakes, throwing its Buffaloes loaded with men into the sea. Two ammunition Buffaloes brewed up and exploded on the beach. Some blew up on mines buried deep in the sand and missed by the clearance sappers. But the second wave of 48th Commandos swarmed up and over the dyke to continue the fight. Even the AGRAs from Breskens giving covering fire fell short. The FOOs directing fire were killed. The little Weasels could not negotiate the impossible mixture of surf and beach obstacles. But the assault went on. In two columns the 25 support craft had come under fire from W13 and W15 at 08.09 hours and a few minutes later from W11 in the south to W17 in the north. Each column comprised three LCG(L), three LCF, three LCS(L), one LCG(M) and three LCT(R) in the northern group and two in the southern. Commander K.A. Sellar commanded the southern flotilla and Lieutenant Commander Leefe, the northern. The four LCTs in the first wave of support on Tare Red beach each carried five Buffaloes crammed with Marine Commandos. They were named *Cherry, Damson, Bramble,* and *Apple*. At 09.00 hours *Damson*, leading *Cherry* by two lengths, ran into heavy fire 600 yards from shore. A shell collapsed the bridge carried by the Churchill AVRE which in turn fell on a Lothian flail tank. An AVRE carrying a large round wooden fascine was set alight by shellfire, other vehicles were damaged. As *Damson* was making water and was also on fire, it was ordered back to Ostend. *Cherry* was hit several times and only 20 yards off Tare Red beach was hit again, was ordered offshore, was hit again and started to run in on Tare White beach. The bridge on top of its AVRE (quite a large target) collapsed on the Lothian flail tank in front but somehow two AVRES, a flail, a gun-Sherman and an armoured bulldozer got off on the beach alongside *Bramble* which was already unloading. Its AVRE bridge was hit, collapsed and jammed the Churchill in the LCT as it was carrying off. *Apple* touched down on Tare White beach, but a soft patch bogged down *all* vehicles that landed and blocked others trying to get ashore.

Then the incoming tide 'drowned' two tanks on the beach. The support squadron engaged the enemy until 12.30 hours when all the commandos were ashore. Captain Pugsley ordered Commander Sellar to break off action and return to Ostend with the few surviving craft. *The Official History of the Canadian Army* records that 'the battered remnants of his gallant squadron slowly withdrew, carrying with them 126 badly wounded officers and men and those of their 172 dead who had not already found graves in the sea.' 82nd Assault Squadron RE had eight craft sunk with 19 casualties. Captain Michael Wilford was one of them, 'The first wave of LCTs carried Paul Bennett's three Buffaloes with a Commando troop aboard, the second myself with four Buffaloes, another Commando troop and their mortars. The OC, Tony Poynder, next with four Buffaloes and command HQ. The second wave had Jim Skelly with five, and Bill Green with four Buffaloes. Soon the shore batteries concentrated their fire on the LCGs (Landing Craft Guns) in the Support Squadron. They were very hard pressed, taking hits from heavy calibre weapons. Once our ramp was let down, all hell was let loose with a mixture of shells, mortar bombs and small arms.'

Captain Aschmann, the German sea commandant, South Holland commented in his *War Diary* that on the evening of 30 October his battery W13 had 1,565 rounds of 15cm shells with another 190 on their way to it. W11 had 1,751 shells with 360 on the way. Both batteries had been firing across the Scheldt on the 30th and 31st. Later all batteries except W17 and W19 fired when a smokescreen was created ahead of Infatuate I, the attack from Breskens towards Flushing. The end result was that by the morning of 1 November W13 and W11 'only' had about 200 shells left per gun. At 10.17 hours, when W13 had done enormous damage, not to the first wave of attack on Tare White, but on the second support wave, it was suddenly out of ammunition. Several 17 pounder anti-tank guns were carried in LCG (M) with solid armour-piercing shot with special heavy armour protection. One of them fired 50 rounds at W15 gun emplacement at short range. Later after the battery's capture, it was seen that the AP shot had penetrated six feet into the ten-foot thick walls. No shells had penetrated inside the casement.

With W13 out of ammunition, W15 partly crippled and Typhoons deluging strongpoints with 10,000 cannon shells and 220 rockets, things looked a little more cheerful. Out of the wreckage of the support flotilla, two Sherman gun tanks, three Sherman flail tanks (with 75 mm guns), two AVRES with petard bombards and one armoured bulldozer crawled slowly into the battle. Sergeant Ferguson in a Sherman Flail put 11 rounds of HE into the Westkappelle radar tower and the town garrison shortly afterwards surrendered. Two flooded and unoccupied batteries were also found. 41st Commandos went through north of the 'gap' in Buffaloes, dismounted beyond the dyke, and occupied Westkappelle. By 11.00 hours the 48th Commandos in scores of small intimate fights had secured much of the dune area to the south and were preparing to capture the non-firing W13 casement battery.

There were three Canadian medical units with the first wave of Commandos to Westkappelle, the 8th and 9th Canadian Field Surgical Units (RCAMC), a section of No 17 Canadian LFA (Light Field Ambulance), and a beach dressing station set up in the sand dunes by Number 10 Field Dressing Station. Major J. Hillsman RCAMC noted 'pinpoints of light sparked from the south batteries. The Germans were opening up at last. The whole line of support craft broke into flame and smoke. Ships blew up and were swallowed in one gulp. Others drifted aimlessly around out of control.' On the second day the medical staff were in a dug-out having lunch when a salvo of shells hit three nearby Buffaloes with seven tons of ammunition, being unloaded by a German prisoner of war. There were many casualties, 20 killed including the German prisoner. Only Captain L. Ptak of the transfusion unit and Major Hillsman were free to help the wounded, 'For the next half hour we lay on our faces in the sand, dressing wounds, stopping haemorrhages and splinting fractures. Constant explosions were blowing sand over us as we worked.' During the next three days of gales the main surgical tent was erected by 40 men on top of the *flat* dyke, most vulnerable to the wind—and to the enemy! Petrol and ammunition dumps surrounded the tent. The dead lay wrapped in blankets on one side of the entrance. German prisoners huddled in the huge crater pits nearby. In the two days Hillsman and his team carried out 52 operations, many by the light of a flickering acetylene lamp. For 12 days and nights the dedicated RCAMC medics—most of the time under fire from the batteries—worked on British and German wounded.

Major Peter Wood, the second in command of the 41st Commandos beached below the fire from the guns of W15 and cleared opposition round the dyke and the western edge of Westkappelle. By 12.30 hours they had captured W15 from the rear taking 120 prisoners of war, and then reached the lighthouse where the coast turns northeast. At 15.00 hours the 41st Commandos approached Domburg, three miles northeast, and captured the powerful W17 battery, meeting many drunken Germans yelling defiance and throwing stick grenades. But the village and powerful W18 held out vigorously.

Lieutenant Colonel J.L. Moulton led the 48th Commandos on to the southern part of the gap at 10.05 hours, captured a large concrete blockhouse, then the radar station, and took strong points W285 and W286. They were then halted by the W13 defences. At 15.45 hours a 15-minute barrage from Canadian guns south of the Scheldt plus Typhoon rockets and bombs enabled the 48th Commandos to take W13 and 70 prisoners of war by the evening.

The great gap in the main sea dyke had now become a rip-tide, 400 yards across with a current running at ten knots. Weasels could make no progress and even the heavier more powerful Buffaloes found progress difficult. The four LCTs carrying the 47th Commando under Lt Colonel C.F. Phillips should have landed south of the gap but in the confusion of battle, landed near the northern shoulder near Westkappelle. By 19.00 hours they assembled in the correct place, 600 yards south of the gap, having lost casualties, and all soaked to the skin by wading or swimming across the rip-tide in the gap.

Lance Sergeant L. A. Wells of the 80th Assault Squadron RE in his LCT carried a troop of 47th RM Commandos perched on top of the ammunition in the second wave. They were due to land on Tare White at 10.45 hours and move south towards Vlissengen. He recalled, 'Captain Saunders OC 3 Troop was hit by a shell splinter and was killed instantly. Captain Oxtoby's Buffalo was in the stern and mine was immediately behind it. I told Les Amos my driver to follow closely (six inches) behind him. The scene ashore was one of absolute devastation. The sea was flooding through the gap in the dyke. The church and most of the village (of Westkappelle) were on fire. Shells were bursting everywhere, tanks were coming to grief. An RTR Buffalo abandoned by its crew was on fire, floating inland, its cargo of ammunition was on fire and popping off in all directions—a mobile fireworks display. Weasels were being swamped by the current. The artillery link to the other side of the Scheldt was in a Weasel that was lost.' Sergeant Wells later moved south past W13 to Zoutelande and guarded 200 German prisoners of war.

By nightfall on 1 November six miles of dunes had been captured by the 4th Special Service Brigade, including the large powerful Domburg (W17) and Westkappelle (W15) and W13 batteries. All three troops of Commandos, the 41st, 48th, 47th and the two troops of the 10th (Inter-Allied) Commandos were ashore. Fifteen of the Buffaloes had been destroyed or were out of action but the Weasels had proved to be almost useless. Three of the armoured bulldozers were 'drowned' in a clay patch, another fell into a bomb crater and sank, two struck mines, one sank and another was taken back to Ostend in a damaged LCT. The sappers of 509th and 510th Field Companies and the 144th Pioneer Company eventually had one surviving bulldozer to help them clear the beaches, obstacles and tracks through the dunes.

The next day a tremendous weight of fire came on to the three beaches from W11 battery south of Zoutelande. Captain G.D. Scarrow RAMC of the Lothians, had set up his RAP on White Beach early on the 1st and wrote in his diary, 'Ambulance and hospital dumps were plastered with fire. LVTs and ammunition still going up in flames. We got a fair number of wounded away in one ship but no sign of a Navy ferry service. We tried to get more wounded away but it was too rough for the LCTs to come in.' For three more days the beaches were closed and the bombardment squadron left at dusk on 2 November. The German prisoners of 70th Infantry Division on the beach began to sing 'Deutschland über Alles'. Perhaps they thought their Führer could still save them?

There were several fields of action on the 2nd. The 200 men (Norwegian, Dutch and Belgian) of the 10th I-A Commandos were facing 600 defenders, still probably tipsy, in Domburg village and W18 battery. The 41st Commandos had moved back down past Westkappelle ready to support the crucial attack on W11. The third operation was north of Flushing, to the east by the Lowlanders trying to link up with their third brigade, still held up in the Sloe Channel and Beveland causeway bridgehead.

SHAEF were putting pressure on Montgomery, Guy Simonds (Crerar was still ill in the UK), and at the very sharp end on Brigadier Leicester. W11 was doing a great deal of damage on the beaches and with W4 and W3 could still seriously damage sea traffic in the Scheldt. Brigadier Leicester ordered the 48th Commandos south to take W287 and then the village of Zoutelande, which they did by 11.00 hours capturing 200 prisoners of war. Then the 47th Commandos passed through and because of the lie of the sand dunes had to advance in single file along the dangerous two-mile 'march' to capture W11. The last 100-yard charge was disastrous against deadly mortar and machine-gun fire. With four out of five troop leaders casualties the adjutant led the survivors into W11 at 22.00 hours. They beat off counterattacks in the night—just. On the 3rd, reorganized and joined by a troop of 48th Commandos, Lieutenant Colonel Phillips cleared a pumping station and, with difficulty, winkled out the defenders of each of the four guns of the W11 battery.

The last battery, W4 fell to Phillips's men, who cleared all defences until they reached the gap in the dyke northwest of Flushing. This was accomplished in the face of gale force winds driving the sand in thick storms. Kapitan Hans Koll, the German Officer Commanding of W4 garrison, on being captured said to Phillips, 'You will shoot me if you think I have not done my duty.' His Führer would have approved of his conduct! The 47th Commandos, after a horrible landing on the 1st and a bloody nose on the 2nd, had 'come good' on the 3rd, persevering and taking every objective asked of them. At the same time on the 3rd, Operation Switchback and Infatuate I were declared officially over.

The German 70th Division had had most of their teeth drawn—the coastal batteries commanding the Scheldt were at long last impotent. Indeed on the morning of the 4th, three brave minesweepers set off through mine-infested waters towards Antwerp (in Operation Calender). It might be thought that with the capture of the rest of the island of Walcheren being imminent, Lieutenant General Wilhelm Daser might have surrendered to overwhelming Allied forces. Not a bit of it. Three more clearance battles remained. R.W. Thompson in *The 85 Days*: 'The last five days on Walcheren were macabre—grisly. It was a microcosm of war; a little island, nine miles by nine, holding the whole hideous story. Invasion, occupation, fortification, bombardment, siege, counter-invasion, destruction—there in Walcheren the land was destroyed, the source of life. The battle was lost, irrevocably. A few men had trickled out through Veere, a few through Vrouwenpolder. But there was no longer an escape route and no hope of one, no hope of relief. It was over. These Germans on Walcheren could do nothing to impede the Allies—they could only drag down more dead with themselves in their own shameful ruin.' Daser's men were not familiar SS troops, nor dedicated Hitler Jugend, they were mostly middle-aged men with stomach complaints. They had admittedly once been veterans of the Russian and other fronts, but confronted by appalling concentration of fire from the air, from the sea and from the land, they still fought on, and on. By 4 November almost 2,000 German troops were in grey, remote Middelburg in the centre of the island where 25,000 Dutch refugees had swarmed in from their flooded villages to join the 25,000 residents. They lived on roof-tops, since many cellars were flooded. There was a shortage of food and drinking water, but Daser did not care.

The 'Funnies' of 79th Armoured Division had had a difficult time, with most of their armour sunk or drowned on the beaches. Major Pocock took the surviving two Shermans, and two Churchill AVRES north to help the Tenth I-A Commandos tackle Domburg. The Buffaloes of 26th Assault Squadron RE helped maintain the 40th and 41st Commandos;

the 77th Assault Squadron RE were with Commando Brigade headquarters; the 80th and 82nd Assault Squadrons were with the 47th and 48th Commandos whilst the 79th Assault Squadron RE assisted medical units on the beaches.

Pocock's four tanks reached Domburg on the night of the 3rd. For three days a terrific fight was waged for the W18 battery and a heavily fortified gun position in woods named 'The Black Hut'. The 41st Commandos now joined the 10th (I-A) but they were faced by massed Oerlikons, *nebelwerfers*, flame-throwers, machine guns, wire and minefields.

On 6 November W18 fell and 300 prisoners of war were taken, and a day later Typhoons dived down on 'The Black Hut' which then surrendered. The two Shermans fired 1,400 rounds of 75 mm HE at point-blank range and 34 boxes of Browning machine-gun ammunition. The AVRES fired 46 boxes of BESA and expended their petard bombs. One AVRE went over such a powerful mine that two of the crew were killed, another wounded. In the four-day fight for W17, W18 and 'The Black Hut' 750 prisoners of war were taken. Brigadier Leicester wrote to Lieutenant Colonel Dallmeyer, the Officer in Command of the 'Funny' contingent, 'The few tanks we got ashore were worth their weight in gold.' The next day the 41st Commandos took the northern W19, the last battery, and the 4th Commandos coming up from the south reached Fort de Haak.

Back on White Beach Captain Sparrow wrote, 'Monday 5th. An LCT got in perfectly and we loaded 70 wounded and 250 prisoners and then pulled out quickly. The wounded had an unpleasant time soaked to the skin even through the German PoW held tarpaulins over them.' On the east coast after non-stop fighting in the causeway battle, on the 4th the Cameronians were relieved by the 5th HLI. The next day the HLI linked up with the 1st Glasgow Highlanders and reached Gronenburg making a substantial bridgehead. Finally on the 6th the Lowlanders advanced through Arnemuiden to the edge of the floods. Beyond was a heavily mined railway and road leading to Middelburg half a mile away to the west.

A Dutch doctor from the civilian hospital in Middelburg brought a message to the 15th Lowland Brigade HQ, that Lieutenant General Daser would probably surrender to a tank force with a commander of senior rank as a face-saving operation. Daser was not to know that the only three surviving tanks of Major Pocock's were finishing off his defiant troops in the casements of W18 and treacherous woods around 'The Black Hut', eight miles to the west over deeply flooded polder.

Eventually Major Dawson of the 7/9th Royal Scots loaded 120 men into 11 Buffaloes of 11th RTR led by Lieutenant V.R. Lowe and commanded by Major Newton Dunne. With a few machine gunners of the Manchesters the convoy left Flushing, via Hoodekerke and Ter Hooge, on 6 November. Absolute surprise was vital so a circuitous route was taken of 10–12 miles on a westerly flank towards Middelburg. At the same time the 4th Battalion KOSB advanced yard by yard along both banks of the Flushing–Middelburg canal pulling German defenders out of their rat-holes and strongpoints amidst fields of Schu mines. Their casualties were heavy. The third attack was to come in from the northeast of the town by the 156th and 157th Lowland Brigades over the Middelburg-Veere canal. Suicide groups in fortified strongpoints of the fanatical survivors of the 64th 'leave' Division from the Scheldt Fortress South, now helped Daser's last stand. At about 16.00 hours on 6 November eight of the 11th RTR Buffaloes (one was blown up, another was entangled in wire, and the third took wounded back) crossed or swam the anti-tank moat round Middelburg and entered the town through a breach in the walls. They hoped they would be sounding and looking like *genuine* tanks. Major Johnson sent the brigade intelligence officer, Captain Jones, and another officer to find General Daser's HQ and demand his surrender. There were 2,000 well-armed German troops still in the town but Major Johnson put on a brave front. Despite the fact that Johnson had 'promoted' himself to 'Lieutenant Colonel', stalemate continued throughout the night as the Germans now gathered in the main town square and sang the 'Horst Wessel' song with enthusiasm. The Dutch civilians in the bars, enthusiastic about their liberation, were firing off discarded weapons. The well-organized Dutch resistance 'tidied up' their tipsy friends. At 03.30 hours the headquarters staff of the 5th HLI of the 157th Lowland Brigade arrived and soon after the 4th Battalion KOSB arrived from Flushing with a company of the 7/9th Royal Scots. The triple attack on Middelburg had worked perfectly. The city fell without a shot being fired with 2,030 German prisoners of war. Twelve casualties were lost when an 11th RTR Buffalo was mined on the way to Middelburg. Later on that day Veere, five miles northeast, surrendered to the 6th Battalion Cameronians who accepted the surrender of 13 officers and 620 well-armed men. In all Lieutenant General Daser and 8,000 of his garrison were marched off to the prison camps. General von Zangen lost 22,000 prisoners in the defence of Adolf Hitler's Fortress Scheldt. Probably another 6,000 lay buried in the ruins of the 60 individual gun casements, in the flooded polders and in the debris of innumerable strongpoints. Although hostilities on Walcheren were officially ended on 8 November, many isolated bodies of Germans were rescued from their marooned, forgotten positions. An island at Gapinge yielded 140 very cold and very hungry Germans ready for the camps with their fibre suitcases already packed.

There were 58,000 Dutch civilians in Middelburg and more than half needed to be evacuated and gave Major General Hakewill Smith, GOC of the 52nd Lowland Division, cause for concern. The flooding that had caused so much chaos to the island hinterland and its long-suffering population, was of course a major contribution to the defeat of Daser's determined garrison. Some batteries were flooded and many were so isolated that supplies and ammunition could not get through. The assault troops could to some extent move by Buffalo and occasionally by Weasel across the flooded polders. Throughout November sappers and troopers did their best for the Dutch but the thousands of mines and booby traps were a deadly menace. It was going to be a long bitter winter.

Clearing Fortress Scheldt had cost the Allies 12,873 casualties, mainly Canadian, but there were many British (and Scottish). The Canadian 3rd Infantry Division had 324 killed in action, 2,077 wounded, with 231 reported missing. Canada's 2nd Infantry Division had 3,500 casualties. In Vitality I and Vitality II, Infatuate I and Infatuate II the Allied casualties were 6,506.

CHAPTER TWENTY-TWO

Operation Calender:
'Delight in getting mines'

THE ROYAL NAVY HAD BEEN MAKING PLANS FOR THE CLEARANCE of the Scheldt Estuary up to the great port of Antwerp 55 miles inland. Admiral Bertram Ramsay had assembled two substantial minesweeping forces. Force A for the actual Scheldt Estuary clearance was commanded by Captain H.G. Hopper RN, Captain Minesweeping, Sheerness. From his headquarters, HMS *St Tudno* he controlled the 157th, 159th and 165th Flotillas of 120-foot British yard minesweepers (BYMS) equipped with both Oropesa sweeps and magnetic sweeps; the 102nd, 110th, 139th and 140th Flotillas of 105-foot minesweepers fitted with magnetic sweeps; the 131st Flotilla (as above but equipped for sweeps in *fresh* water); the 15th and 19th Flotillas, motor launches equipped with Oropesa sweeps; the 197th, 198th and 199th Flotillas (from Ostend), which were Motor Fishing Vessels (MFV) equipped with magnetic sweeps; and the 704th Flotilla LCP(L) with snag line sweeps.

Force B was commanded by Captain T.W. Marsh RN, Captain Minesweepers, Harwich and was entrusted with the clearance of the Zeebrugge-Ostend channel. His force consisted of the 165th MS Flotilla and five MMS under command of Commander Spencer Stammwitz, Commander Minesweeping, Belgium. They were to clear the freshwater section of the Scheldt from Walsoorden to Antwerp.

There were three types of mine; moored mines activated by contact with a ship's hull, and ground mines resting on the bottom, activated by the noise of propellers as the magnetic field of the ship passed overhead.

The new 'oyster' mines were activated by water pressure from ships passing and were almost unsweepable. The minesweepers were small shallow-draft craft and operated in a V-shaped movement, with the flotilla taking station within the spread of the sweep of the next vessel ahead. The leader of course was at risk! To sweep moored mines, wire sweeps (Oropesa) spread in the vessels wake, were controlled in depth, and cut the cables of the mines. On the surface they could be destroyed by rifle fire. To sweep magnetic mines pairs of sweepers towed floating cables, between which an electric pulse passed through the water, setting off the mine's firing mechanism. Acoustic mines were dealt with by electrically operated hammers, whose noise, it was hoped, would operate the firing mechanism of the mine at *a safe distance in front*. Sometimes grenades were thrown into the sea to set off floating mines. Wire cutting could not be used at the same time as the magnetic sweep, but the acoustic hammer could be used at any time. Commander A. Kimmins RN described the dangerous business of minesweeping and the men aboard the sweepers. 'What struck me most about them was firstly their persistent delight in getting mines...and secondly their amazing stamina. They were such long, long days; sometimes desperately exciting with a record catch; but always long, always tiring, and always nerve-racking. Never a moment without the constant threat of what might suddenly happen, and then, often just when it was least expected, it did; the sudden jarring impact sometimes enough to knock you off your feet; the roar of the explosion, and as the great plume of mud and water subsided, the cheers of all the crew at the thought of another white chevron to be chalked up on the funnel. Down in the engine room were two men who, with that first violent impact, had instinctively grasped a handrail and being unable to see, could not be sure how close it really was.'

On 1 November Admiral Ramsay ordered Force B to try to reach Breskens. Next morning three Belgian sweepers left for Ostend but came under heavy fire from the Zeebrugge battery. They were hit, but had no casualties, swept five ground mines and returned safely. Early on 3 November in darkness the force reached Breskens safely, despite fire from the Flushing battery. The combined force of six Belgian and seven British detailed for the Breskens—Flushing route were now ready for Operation Calender. The next day Commander Stammwitz led his six sweepers of 19th Flotilla from Breskens into Antwerp having detonated five magnetic mines in the Walsoorden channel and swept the last five miles from Hansveerde. The British seven swept a channel three cables wide between Breskens and Flushing and detonated nine ground mines.

The target date for the final and complete clearance of the Scheldt was estimated at 28 days, although days of heavy weather might delay this plan. During Calender more than 80 ships each day used Ostend Harbour. All the local fishing boats assembled at Terneuzen, having been laid up during the war. They were individually vetted by security officers, set sail for Zeebrugge and were despatched to their home ports to resume fishing again.

The Royal Navy during November suffered losses. Lieutenant Commander Clayton RNR saw ML 916 blown up on an acoustic mine sweeping down to Terneuzen. The whole ship was blown into the air and disintegrated; there were only two survivors. LST 420, the minesweeper *Hydra* and HMS *Duff* were mined and LST 321 hit by a torpedo. Bad weather on the 7th and 9th delayed sweeping but most days there was a 'tally'. On 4 November 64 mines were detected and destroyed, on 8 November, 23, on the 9th there were 13, and during the next nine days a further 71 were destroyed.

On the 21st an optimistic view was taken after three days of negative findings. But on the 22nd and 23rd another nine mines were found. On the 26th Captain Hopper again reported Operation Calender completed and that the risk of odd mines appearing must be accepted. By then 229 ground mines and 38 moored mines (but no 'oysters') were detonated or swept. The first three coasters reached Antwerp that day and two days later, the 28th, the first Liberty ship convoy of 19 ships (16 over 7,000 tons) arrived safely led by the Canadian-built *Fort Cateraqui*. Captain Hopper led the convoy in, and in a small welcome ceremony by Admiral Ramsay and the Burgomeister of Antwerp, it was noted, sadly, afterwards that no representative of the First Canadian Army was present.

It looked as though the long 85-day campaign to clear the Scheldt and open Antwerp harbour was over. In a sense that was true, since by the end of November, daily landing of stores was running at 5,528 tons from British ships and 5,435 tons from American ships. At the end of December 10,000 British vehicles had been landed, plus 268,534 tons of British stores and 428,995 tons of US stores. In addition, with PLUTO now working, 182,653 tons of petrol, oil and lubricants were also shipped in. The targets set were 17,500 British and 22,500 US daily tonnage. By the end of December 4 *million* square yards of harbour quays and *bassins* had been swept, with 120 mines found.

Nevertheless after Operation Calender, casualties and incidents occurred. On 30 November, HMS *Stevenstone* was mined, SS *Frances Ashbury* on 3 December, the Belgian tug *Orion* blown up near Hoboken and SS *Samsip* on the 7th. A score of Luftwaffe planes dropped mines on the 8th in the main anchorage. The first Belgian ship *Belgian Sailor* docked on 13th, the SS *War Niwan* on 16th. On the 22nd and 23rd attacks were made by German midget submarines and human torpedoes and in a battle with German E-boats from the Dutch ports three E-boats were sunk, two badly damaged. A midget submarine torpedoed SS *Allan-a-Dale* and sank it on the 23rd; and three days later three more midget submarines were sunk. A British port construction company had arrived on 12 September, a week after the port's capture. A huge Belgian workforce of about 26,000 was employed by British and American forces engineer units. By the time the first convoy arrived on 28 November, 219 out of 242 shipping berths were cleared, about 600 cranes were in working order and all the many lock, road and rail bridges in the port were repaired.

Adolf Hitler had realized that when Antwerp fell on 4 September, by one means or another he had to neutralize its use and/or destroy the harbour facilities. It was a huge target with 30 miles of wharves, 632 operating hoists and cranes and 186 acres of warehouses and oil storage facilities. There were more than 50 miles of rail track, of which the Germans had removed 35 miles and 200 points and crossings.

The bombardment thus began on 19 October, when the first V-2 ballistic missile hit Antwerp and the first V-1 flying bomb came on the 23rd. In December 224 V-1s and 220 V-2s caused heavy casualties of 561 killed and 1,407 wounded, with 154 people missing, believed killed. By the end of March 1945 when the bombardment ceased, 1,214 V-weapons fell on the 36 square miles of greater Antwerp. They killed about 3,000 people, mainly civilians, wounding another 12,000. 302 V-weapons fell in the docks, sinking two large ships and 58 smaller ones. Kruisschans Lock was damaged and the Hoboken POL installations were twice hit. On 12 December a V-2 hit the Rex Cinema, killing 242 soldiers, many on short leave, and 250 civilians, with 500 others badly wounded.

Hitler deployed fully half his V-weapon resources on the Antwerp target—a diminishing figure as the V-weapon bases were overrun, except those in northern Holland.

Brigadier General C.H. Armstrong was the US officer commanding a substantial anti-aircraft defence force of 22,000 deployed on the outskirts of Antwerp. Amongst the formations was the 86th HAC (Honourable Artillery Company), Heavy Anti-Aircraft Regiment. There were 336 heavy guns, 188 light anti-aircraft guns and 72 searchlights. The defences shot down 2,394 V-weapons in the five-month bombardment.

By the end of April the Americans were discharging 25,000 tons a day and the British over 10,000 tons daily through Antwerp. Hitler's V-1s, V-2s, E-boats and submarines had failed abysmally to check the huge momentum of the Allied supply—now that the Fortress Scheldt had been demolished. But it had been a close run thing.

CHAPTER TWENTY-THREE

A Kind of Odd-Job Formation

BRIGADIER BILL WILLIAMS, MONTGOMERY'S HEAD OF INTELLIGENCE told the author, Richard Lamb, 'Monty's handling of the Canadians was strange. He did not like Crerar whom he used to describe as more of a Quartermaster General than a Field Commander. With hindsight I feel Monty was astonishing in his relationship with all his Dominion troops. He ordered them around like British troops, ignoring the devolution of the British Empire....he was completely out of date. Still, he handled them well in battle.' Crerar and Montgomery crossed swords vigorously over the 'return to Dieppe' affair. On 3 September the day before the capture of Antwerp, Crerar was given orders: 'Canadian Army will clear the coastal belt [by capturing Le Havre, Dunkirk, Calais, Boulogne, Zeebrugge, etc.] and will then remain in the general area of Bruges-Calais until the maintenance situation allows of its employment further forward.' It seems incredible that Montgomery, now a field marshal and only responsible for the British and Canadian Armies did not realize with all the Ultra information available that *every* coastal fortress would be very heavily defended indeed. Montgomery knew that the US Army needed three weeks, with massive air and sea support, to subdue Cherbourg. And then the dismissive sign-off phrase 'maintenance situation allows of its employment further forward'. Chester Wilmot wrote in his *Struggle for Europe*, 'The Canadian flank was allowed to languish' and in Horrocks' book *Corps Commander*, he mentions that 'The Canadian Army was treated as a *kind of odd-job* organisation and thus given a very low claim to supplies.' In mid-September the 5th Canadian Brigade (and probably the others) had their 25 pounder field-gun regiments rationed to three rounds per gun per day, and for their heavy mortar companies only five rounds per 4.2-inch mortar per day. A barrage for a regimental attack might need between 100 and 200 rounds per gun! When Eisenhower eventually persuaded Field Marshal Montgomery to take the Scheldt clearance seriously, he promised the Canadian First Army maximum support. And did they receive it?

The Royal Navy, as one might expect were magnificent. Their three warships bombarded Walcheren when required. They provided the intrepid brigade of Royal Marine Commandos who were the mainspring for Infatuate 1 and Infatuate II, and finally flotillas of 100 minesweepers, which swept and reswept the 55 miles of mine-strewn river before leading the first convoy into Antwerp in Operation Calender.

The Scottish 52nd Lowland Division in their first battle actions performed with distinction in South Beveland and Walcheren. The British 79th Armoured Division with their 'Funny' zoo of formidable armour—flails, Crocodiles, AVRES, Buffaloes and Terrapins—did all they were asked in the Breskens pocket, including fetching and carrying to South Beveland and Walcheren, and eventually a few survivors helped the Marine Commandos at Westkappelle and Domburg. RAF Bomber Command did its best and dropped over 10,000 tons of bombs, but its top brass were unhelpful.

Air Chief Marshal 'Bomber' Harris boasted that he could, 'Capture Walcheren with his batman after all the bombs that had been dropped on it.' He conveniently forgot that 98 per cent of the bombs dropped failed to do any damage to the casemented batteries, although, to be fair, the breaching of the coastal dykes was most successful.

Air Chief Marshal Sir Charles Portal, Chief of Air Staff, wrote to General Eisenhower in mid-October, 'I believe that the constant application of the heavy bombers to the [Canadian] land battle, *when it is not essential*, and its only purpose is to save casualties, must *inevitably lead to demoralisation of the Army.*' A statement that might have come straight out of *Alice in Wonderland*!

And Air Chief Marshal Lord Arthur Tedder, Eisenhower's second in command, wrote back to Portal, 'We are now I am afraid beginning to see the results in precisely that demoralisation of which you speak. The repeated calls by the Canadian Army for heavy bomber effort to deal with a part-worn battery on Walcheren, and the evacuation of Breskens because of intermittent harassing fire from this battery is in my opinion only too clear an example. It is going to be extremely difficult to get things back on a proper footing.' Tedder vetoed the bombing of Flushing town and batteries (and its inhabitants) and openly said that the Canadian Army was 'drugged with bombs'. On 24 October Tedder with Eisenhower's approval forbade further heavy bombing attacks on Walcheren. In Infatuate II the powerful W15 battery fired at the Royal Marine Commandos at point-blank range, the W13 at close range and the W11 at longer range. It is a pity that the gallant air commanders were not there to see the support squadron being torn to pieces. Moreover W17 fired across the western tip of the island, and the Flushing batteries commanded the sea area towards Breskens.

General Crerar and Lieutenant General Guy Simonds very much hoped for some airborne support to drop even small forces by parachute or glider to help neutralize some of the powerful batteries immune to bombs or shells. On 13 September Montgomery wrote to General Crerar. 'The *whole energies* of the Army will be directed towards operations designed to enable full use to be made of the port of Antwerp. Airborne troops are available to co-operate.' They were not.

On 11 September Lieutenant General Lewis Brereton, GOC First Allied Airborne Army had to consider ten possible airborne operations. Bearing in mind the heavy losses in the D-Day landings in the Cotentin peninsula from flak and by drowning in the flooded marshlands, he was perhaps understandably cautious. He wrote in his diary. 'I refused Operation Infatuate on Walcheren because of intense flak, difficult terrain which would prevent glider landings, excessive losses likely because of drowning, *non-availability of US* troops and the fact that the operation is an *improper* use of airborne forces.' Walcheren was considered to be a minor side-show!

For the record, both in the Sicily assault and the D-Day landings American airborne divisions were dropped in widespread confusion and rarely near their scheduled objectives. The coastal batteries along the Scheldt needed pin-point dropping of airborne troops. The penalty would have been severe. The early winter temperatures in flooded polders or the North Sea would have taken their toll. Monty wanted the airborne command to take a risk. Brereton refused.

CHAPTER TWENTY-FOUR

The Logistical War of Supply and Demand

BY THE AUTUMN OF 1944 IT WAS CLEAR THAT THE AMERICAN forces, if they were to keep up pressure on the Rhineland, urgently needed far more supplies. By February 1945 General Eisenhower's command in northwest Europe (Americans, British, Canadians and Poles) would rise to 84 divisions plus 285 air squadrons. The men-at-arms to feed and equip would rise from 2.6 million in November 1944 to 3.4 million in April 1945. The four armies when they were advancing, needed one million gallons of petrol per day. Pipelines under the ocean (PLUTO) could not yet cope with this huge requirement.

The pipeline from Cherbourg had reached Chartres by 12 September. R.G. Ruppertal's *Logistical History of NW Europe Operations* states that in the month of November 1944, no less than 2 million tons of supplies, petrol, oil and lubricants, ammunition, food, etc. were landed. About 600 tons were needed per day per division (plus the many independent brigades), plus requirements for the air force units, and the enormous administrative back-up of the British, American and Canadian armies. The humanitarian decision to supply the Parisian region and parts of liberated Holland further required a minimum of 2,600 tons per day.

In September the issue was clear to General Eisenhower and to General Bradley, his commander in the field. Cherbourg was on stream with 14,500 tons per day (tpd) and Omaha/Utah 10,500 tpd but St Malo and Brest were closed and Lorient and St Nazaire neutralized and invested. Overlord plans had counted by D+90 (6 September) on 14,000 tons a

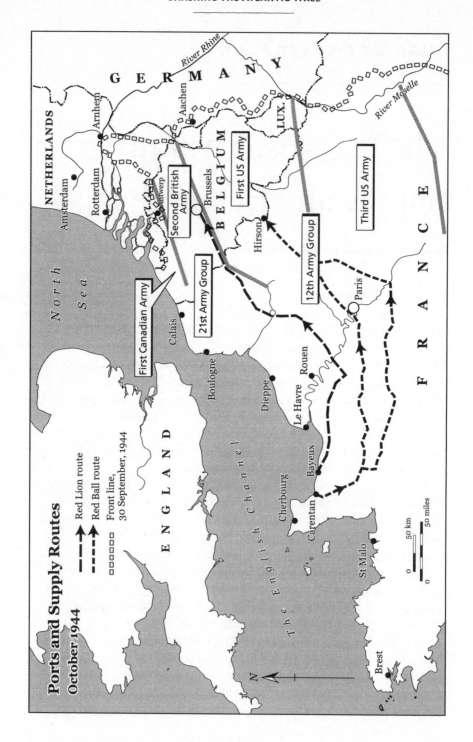

Ports and Supply Routes
October 1944

Red Lion route
Red Ball route
Front line,
30 September, 1944

day from the Brittany ports. The autumn gales were threatening Cherbourg and Utah/Omaha productivity. Eisenhower organized airlifts. The American Red Ball Express had delivered 75,000 tons to the Chartres area by 5 September. The route was extended from Bayeux to Hirson, 50 miles south of Brussels, for the US First Army and to Chalons for the US Third Army. An average round trip was 714 miles, which took about 70 hours. The 1,500 trucks carried between 7,000 and 8,000 tons per day. The White Ball route was opened from Le Havre and Rouen, on 6 October and it ran until 10 January. As rail transport was repaired and improved, on 16 November Red Ball Express ceased operations. On the same day the Normandy beaches supply route also closed. Besides Cherbourg, Dieppe was unloading 7,000 tpd, Le Havre 5,000, Boulogne 11,000 and Ostend 5,000.

Eisenhower had agreed—perhaps reluctantly—for Operation Market Garden to go ahead, even though he was getting very anxious indeed about supplies. There was only one possible answer. Antwerp with its potential of 40, 000 to 60,000 tons per day was absolutely vital. He tried several times to get this message through to Field Marshal Montgomery.

During the week before Market Garden, in mid-September, General H.D.G.Crerar, GOC Canadian First Army was signalled by Montgomery, '6 September. It looks as though the port of Antwerp may be unusable *for some time* as the Germans are holding islands at the mouth of the Scheldt. *Immediate* opening of some port north of Dieppe essential for rapid development of my plan, and I want Boulogne badly. What do you think the chances are of getting it soon?'

Boulogne was captured on 22 September and was opened on 12 October, i.e. five weeks after the message to Crerar. Supplies rapidly built up to landing 11,000 tons per day, and POL arrived too via PLUTO. Three days later Montgomery cabling to Eisenhower was sure that, 'With one good Pas de Calais port, 1,000 tons a day airlift and additional road transport, I can reach Munster and that with Dieppe, Boulogne, Calais [captured 30 September, open only on 20 November for personnel] and Dunkirk [never captured], plus 3,000 tons a day from Le Havre [taken 12 September, open 9 October with unloading rising from 3,650 in mid-October to 5,000 in November], we can reach Berlin.' On 9 September Montgomery, out of character, was wildly optimistic and unrealistic. Of the five Channel ports he was counting on, only Dieppe that day was 'producing'. He knew what had happened at Cherbourg and St Malo when their harbours had been pulverized. In his memoirs the field marshal wrote *after* the end of hostilities, 'We had both feet off the ground, relying on opening up the

Channel ports, particularly Dieppe, before our accumulated stocks became exhausted. But administrative risks have to be taken in war as well as tactical ones; the point to realise is that a Commander requires a nice judgment to know when risks are justifiable and when they are definitely not so.' They are words written rather blandly with the benefit of hindsight, without an apparent thought for the hard-pressed American allies. Prime Minister Winston Churchill noted in October, 'The Americans had all but outrun their supplies in the lightning advances of September and a pause was essential to build up stocks and prepare for large scale operations in November.' Certainly Lieutenant General Hodges US First Army was totally grounded as were another three divisions at the beachheads, so too was the British VIII Corps.

General Omar Bradley, GOC US 12th Army Group, and the senior American fighting general wrote in his memoirs, 'Of all the might-have-beens in the European campaign, none was more agonising than the failure of Monty to open Antwerp.'

Field Marshal Montgomery failed to grasp the importance of the logistical problem—not only for his Canadian First and British Second Armies—but also for his 'rivals' Generals Patton, Nevers and Bradley. He had also failed to grasp an immense tactical opportunity. When 11th Armoured Division captured Antwerp town and the port areas on 4 September, their GOC Major General Pip Roberts was not aware of the prize around the corner. Nor was Lieutenant General Brian Horrocks the Corps Commander; and nor did the army commander, General Dempsey and Field Marshal Montgomery choose to be aware. The German General Gustav von Zangen, commanding the Fifteenth Army, in spite of constant Allied air attack, succeeded in extricating 80,000 troops, 600 guns and all their vehicles. Tubby General Eugen-Felix Schwalbe was responsible for the evacuation of most of the German Fifteenth Army, mostly at night, to avoid bombing by the RAF's 84th Group. Using a Siebel ferry, 16 small Rhine boats, three large rafts and two large Dutch civilian ships they plied non stop between Breskens and Flushing. They escaped to fight again in the Peel country of northern Holland—a nebulous region extending west of the River Maas to Helmond-Venraid-Boxtole and in the defence of the Siegfried Line. Without doubt these troops helped prolong Adolf Hitler's desperate defence of the Third Reich. Enigma/Ultra had revealed the information of the Fifteenth Army's whereabouts and their audacious route to escape across the Scheldt, east through Beveland and through the isthmus to safety. There was a 'window of opportunity' when British or Canadian or American troops could have moved 15 miles northwest of Antwerp to Woensdrecht and blocked von Zangen's retreat. But they did not even contemplate the idea. All the 'top brass' had their eyes focused on Market Garden, hypnotized by Montgomery's promise to get a firm bridgehead over the Rhine. By the time the gallant survivors of the airborne drop in Arnhem were being brought out to safety, the opportunity to thwart von Zangen had come and gone.

During the crisis of supply, combined air forces airlifted 23,000 tons in the four-week period to 16 September. It was proof of the desperate need by the American armies. The USAAF flew in 20,000 tons and the RAF 2,850; but 2,600 were sent to the Parisian civilian relief, 12,800 to 12th US Army Group and 7,000 to 21st Army Group.

Did Adolf Hitler's well-defended fortress-ports significantly delay Allied progress towards the frontiers of the Third Reich in the autumn of 1944? Certainly in Brittany German resistance and destruction went according to the Führer's directives. The eccentric von Aulock in St Malo, General Ramcke in Brest, General Wilhelm Farmbacher in Lorient and Admiral Schirlitz at La Rochelle denied the Americans any use of those ports. Lieutenant General Karl-Wilhelm Schlieben delayed the Allies considerably in Cherbourg. It was D+90 before substantial supplies were being landed.

Admittedly the failure to fortify Dieppe was probably an error but destruction of the harbour meant a delay until D+90 when supplies were landed. Although Le Havre was captured in two days by a truly massive all-arms assault, it was not until mid-October that reasonable supplies could be cleared. So Colonel Eberhardt Wildermuth was responsible (with the RAF and Royal Navy bombing and shelling) for a considerable delay. Boulogne under Lieutenant General Heim put up a spirited defence, but supplies came through and were landed eventually on 12 October. Calais, guarded by Lieutenant Colonel Ludwig Schroeder, also put up a determined defence. It was not until 20 November that Allied personnel could use the port. Dunkirk held out and was 'masked', and after Ostend was taken three weeks' work was required to clear the harbour before supplies and POL came through at the end of September.

Almost certainly Adolf Hitler made a significant mistake in not turning Antwerp into a designated fortress-port on a scale similar to Brest. He knew that the Breskens pocket, South Beveland and Walcheren Island would cause great and painful delay to the Allied advance to clear Antwerp. But Major General Graf Stolberg-zu-Stolberg, with insufficient defences, put up a lacklustre defence in Antwerp and was simply overwhelmed by the head-long rush of 11th Armoured Division. If Hitler had ordered the

Todt organization to deploy their fortress-building skills in Antwerp, and if the plans to demolish all the key features of the gigantic port had been more efficient, then again plans to advance to the Siegfried Line and the Ruhr would have had to be delayed, perhaps to the spring of 1945. Nevertheless General Daser, General Eberding, Colonel Rheinhardt, General Ferdinand Heim and Colonel von der Heydte 'bought' their Führer nearly three months of valuable time. Hitler belatedly turned 50 per cent of the effort of his V-weapons on to Antwerp without noticeable success. But when a month after Antwerp was open Field Marshals Walther Model and von Rundstedt unleashed their panzer armies in Operation Watch on the Rhine, in the Ardennes, Liège (a major US supply point) and Antwerp were the two key objectives. After the war Major General Knut Eberding, the Breskens pocket GOC, admitted that, 'We prevented as long as possible the use of the port of Antwerp for the Allied force because the decision for the offensive in the Ardennes *depended on the non-function of the port of Antwerp for the Allies.*' As it was, the Americans had immense losses of POL, arms, ammunition and transport as many supply depots were overrun in the four weeks of the Ardennes 'Battle of the Bulge'. Churchill wrote, 'Rundstedt's great force (10 panzer and 14 infantry divisions) was intended to break through our weak centre in the Ardennes..... cut the Allied line in two, seize the port of Antwerp *and sever the lifeline of our northern armies.*'

History of course is made up of 'Ifs'. *If* Montgomery had concentrated his efforts, including an airdrop, on clearing the Scheldt and opening Antwerp earlier. Lieutenant General Brian Horrocks, GOC XXX Corps wrote in his memoirs, '*If* we had taken the chance and carried straight on with our advance instead of halting in Brussels [and Antwerp] the whole course of the war in Europe might have been changed. On 3 September we still had 100 miles of petrol per vehicle and one further day's supply within reach.' And he continued, '*If* I had ordered General Roberts not to liberate Antwerp, but to by-pass the town on the east, cross the Albert Canal and advance only 15 miles NW towards Woensdrecht we should have blocked the Beveland isthmus and cut the main German escape route. The only troops available to bar our passage northwards was the German 719th Division of elderly gentlemen guarding the north coast of Holland, a battalion of Dutch SS and a few Luftwaffe detachments. A meagre force strung out on a 50 mile front along the canal.' *If* Adolf Hitler had fortified Antwerp and made sure of its total destruction if and when captured. *If* the considerable supplies being unloaded at Antwerp in late November and early December had *not* been available to the Allied forces (19,000 tons a day), perhaps the Battle of the Ardennes might have ended up in the suburbs of Antwerp... and so on.

'Rain, cold and mud dominated the battlefield. The tanks fell back, practically useless in this morass. The infantry came forward. An amphibious warfare developed; first the flooding, then the landings at Walcheren. Then the mopping up on the south bank.' Alan Moorehead in *Eclipse* continued, 'This was fighting in conditions which divorced the life of the fighting soldier from anything which the civilian at home could understand or imagine; a business of filth and danger in the mud. The thing was done at last by November.' But it was the 'water rats' of the 'Cinderella Army' on the eastern flank and the 'step-children' on the Brittany flank who were the real heroes, albeit without the honour, the glory and the headlines.

CHAPTER TWENTY-FIVE

The Verdronken Land:
The Drowned Land

IN OCTOBER THE AMERICANS IN BRITTANY SURROUNDED THE HUGE ports of Lorient and St Nazaire, and port clearance teams wrestled in vain attempting some sort of clearance of Brest Harbour in their 'mousetrap' or 'step-children' war. On the eastern flank the Canadians and British struggled in appalling conditions. R.W. Thompson in *The 85 Days* describes the pitiless polder lands called by the Dutch peasants the *verdronken land*—their drowned land, 'Under a sky like the inside of an oyster shell, the land lay like a map to the sand banks and the sea, colourless and featureless, save for the everlasting dykes, the low shapes of barns and of small farmsteads in which the silent dour folk sheltered with their livestock against the bitter winds. Such crops as there were had been harvested and much was hidden from enemy and friend. War was alien to them, a monstrous inexplicable evil that had afflicted them for four years.' Thompson describes those men fighting the 'Cinderella War' going into action: 'The leading battalions splayed out left and right like the fingers of two hands resolving themselves at the tips, into individuals who must walk and eat, rest and sleep with death. To them war was a series of barns, road junctions, slit-trenches, strongpoints and mines, the objectives of day after day. Their horizon was limited by their field of vision.' And as the sappers led the single files of the infantry looking for the mines that the German defenders had seeded everywhere, the platoon sections moved as fast as they could—which in the polder meant very slowly indeed—spread out, cursing the lack of cover: 'The sudden stutter of a Spandau and the menacing crackle of exploding mortar bombs brought them instantly to their knees and bellies in the sodden dykes, whilst their young leaders, raw 2nd lieutenants or platoon sergeants kept their eyes ahead, seeing the enemy, striving to pin-point a target for attack.'

The Canadians had suffered immense losses in the Normandy campaign and by autumn 1944 the original company and platoon leaders had, almost to a man, become casualties. So their inexperienced replacements, in the *verdronken land* were almost inevitably doomed as well. When men crumpled suddenly in the polder fields or by the road sides, or by the side of a dyke winkling out von der Heydte's parachute troops, General Daser's Wehrmacht (the stomach division), Colonel Rheinhardt's garrison troops in Flushing, or General Eberding's professional 'leave' division men in the Breskens pocket, the RAMC jeeps came swiftly forward and the wounded were lifted carefully by brave men, seemingly unaware of the snipers, the mortars and bursting shells. All this in winds blowing at least half a gale, and cold bitter driving rain. There was more. There was now a determined hatred, as Thompson put it, 'growing to an absolute loathing for the Germans had mined and booby-trapped the bodies of their dead. The bloated bodies in the mud of the polders and lolloping face down like filthy grey bags in the dark waters of the dykes had proved as dangerous dead as alive.' There was no quarter; the mines touched off explosions of mud shot through with fragments of steel. The awful Schu mines blew off feet as the poor bloody infantrymen crawled through the swamps and left men staring at their shattered stumps. In this hell on earth the field marshals and the generals and the admirals and the air force commanders disputed and argued. William Shakespeare got it right in his *King Henry V*: 'From this day to the ending of the world, but we in it shall be remembered. We few, we happy few, we band of brothers. For he today that sheds his blood with me, shall be my brother.'

And how had it looked to the survivors? In Brittany just before the capture of Brest Lieutenant Charles Cawthorn wrote, 'The brief fight for relatively minute stakes in an ordinary hedge-enclosed field outside la Trinité, Brittany on a cloudy August afternoon 1944 was a microcosm of war at all times and levels. It encompassed misconception, chance, rashness, violence, courage, despair, victory and defeat—all monitored by death. Clashes between nations hold no more, or no less.' And Private First Class Leon Standifer, of the US 94th Infantry Division, noted from outside Lorient, 'We were being shelled and shot at nearly every day but with caution and luck, I would get through the war without a wound. I was satisfied to stay around Lorient rather than being fed into the meat grinder of riflemen fighting at the German border: playing nursemaid to 25,000 Germans on a lonely submarine base on the Atlantic coast. "War's desolation" took on a new meaning—wet, cold, isolated and dismal.'

When the 'Vitalities' and 'Infatuates' were over on the eastern flank, Major D.J. Goodspeed, Royal Regiment of Canada watched on 1 November as, 'a long line of weary muddy infantrymen plodded slowly back down the road that would take them to Hofstade, a sleepy little Dutch town near Mechelen. The men were indescribably dirty. They were bearded, cold, as it is only possible to be cold in Holland in November and wet from having lived in water-filled holes in the ground for 24 hours a day. Their eyes were red-rimmed from lack of sleep and they were exhausted from their swift advance on foot under terrible conditions. Yet all ranks realised with a certain grim satisfaction that a hard job had been well and truly done.'

The enemy had lost, but he had won a great deal of time to reinforce the Siegfried Line defences. Another two or three weeks of delay and Operation Watch on the Rhine, the great Ardennes counterattack might have reached Antwerp and cut off the Allied armies.

Captain Stanley Briggs, HLI of Canada wrote a poem 'Strange Harvest' which was a tribute to the Canadian 3rd Division. The last verse was

Dip gently your scythe, good reaper now
O'er the fields of the hallowed dead
for young men fought and young men died
Near the sea, where the earth is red.

The 'water rats' in the *verdronken land*—the Canadians, British, Scottish and Americans of the Cinderella armies had struggled in an alien land far, far away from home.

BIBLIOGRAPHY

Bercuson, David, *Battalion of Heroes* (Calgary Highlanders), Calgary Highlanders Regt. Foundation, 1994

Bird, Will R., *No Retreating Footsteps* (North Nova Scotias), Kentville, 1983

Bird, Will R., *History of North Shore Regiment*, Brunswick Press, 1963

Blumenson, Martin, *Breakout and Pursuit*, Officer of Chief Military History, Washington DC, 1989

Bradley, Omar, *A General's Life*, Simon & Schuster, NY, 1983

Breuer, William B., *Hitler's Fortress Cherbourg*, Stein and Day, NY, 1984

Cawthon, Charles, *Other Clay* (29th US Division), University Press, Colorado, 1990

Chazette, Alain, *Atlantikwall*, Heimdal, Bayeux, 1995

Collins, J. Lawton, *Lightning Joe*, Louisiana State University, Baton Rouge, 1979

Delaforce, Patrick, *Black Bull* (11th Armoured Division), Sutton, 1996

Delaforce, Patrick, *Polar Bears* (49th W.R. Division), Sutton, 1996

Delaforce, Patrick, *Churchill's Secret Weapons* (79th Armoured Division), Hale, 2000

Delaforce, Patrick, *Monty's Highlanders* (51st Division), Donovan, 1998

Fouque, R., *La Cité-Bastion de St Malo*, St Malo, 1945

David Fraser, *Knight's Cross:Rommel*, HarperCollins, 1993

Glanville, R., *Highland Light Infantry of Canada*, HLI of Canada Assoc., 1951

Greenhouse, Brereton, *Semper Paratus* (Royal Hamilton LI), RHLI Historical Assoc. 1977

Hart, Liddell, *The Other Side of the Hill*, Cassell, 1951

HMSO, *Campaign NW Europe 1944*, HMSO, 1944

Irving, David, *Hitler's War*, Hodder & Stoughton, 1977

Moorehead, Alan, *Eclipse*, Hamish Hamilton, 1945

Morgan, Frederick, *Overture to Overlord*, Hodder & Stoughton, 1950

Moulton, J.L., *Battle for Antwerp*, Ian Allen, 1978

Patton, George, *War as I Knew It*, Houghton Mifflin, Boston, 1947

Queen-Hughes, R.W., *Whatever Men Dare* (Queen's Own Cameron Highlanders), Bulman Press, 1960

Rondel, Eric, *III Armée US de Patton en Bretagne*, Club 35, Fréhel, 1994

Speer, Albert, *Inside the Third Reich*, Weidenfeld & Nicholson, 1970

Standifer, Leon, *Not in Vain* (94 US Infantry Division), Louisiana State Press, Baton Rouge, 1992

Thompson, R.W., *The 85 Days*, Hutchinson, 1957

Trevor-Roper, H.R., *Hitler's War Directives*, Sidgwick & Jackson, 1964

Walther Warlimont, *Inside Hitler's HQ*, Weidenfeld & Nicholson, 1964

Whitaker, Denis, *Battle for the Scheldt* Souvenir Press, 1985

Williams, Jeffery, *Long, Left Flank*, Leo Cooper, 1970

Williams, Jeffrey, *Princess Patricia's L.I.*, Leo Cooper, 1972

GLOSSARY

AA	Anti-aircraft guns
Abwehr	German armed forces intelligence unit
AF barges	German AA/Flak barges
AFV	Armoured fighting vehicle
AGRA	Army group royal artillery
ANCXF	Allied Naval Commander, Expeditionary Force
AOP	Air observation point (often from Auster plane)
AP	Armour-piercing shell
APC	Armoured personnel carrier
AVRE	Armoured vehicle Royal Engineers (usually Churchill tank)
BESA	British small arms ammunition
BUFFS	Royal East Kent (flame-thrower tanks) regiment
BUFFALOES	British nickname for US LVT carrying infantry or small vehicles
Brew-up	Army slang for tea-making, or destruction/burning by enemy fire
BYMS	British yard mine sweeper
Cab rank	Army slang for RAF fighter planes in the air 'on call'
CIGS	Chief of Imperial General Staff
Conger	Rocket-launched mine-sweeping device
COSSAC	Chief of Staff to Supreme Allied Commander
CO	Commanding Officer
CRA	Commander Royal Artillery (usually a Brigadier)
Crabs	Sherman tank with revolving flail with chains to 'flog' a path through a minefield
Crocodile	Flame-throwing apparatus on a Churchill gun-tank with oil carried in a trailer
DD	Duplex-drive Sherman amphibious tank
D-Day	First day of any military operation
DSC	Distinguished Service Cross
DSO	Distinguished Service Order
DUKW	Duplex-drive amphibious truck
E-boat	Small fast German torpedo boat (*S-boot*)
Element C	German underwater beach obstacle

Fascines	Large bundle of sticks carried on AVREs to fill trenches, ditches or craters
Festa	German fortress-garrison artillery troops
Festung	German fortress
FFI	*Forces Françaises de l'interieur* (French Resistance movement)
FTF	Napalm flame oil
Flails	See Crabs; another name for mine-clearing Sherman tanks
Flak	German anti-aircraft gunfire
Flog	Army term for beating a lane through a minefield by Crabs
FOO	Forward observation officer
Funnies	British generic term for specialized armour of 79th Armoured Division
GHQ	General Head Quarters
GOC	General Officer Commanding
GSO	General Staff Officer (grades I, II or III)
HAA	Heavy anti-aircraft guns
HE	High explosive
HLI	Highland Light Infantry
HQ	Head Quarters (command group)
H-Hour	Key time for launch of military operation
i/c	In charge
Invest	Surround closely enemy objective (usually a town)
IR	German infantry regiment
Kangaroo	Turretless tank for transporting infantry
KIA	Killed in action
KSLI	King's Own Shropshire Light Infantry
KOSB	King's Own Scottish Borderers
KOYLI	King's Own Yorkshire Light Infantry
Kriegmarines	German (war) marine troops
LCA	Landing craft assault
LCF	Landing craft flak (AA)
LCI	Landing craft infantry
LCP	Landing craft personnel
LCT	Landing craft tanks
LSI	Landing ship infantry
LST	Landing ship tanks
LVT	Landing vehicle tracked (Alligator)

Lodgement	Initial landing or break-in
Luftwaffe	German airforce
MAA	German marine artillery
Mask	Screen a military objective without attacking it
Mark	i.e. IV, V, model type of AFV
MFV	Motor fishing vessel
MG	Machine gun
ML	Motor launch
MS	Mine sweeper
MTB	Motor torpedo boat
Mulberry	Artificial harbours towed to Normandy beaches
Napalm	Flame-throwing oil
Nebelwerfer	German multi-barrelled mortar
Neptune	Naval assault phase of Overlord
NCO	Non-commissioned officer
NOIC	Naval officer in charge (ports, beaches)
Obwest	*Oberfohlshaber*, senior commander German Army Group West
OC	Officer commanding
Oerliken	Swedish-made AA machine gun
OKH	German High Command of the Army
OP	Observation post
OR	Other rank (Army)
Orepesa	Wire sweep trailed behind minesweeper to cut cables of moored mines
Organisation Todt	The complex fortifications of the West Wall
Ost (truppen)	Non-German volunteer troops from east European countries
Overlord	General plan for liberation of NW Europe
Petard	Spigot mortar bomb fired from AVRE
Pdrs	Pounders, i.e. 25 pounds weight of shell
PLUTO	Pipeline under the ocean (oil supply from UK to the Continent)
POL	Petrol, oil, lubricant supplies
POW	Prisoner of war
PT	American patrol torpedo boat
Priests	105 mm self-propelled gun on Sherman chassis
RA	Royal Artillery
RAC	Royal Armoured Corps (tank regiments)

RAF	Royal Air Force
RAP	Regimental aid post
R-boat	Type of German E-boat
RE	Royal Engineer
RN	Royal Navy
RNVR	Royal Navy Volunteer Reserve
RTR	Royal Tank Regiment
Schu	German mine, wooden case, exploded metal balls at foot height
S-boat	Type of German E-boat
SDG&H	Stormont, Dundee and Glengarry Highlanders (Canadian)
SHAEF	Supreme HQ Allied Expeditionary Force
Siegfried Line	Defensive line of forts on German frontier
SP	Self-propelled (gun, halftrack etc.)
SSEF	Support Squadron Eastern Flank
TACHQ	Forward tactical formation HQ
TAF	Tactical forward RAF formation
Terrapins	Amphibious truck with eight wheels carrying infantry, POL etc.
TPD	Tons per day, loaded/unloaded, of military supplies
U-boat	German submarine
Wasp	Small tracked flame thrower
Weasel	Small tracked amphibious jeep
Wehrmacht	German armed forces
West Wall	German fortifications extending from Luxembourg in the north to Switzerland in the south – opposite the French equivalent, the Maginot Line

CANADIAN FORCES

2nd Canadian Division

4th Brigade: Royal Regiment of Canada: Royal Hamilton Light Infantry; Essex Scottish Regiment.

5th Brigade: Black Watch (Royal Highland Regiment) of Canada; Le Régiment de Maisonneuve;The Calgary Highlanders.

6th Brigade: Les Fusiliers Mont-Royal; The Queen's Own Cameron Highlanders of Canada; The South Saskatchewan Regiment

3rd Canadian Division

7th Brigade: Royal Winnipeg Rifles; Regina Rifle Regiment; 1st Bn The Canadian Scottish Regiment.

8th Brigade: The Queen's Own Rifles of Canada; Le Régiment de la Chaudière; The North Shore (New Brunswick)Regiment.

9th Brigade: Highland Light Infantry of Canada; The Stormont, Dundas & Glengary Highlanders, The North Nova Scotia Highlanders

4th Canadian Armoured Division

4th Armoured Brigade: 21st, 22nd & 28th Armoured Regiments.

10th Infantry Brigade: The Lincoln & Welland Regiment; The Algonquin Regiment; The Argyll & Sutherland Highlanders of Canada (Princess Louise's)

INDEX

Resistance
  Belgium 121-3, 134
  France 25
  Netherlands 205
  see also French Forces of the Interior
    (FFI)
Reynaud, Paul 75
Rheinhardt, Colonel Gustav 192, 193
Rhine, River 126
Riantec 108
Richter, Kapitan zur See Eugen 93
Ridgway, Major General Matthew 61, 62, 75
Rilland 184
Ritchie, Lieutenant Colonel Bruce 173, 185
RMK demolition mine 143
Roberts 196
Roberts, Lieutenant Colonel (Manitoba
    Dragoons) 134-5
Roberts, Major General Pip 121, 218, 220
Robertson, General 104
Robinson, Colonel Warren 71
Rockingham, Brigadier 148, 178-9, 181
Rohrbach, Lieutenant Colonel Helmuth 70,
    74
Rommel, Field Marshal Erwin
    Cherbourg 62-3, 73, 74, 78
    command in west 41-2
    defences 34-5, 36-7, 60
    St Nazaire 110
    suicide 79
Roosevelt, President 47, 48, 90
Rouen 50, 114-16
Roundup, Operation (cross-Channel attack
    plan) 45
Rowley, Lieutenant Colonel Roger 180-1
Royal Air Force (RAF) 213-14
    bombing of Brest 92
    Boulogne 146, 147, 151
    Breskens pocket 167
    Brest 97, 101
    Calais 156, 158
    Le Havre 138-9, 140
    Neptune Naval Operation Orders 53-4
    Walcheren Island 166, 167, 174, 190, 196
Royal Marines (RM) 213, 214
    4th Commandos 182, 204
    10th I-A Commando 192, 197, 201, 202,
      203-4
    30th Assault Unit (RN/RM joint unit)
      59, 64-6, 72-4, 94-6, 142-3
    40th Commando 203-4
    41st Commando 195-6, 197, 200, 201-2,
      203-4
    47th Commando 195-6, 201-3
    48th Commando 132, 195-6, 197-8, 200-2
    Infatuate II 195-203
Royal Navy 213
    30th Assault Unit (RN/RM joint unit)
      59, 64-6, 72-4, 94-6, 142-3
    Calender, Operation 207-11
    Forward Interrogation Unit 151
    Infatuate II 194-5, 196
    naval port clearance parties ('P' parties)
      54-8, 76-7

Neptune planning 52-9
Port Clearance Party Number 1571 54,
    76, 116, 119, 143
Port Clearance Party Number 1572 54,
    76, 123
Port Clearance Party Number 1573 54, 76
Port Clearance Party Number 1574 54,
    135, 151, 160
Port Clearance Party Number 1686 119
Walcheren Island 191
Rudder, Lieutenant Colonel J.E. 106
Rundstedt, Field Marshal von 25, 78, 174
    Antwerp 125
    Ardennes Offensive 220
    command in West 41
    defences 26, 28-9, 36-7, 42, 112-13
    predictions of Allied landing sites 40
Rupembert 146
Russell, Brigadier J.D. 186
Rutter, Operation (Dieppe landings) 25, 45-6
Ryles, Major Nigel 104

St Benoit-des-Ondes 82
St Briac-sur-Mer 84
St Etienne-au-Mont 145, 146
St Ideuc 82, 83, 85
St Joseph's Hill 83
St Lo 79, 81
St Lunaire 84
St Malo 27, 60, 79-89, 92
St Mathieu 101
St Michel-en-Greve 82
St Nazaire 10, 93, 106, 110, 222
    commando raid 24
    defences 100
    Overlord planning 50, 80
St Thoan 96
HMS *St Tudno* 207
St Valéry-en-Caux 137
Sandvliet 171
Sangatte 154, 156-7
Sattler, Major General Robert 75
Saunders, Lieutenant (Buffs) 157-8
Scaife, Lieutenant 181
Scanlon, Staff Sergeant George 104
Scarrow, Captain G.D. 202
Scheldt Estuary 120, 161-8
    Angus, Operation 169-74
    Breskens pocket 175-82
    Calender, Operation 207-11
    logistics 217
    Vitality I 183-6
    Vitality II 187-9
Scheldt Fortress South 163-7, 175-82
Scheldt, River 122, 123-6
Schilling, Colonel 160
Schirlitz, Admiral von 110, 219
Schlieben, Lieutenant General Karl-
    Wilhelm von 64, 68-71, 73-5, 78, 219
Schmidt, Adjutant Colonel 26
Schoondijke 175, 180, 181
Schouwen 166
Schroeder, Lieutenant Colonel Ludwig 154-
    5, 158-9, 219